Student Activity Guide

Managing Your Personal Finances

SEVENTH EDITION

Joan S. Ryan, M.B.A., Ph.D., C.M.A.

Clackamas Community College
Oregon City, Oregon

Christie Ryan, MA, LMHC

Institute for Family Development
Vancouver, WA

✱ Cengage

Australia • Brazil • Canada • Mexico • Singapore • United Kingdom • United States

For product information and technology assistance, contact us at **Cengage Customer & Sales Support, 1-800-354-9706 or support.cengage.com.**

For permission to use material from this text or product, submit all requests online at **www.copyright.com.**

ISBN: 978-1-305-08135-2

Cengage
200 Pier 4 Boulevard
Boston, MA 02210
USA

Cengage is a leading provider of customized learning solutions with employees residing in nearly 40 different countries and sales in more than 125 countries around the world. Find your local representative at: **www.cengage.com.**

To learn more about Cengage platforms and services, register or access your online learning solution, or purchase materials for your course, visit **www.cengage.com.**

Printed in the United States of America
Print Number: 07   Print Year: 2023

Contents

Name _____

1 section:
vocabulary

Fill in the missing word(s) in the space provided at the right.   **Answers**

Example: A face-to-face meeting with a potential employer is a(n) _____.   0. __job interview__

1. The process of gathering and analyzing data and summarizing it into
   useful information is known as _____.   1. _____

2. A listing of your work experience, education, abilities, interests, and
   other information that may be of interest to an employer is a(n) _____,
   also known as a CV or a personal data sheet.   2. _____

3. A(n) _____ is a data mining system that gathers and stores information
   electronically about what is purchased and grants reward or points that
   can be redeemed.   3. _____

4. Forms of electronic communication through which users create online
   communities to share information are known as _____,   4. _____

5. Actively seeking new knowledge and skills over time is known as _____.   5. _____

6. An economic event where jobs are eliminated, because company
   revenues are falling while costs are rising is known as _____.   6. _____

7. The largest and fastest growing sector of the job market is in the _____
   industry.   7. _____

8. A(n) _____ is a list of strengths, weaknesses, and plans of action for
   improvement.   8. _____

9. During _____, an employee learns new and different skills so that he or
   she can retain employability.   9. _____

10. Employers may ask for _____, or people who have known you for a year
    or more and can provide information about your skills, character, and
    achievements.   10. _____

11. In the United States, job opportunities are determined by consumer _____. 11. _____

12. When an employee advances to a higher level of skill to increase his or
    her usefulness to an employer, the employee is _____.   12. _____

13. School records that include a listing of courses taken are called _____. 13. _____

14. A(n) ___ goal is one you expect to reach in a few days or weeks.   14. _____

15. To cope with ___, there are three things you can do: accept it, reject it,
    or ignore it; progress cannot be stopped.   15. _____

16. A(n) _____ takes the risks of being self-employed and owning a business. 16. _____

17. A(n) _____ is a small business that will grow and eventually become a
    corporation.   17. _____

18. A(n) _____ is a formal document that outlines the route a business will
    take to earn and grow revenues.   18. _____

section:
review questions

After each of the following statements, circle *T* for a true statement or *F* for a false statement.

		Answers	For Scoring
1. Careers in the digital age are not affected by technology and innovation.		T F	1. _____
2. Data mining can occur without your permission and can result in negative consequences for consumers.		T F	2. _____
3. Most customer loyalty programs bring worthwhile benefits to consumers.		T F	3. _____
4. New technology will require many workers to upgrade and retrain or be unemployable.		T F	4. _____
5. A person going into business (entrepreneur) has many sources of information or assistance to help him or her.		T F	5. _____
6. Having another person objectively assess your strengths and weaknesses is one way to help clarify your self-assessment.		T F	6. _____
7. New jobs and careers are created when the economy is growing and new products and services are being produced.		T F	7. _____
8. A resume should contain extensive personal information, including your age, ethnicity, and marital status.		T F	8. _____
9. When preparing for a job interview, it is important to do company research to find out about the company's history and what it makes or sells.		T F	9. _____
10. While long-term planning is necessary for businesses, long-term goals are not an essential part of an individual's career planning.		T F	10. _____

On the line at the right of each sentence, print the letter that represents the word or group of words correctly completing the sentence or answering the question.

1. A business that the owner intends to keep small but is a full-time job is a(n) (a) side business, (b) lifestyle business, (c) venture business, (d) entrepreneurship.   _____ 1. _____

2. Something you will achieve in the next few months or years is a(n) _____ goal. (a) short-term, (b) intermediate, (c) long-term, (d) self-employment   _____ 2. _____

3. Which of these is not a government publication? (a) *Occupational Outlook Handbook*, (b) *Dictionary of Occupational Titles (DOT)*, (c) *Business Periodicals Index*, (d) *Monthly Labor Review*   _____ 3. _____

4. All of the following are parts of a resume except (a) career objective, (b) transcripts, (c) references, (d) education.   _____ 4. _____

5. Contact with a potential employer after a job interview is called (a) job analysis, (b) self-assessment, (c) follow-up, (d) company research.   _____ 5. _____

6. The management of data storage and retrieval is known as (a) data warehousing, (b) data mining, (c) web mining, (d) social media.   _____ 6. _____

7. Knowledge and skills obtained from working in a career field is known as (a) Plan B, (b) upgrading, (c) retraining, (d) experience.   _____ 7. _____

3 section:
problem solving

Activity 1.1 Social Media and the Internet

Directions: Consider how you use social media websites, personal blogs, and other forms of communication on the Internet. Answer the questions that follow, based on the types of information you post about yourself and others and steps you take to protect your privacy and that of others.

1. What social media websites do you visit regularly?

2. How do you access these sites (smartphone, tablet, computer)? List all that apply.

3. Why did you choose these particular sites or forms of communication on the Internet?

4. How have you benefited from use of social media?

5. Describe any negative consequences you have experienced from your social media postings?

6. What do you do to protect your privacy (to thwart the efforts of data miners and other users of information who can profit from selling information about you that you have provided voluntarily)?

7. Do you feel that social media website postings are secure from those who would use information against you and others? Why or why not?

Activity 1.2 *O*Net* **Research**

Directions: Go to the O*NET website (www.online.onetcenter.org). Click on the "Find Occupations" link. Find the category called "Job Family" and click on the pull-down list of occupational groups. Choose a career category and hit the GO button. You will see a long list of career or job titles. Click on one of these and answer the following questions.

Occupation _____

1. What are some tasks this career requires?

   _____

   _____

   _____

2. List two or more skills required of this career.

   _____

   _____

   _____

3. List two or more abilities required of this career.

   _____

   _____

   _____

4. List two work activities.

   _____

   _____

5. List two work styles.

   _____

   _____

6. List one work value.

   _____

   _____

7. What are the (a) median wages, (b) employment trends, and (c) projected growth?

   _____

   _____

   _____

   _____

   _____

Activity 1.3 Self-Assessment Inventory

Directions: Complete the following self-assessment inventory. Provide statements about yourself that are accurate at present.

SELF-ASSESSMENT INVENTORY		
Strengths	**Weaknesses**	**Plan of Action**

Ask a counselor or teacher to initial here, showing that he or she read your self-assessment inventory and made comments.

Initials of counselor or teacher:

Comments of counselor or teacher: _____

_____

_____

_____

_____

Activity 1.4 Job Application

Directions: Complete the following job application (or one that you pick up from a local business). Answer questions appropriately. If there is a question that is not applicable, use N/A or a dash (—) to indicate that you choose not to answer the question.

JOB APPLICATION

Date: ____/____/____   Job you are applying for: _____   ☐ Full Time   ☐ Part Time

First Name: _____   Middle Initial: _____   Last Name: _____

Mailing Address: _____   City: _____   State: _____   Zip: _____

Home Phone: (____)_____   Work Phone: (____)_____

Have you worked for this company before? ☐ Yes ☐ No   From: _____ To: _____ **What location?** _____

Your name at that time: _____   Position when you left: _____

If you are under 18, give your birthdate: ____/____/____ and work permit number (if applicable): _____

Date available for work: _____

START WITH CURRENT OR LAST EMPLOYER—INCLUDE MONTH AND YEAR IN DATES

FROM Mo. Yr.	COMPANY		POSITION HELD	BEGINNING PAY
TO Mo. Yr.	STREET and NUMBER	CITY and STATE		ENDING PAY
SUPERVISOR'S NAME TITLE		REASON FOR LEAVING		
FROM Mo. Yr.	COMPANY		POSITION HELD	BEGINNING PAY
TO Mo. Yr.	STREET and NUMBER	CITY and STATE		ENDING PAY
SUPERVISOR'S NAME TITLE		REASON FOR LEAVING		
FROM Mo. Yr.	COMPANY		POSITION HELD	BEGINNING PAY
TO Mo. Yr.	STREET and NUMBER	CITY and STATE		ENDING PAY
SUPERVISOR'S NAME TITLE		REASON FOR LEAVING		

MAY WE CONTACT YOUR PRESENT EMPLOYER? ☐ Yes   ☐ No

SCHOOL NAME	ADDRESS	FROM	TO	DEGREE/DIPLOMA
HIGH SCHOOL				DIPLOMA ☐ Yes ☐ No TYPE:
BUSINESS/VOCATION SCHOOL				DIPLOMA ☐ Yes ☐ No TYPE:
COMMUNITY COLLEGE/UNIVERSITY				DIPLOMA ☐ Yes ☐ No TYPE:
UNDERGRADUATE COURSEWORK EMPHASIS				CUM GPA
GRADUATE COURSEWORK EMPHASIS				CUM GPA

I understand that any offer of employment is conditioned upon the satisfactory completion of this verification process and that the company will hire only those individuals who are legally authorized to work in the United States and who present acceptable proof of their lawful employment status and identity.

_____   _____/_____/_____
        SIGN HERE   **DATE**

Activity 1.5 Values and Lifestyle

Directions: To complete this activity, record your answers to the questions in the space provided. Because answers are individualized and personal, there are no right or wrong answers; but you must be honest and truthful for this activity to be of value to you.

1. Rate the following items as important, not sure, or unimportant to you at this time in your life or as a goal for you:

	Important	Not Sure	Unimportant
a. Possessing wealth, making lots of money	_____	_____	_____
b. Attaining fame and power	_____	_____	_____
c. Being attractive and liked by others	_____	_____	_____
d. Having good health; being physically and mentally fit	_____	_____	_____
e. Being honest; having a good reputation	_____	_____	_____
f. Helping others	_____	_____	_____
g. Participating actively in my faith	_____	_____	_____
h. Trying to be a good student in school and/or athletics	_____	_____	_____
i. Getting top grades and learning many subjects	_____	_____	_____
j. Having many friends	_____	_____	_____
k. Working hard to help support my family	_____	_____	_____

2. Can you think of any other values? Why are these values important to you?

_____

_____

_____

_____

_____

_____

_____

_____

_____

_____

_____

3. The following three items are examples of what society values. Name three additional values of society, and then rate the importance of all six values to you.

	Important	Not Sure	Unimportant
a. Education (a college degree)	_____	_____	_____
b. Wealth and fame	_____	_____	_____
c. Beauty and attractiveness	_____	_____	_____
d. _____	_____	_____	_____
e. _____	_____	_____	_____
f. _____	_____	_____	_____

4. From the list of work activities given here, circle those that appeal to you, and then try to think of at least three occupations that would include these types of activities.

performing indoor work	working at various tasks	working alone
doing physically inactive work	working with others	meeting deadlines
following directions	doing manual work	working with tools
analyzing and recording	performing routine tasks	leading and directing people
doing physically active tasks	helping others	presenting or speaking to people
being creative	performing self-motivated tasks	creating and designing activities
performing outdoor work	memorizing	

Three occupations _____

_____

5. Read through the activities listed in the three columns below. Choose the one activity from each column that would interest you the most and circle it.

ACTIVE	**INACTIVE**	**INTELLECTUAL**
playing sports	painting a picture	keeping scores
cooking meals or snacks	watching television	reading a book
attending a dance	singing songs	writing a letter
doing exercises (jogging)	listening to music	helping someone

How can the interests that you have circled be of benefit to you in the type of work you would like to do?

_____

_____

List three of your favorite activities in order of preference. Beside each activity, note how many times you engage in this activity each week. Then list activities you'd like to do more of but don't have the time, energy, or financial ability to do so.

_____

_____

_____

6. Rate yourself as to how well you think you have or have not developed each of the following personality traits:

	Almost Always	**Occasionally**	**Never**
a. I am at work (or in class) on time	_____	_____	_____
b. I am friendly and enthusiastic	_____	_____	_____
c. I care about others' problems	_____	_____	_____
d. I am dependable and get my work done	_____	_____	_____
e. I can take a joke	_____	_____	_____
f. I am neat, clean, and well dressed	_____	_____	_____
g. I help someone every day	_____	_____	_____
h. I put forth my best efforts	_____	_____	_____
i. I am thrifty and not wasteful	_____	_____	_____
j. I eat good, nutritious food most of the time	_____	_____	_____
k. I am enthusiastic about life	_____	_____	_____

Activity 1.6 Goals Checklist

Directions: Fill in the blanks in the following checklist, using textbook information and your personal life.

CHECKLIST
Week of: _____

Short-term goals (today/this week)   **Accomplished**

1. _____

   _____   _____

2. _____

   _____   _____

3. _____

   _____   _____

4. _____

   _____   _____

5. _____

   _____   _____

Intermediate goals (next month/year)

1. _____

   _____   _____

2. _____

   _____   _____

3. _____

   _____   _____

Long-term goals (future)   **Things to do now**

1. _____   _____

   _____   _____

   _____   _____

   _____   _____

   _____   _____

2. _____   _____

   _____   _____

   _____   _____

   _____   _____

Activity 1.7 Entrepreneurship

Directions: To complete this activity, record your answers to the questions in the space provided. Because answers are individualized and personal, there are no right or wrong answers; but you should be honest and truthful for this activity to be of value to you.

1. Have you ever considered opening/running your own business? If so, what businesses have you considered as possibilities?

   _____
   _____
   _____
   _____
   _____
   _____

2. Do you have the characteristics of a successful entrepreneur? Consider the list on page 29 in Chapter 1 of your textbook. Are there characteristics you fill completely? Are there characteristics you need to improve?

   _____
   _____
   _____
   _____
   _____
   _____

3. Visit the Small Business Administration (SBA) website and read an article that interests you. Briefly summarize the article and explain how it is useful to a new business owner or someone considering opening a small business.

   _____
   _____
   _____
   _____
   _____

4. Interview a small business owner, or read about one in a periodical or online. What were some of the lessons he or she learned when starting and operating a small business?

   _____
   _____
   _____
   _____
   _____

2 Pay, Benefits, and Work

Name _____

1 section: vocabulary

Fill in the missing word(s) in the space provided at the right.

Answers

Example: A standard workweek is 40 hours in a _____-day period of eight hours each day.

0. _____five_____

1. A form of employee compensation, _____ are in addition to your paycheck.

1. _____

2. Amounts, both required and optional, subtracted from gross pay are called _____.

2. _____

3. When deductions are subtracted from gross pay, what is left is known as _____.

3. _____

4. Profit sharing is a way to encourage employees to strive for higher levels of performance, and is known as a(n) _____.

4. _____

5. A group of people working in the same or similar occupations, organized for the benefit of all, is a(n) _____.

5. _____

6. The main function of unions is _____, which is the process of negotiating an employment contract for union members.

6. _____

7. The principle of _____ states that the person who has worked the longest should be the last to be laid off.

7. _____

8. The American Bar Association is an example of a(n) _____, which is very similar to a union.

8. _____

9. An effort made to influence legislation in a way that benefits a profession is known as _____.

9. _____

10. The total amount earned before deductions are subtracted is called _____.

10. _____

11. A person is _____ when he or she is entitled to the full retirement account balance when employment is terminated.

11. _____

12. A type of work schedule that allows employees to choose their working hours outside of core time periods is known as _____.

12. _____

13. _____ is a technique used to train employees to be efficient in more than one specialized area.

13. _____

14. When two people share what was originally a full-time position, it is called _____.

14. _____

15. A formal process known as _____ uses a neutral third party with expertise in legal issues to make a formal decision that has the same effect as a court order.

15. _____

2 section:
review questions

After each of the following statements, circle *T* for a true statement or *F* for a false statement.

	Answers	For Scoring

1. If the regular rate of pay is $9 an hour, the overtime rate is
   $13.50 an hour.   T F   1. _____
2. Employers must contribute matching amounts of Social Security and
   Medicare taxes into each employee's account.   T F   2. _____
3. Net pay is the result when you subtract required and optional deductions
   from gross pay.   T F   3. _____
4. Some types of deductions may be withheld from your paycheck
   without your written consent because they are required by law.   T F   4. _____
5. Employee benefits and incentives are offered by companies to improve
   morale and working conditions.   T F   5. _____
6. Profit sharing is an employee benefit required of all employers.   T F   6. _____
7. Job sharing is a job design in which employees are trained to do
   more than one specialized task.   T F   7. _____
8. The main function of unions is mediation to help settle disputes.   T F   8. _____
9. The American Bar Association is a professional organization for
   lawyers.   T F   9. _____
10. Lobbying is an illegal activity engaged in by many unions and
    professional organizations.   T F   10. _____

On the line at the right of each sentence, print the letter that represents the word or group of words correctly completing the sentence or answering the question.

1. Which of the following is not considered a required deduction? (a) federal
   income tax, (b) savings deposits, (c) state tax, (d) Social Security tax   _____ 1. _____
2. Employee incentives include all of the following except
   (a) employee discounts, (b) income tax deductions, (c) wellness programs,
   (d) profit sharing.   _____ 2. _____
3. A company plan whereby employees receive a portion of the earnings of
   the company is called (a) profit sharing, (b) leave of absence, (c) sick pay,
   (d) retirement plan.   _____ 3. _____
4. A company allowance for full-time employees whereby they are paid even
   though they are absent for a set number of days for illness is called
   (a) profit sharing, (b) leave of absence, (c) sick pay, (d) retirement plan.   _____ 4. _____
5. Railroad employees would belong to a(n) _____ union. (a) craft,
   (b) industrial, (c) public employee, (d) professional   _____ 5. _____
6. Teachers and police officers would belong to a(n) _____ union. (a) craft,
   (b) industrial, (c) public employee, (d) arbitration   _____ 6. _____
7. The major function of unions is (a) collecting dues, (b) conducting
   strikes, (c) bargaining, (d) having meetings.   _____ 7. _____
8. A technique for training employees to be efficient in more than one
   specialized area is called (a) core time period, (b) job rotation,
   (c) flextime, (d) job sharing.   _____ 8. _____
9. A decision facilitated by a neutral third party is called (a) lobbying,
   (b) seniority, (c) bargaining, (d) mediation.   _____ 9. _____

3 section:
problem solving

Activity 2.1 Computation of Gross Pay

Directions: Based on the information given in the following problems, compute the gross pay.

1. Regular hours worked: 40   Overtime hours worked: 8   Regular rate of pay: $7.75 per hour

2. Regular hours worked: 40   Overtime hours worked: 4   Regular rate of pay: $7.80 per hour

3. Hours worked: 46   Regular rate of pay: $7.82 per hour

4. Regular salary: $984 per month   Overtime rate: $10.39 per hour (14 hours overtime to be paid)

5. Hours worked: 51   Overtime hours worked: 11   Regular rate of pay: $7.35 per hour

6. Regular salary: $1,100 per month   Overtime rate: $10.38 per hour (20 hours overtime to be paid)

7. Annual pay: $22,200. Calculate monthly pay.

8. Annual pay: $14,900. Calculate monthly pay.

Activity 2.2 Withholding Taxes

Directions: Using the withholding tax tables for federal and state taxes on pages 38–39 of your textbook, complete the following phrases. Then answer the questions that follow.

1. For a single person, 0 allowances, who made $185 last week

   State withholding tax: _____   Federal withholding tax: _____

2. For a single person, 1 allowance, who made $185 last week

   State withholding tax: _____   Federal withholding tax: _____

3. For a single person, 0 allowances, who made $295 last week

   State withholding tax: _____   Federal withholding tax: _____

4. For a single person, 1 allowance, who made $295 last week

   State withholding tax: _____   Federal withholding tax: _____

5. Explain how withholding taxes works; that is, on what are the taxes based? Why do some people have more taxes withheld than others, even if they have identical amounts of gross pay?

   _____

   _____

   _____

   _____

   _____

   _____

6. If you discover that you are receiving a large tax refund at the end of each year, what can you do to reduce this amount so that you have more money to save throughout the year?

   _____

   _____

   _____

   _____

   _____

   _____

Activity 2.3 Employee Withholding Sheet

Directions: Complete the following Employee Withholding Sheet from the information given.

Michael Anderson, Social Security No. 999-00-3691, works for a weekly paycheck. He is single and claims no allowances. Last week he worked five days, for a total of 46 hours. His regular rate of pay is $7.80 an hour.

In addition to required deductions and Social Security and Medicare taxes, he also has insurance withheld of $16 a week and puts 4 percent of his gross pay into a retirement account. Use the state and federal tax withholding tables on textbook pages 38–39.

EMPLOYEE WITHHOLDING SHEET

Employee Name_____ Social Security Number _____

Pay Period: ☐ weekly   ☐ biweekly   ☐ monthly

Number of Allowances: _____   ☐ married   ☐ single

GROSS PAY

    1. Regular Wages: _____ hours at $_____ /hr. = $_____

or

    2. Regular Salary: =   _____

    3. Overtime: _____ hours at $_____ /hr. =   _____

    GROSS PAY . . . . $_____

REQUIRED DEDUCTIONS

    4. Federal Income Tax (use tax tables) . . . . $_____

    5. State Income Tax (use tax tables) . . . . $_____

    6. Social Security Tax (use 6.2% × gross pay) . . . . $_____

    7. Medicare Tax (use 1.45% × gross pay) . . . . $_____

OTHER DEDUCTIONS

    8. Insurance . . . . $_____

    9. Union Dues . . . . $_____

    10. Credit Union . . . . $_____

    11. Savings . . . . $_____

    12. Retirement . . . . $_____

    13. Charity . . . . $_____

    14. Other: _____ . . . . $_____

    _____ . . . . _____

    TOTAL DEDUCTIONS (total lines 4 through 14) . . . . $_____

    NET PAY (subtract total deductions from gross pay) . . . . $_____

Activity 2.4 Employee Withholding Sheet

Directions: Complete the following Employee Withholding Sheet from the information given.

Phyllis White, Social Security No. 999-00-3288, receives a weekly paycheck. She is single and claims one allowance. Last week she worked five days for a total of 44 hours. Her regular rate of pay is $8.10 an hour.

In addition to the required deductions, she also saves $20 a week and sets aside 5 percent of her gross pay into a retirement account.

EMPLOYEE WITHHOLDING SHEET

Employee Name _____ Social Security Number _____

Pay Period: ☐ weekly   ☐ biweekly   ☐ monthly

Number of Allowances: _____   ☐ married   ☐ single

GROSS PAY

    1. Regular Wages: _____ hours at $_____ /hr. = $ _____

or

    2. Regular Salary: =   _____

    3. Overtime: _____ hours at $_____ /hr. =   _____

    GROSS PAY .... $ _____

REQUIRED DEDUCTIONS

    4. Federal Income Tax (use tax tables) .... $ _____

    5. State Income Tax (use tax tables) .... $ _____

    6. Social Security Tax (use 6.2% × gross pay) .... $ _____

    7. Medicare Tax (use 1.45% × gross pay) .... $ _____

OTHER DEDUCTIONS

    8. Insurance. .... $ _____

    9. Union Dues. .... $ _____

    10. Credit Union. .... $ _____

    11. Savings. .... $ _____

    12. Retirement. .... $ _____

    13. Charity. .... $ _____

    14. Other: _____ .... $ _____

    _____ .... _____

    TOTAL DEDUCTIONS (total lines 4 through 14) .... $ _____

    NET PAY (subtract total deductions from gross pay) .... $ _____

Activity 2.5 Employee Withholding Sheet

Directions: Complete the following Employee Withholding Sheet from the information given.

Terry Peterson, Social Security No. 999-00-2838, receives a weekly (4 times/month) paycheck. He is single and claims three allowances. His monthly salary is $1,600.

In addition to the required deductions, he also pays insurance premiums of $18 a week and sets aside 5 percent of his gross pay for retirement each week.

EMPLOYEE WITHHOLDING SHEET

Employee Name_____ Social Security Number _____

Pay Period: ☐ weekly   ☐ biweekly   ☐ monthly

Number of Allowances: _____   ☐ married   ☐ single

GROSS PAY

    1. Regular Wages: _____ hours at $_____ /hr. = $_____

or

    2. Regular Salary: =   _____

    3. Overtime: _____ hours at $_____ /hr. =   _____

    GROSS PAY . . . . $_____

REQUIRED DEDUCTIONS

    4. Federal Income Tax (use tax tables) . . . . $_____

    5. State Income Tax (use tax tables) . . . . $_____

    6. Social Security Tax (use 6.2% × gross pay) . . . . $_____

    7. Medicare Tax (use 1.45% × gross pay) . . . . $_____

OTHER DEDUCTIONS

    8. Insurance . . . . $_____

    9. Union Dues . . . . $_____

    10. Credit Union . . . . $_____

    11. Savings . . . . $_____

    12. Retirement . . . . $_____

    13. Charity . . . . $_____

    14. Other: _____ . . . . $_____

    _____ . . . . _____

    TOTAL DEDUCTIONS (total lines 4 through 14) . . . . $_____

    NET PAY (subtract total deductions from gross pay) . . . . $_____

Activity 2.6 Employee Benefits and Incentives

Directions: Interview two people who are working full time and have employee benefits and incentives. Ask them the following questions and then write a one-paragraph summary of your findings.

INTERVIEW #1 Job Title: _____

Do you belong to a union? _____   If so, which one: _____

Check the employee benefits and incentives that you receive:

_____ Sick Leave (if so, how many days a year) _____

_____ Personal Leave (if so, how many days a year) _____

_____ Paid Vacation (if so, how many days a year) _____

_____ Paid Holidays (if so, how many days a year) _____

_____ Profit Sharing or Stock Options

_____ Retirement Plan, such as 401(k)

_____ Annual Bonus

_____ Health Insurance

_____ Group Disability and Life Insurance

_____ Group Dental and Vision Insurance

_____ Other: _____

Of all the employee benefits and incentives you receive, which one is the most valuable to you? Why?

_____

_____

INTERVIEW #2 Job Title: _____

Do you belong to a union? _____   If so, which one: _____

Check the employee benefits and incentives that you receive:

_____ Sick Leave (if so, how many days a year) _____

_____ Personal Leave (if so, how many days a year) _____

_____ Paid Vacation (if so, how many days a year) _____

_____ Paid Holidays (if so, how many days a year) _____

_____ Profit Sharing or Stock Options

_____ Retirement Plan, such as 401(k)

_____ Annual Bonus

_____ Health Insurance

_____ Group Disability and Life Insurance

_____ Group Dental and Vision Insurance

_____ Other: _____

Of all the employee benefits and incentives you receive, which one is the most valuable to you? Why?

_____

_____

chapter 3 Income Tax

1 section: vocabulary

Fill in the missing word(s) in the space provided at the right.

Answers

Example: Money in this country is collected from citizens and redistributed according to priorities determined by _____.

0. ___Congress___

1. Incoming taxes, which are treated as income by the government, are called _____.

1. _____

2. A tax that increases in proportion to increases in income is known as a(n) _____ tax.

2. _____

3. After the standard deduction and exemptions are subtracted from adjusted gross income, you arrive at your _____ income.

3. _____

4. In order to avoid itemizing deductions, a person may elect to take the _____, which is a flat amount.

4. _____

5. Money paid to a former spouse (which is taxable income) for that person's support is called _____.

5. _____

6. Money paid to a former spouse (which is not taxable income) for the support of dependent children is called _____.

6. _____

7. Expenses that can be subtracted from adjusted gross income to determine your taxable income are called _____.

7. _____

8. The amount remaining when adjustments are subtracted from gross income is called _____.

8. _____

9. When all sources of taxable income are added together, the total is called _____ income.

9. _____

10. An amount that can be subtracted from your income for each person who depends on your income to live is a(n) _____.

10. _____

11. A(n) _____ tax allows a higher-income person to pay a lower percentage of income in taxes than a lower-income person.

11. _____

12. To intentionally fail to pay taxes owed is to commit a serious crime called _____.

12. _____

13. A tax system that is based on _____ requires all citizens to be responsible for preparing and filing their tax returns on time and paying taxes due.

13. _____

14. A type of tax for which the rate stays the same regardless of income is called _____.

14. _____

15. A(n) _____ is an amount subtracted directly from tax owed.

15. _____

16. An administrative agency of the federal government that collects taxes and enforces tax laws is the _____.

16. _____

17. An examination of tax returns by the IRS is called a(n) _____.

17. _____

2 section:
review questions

After each of the following statements, circle *T* for a true statement or *F* for a false statement.

	Answers	For Scoring
1. The income tax is an example of a progressive tax.	T F	1. _____
2. Unemployment compensation benefits received are taxable to the person who receives them.	T F	2. _____
3. The power to levy federal income taxes rests with the U.S. Congress.	T F	3. _____
4. You may not use short Form 1040EZ for a joint return if your total taxable income is $20,000 or more.	T F	4. _____
5. Only a married person is considered a head of household.	T F	5. _____
6. Child support is taxable to the person receiving it and is deductible to the one paying it.	T F	6. _____
7. Money received in the form of wages, tips, salaries, or interest is taxable income.	T F	7. _____
8. A taxpayer's filing status is unrelated to his or her marital status.	T F	8. _____
9. The Internal Revenue Service is an agency of the Department of the Treasury.	T F	9. _____
10. You can file an amended tax return (1040X) if you discover you made an error.	T F	10. _____

On the line at the right of each sentence, print the letter that represents the word or group of words correctly completing the sentence or answering the question.

1. To compute your tax liability, turn to the tax tables and look up the amount called (a) take-home pay, (b) gross income, (c) adjusted gross income, (d) taxable income.   _____ 1. _____

2. Which of these is a form of flat tax? (a) income tax, (b) sales tax, (c) property tax, (d) excise tax   _____ 2. _____

3. Tax returns must be filed by _____ of the following year. (a) January 1, (b) January 31, (c) April 15, (d) December 31   _____ 3. _____

4. As an alternative to itemizing deductions, taxpayers may (a) file Form 1040EZ, (b) file Form 1040A, (c) claim the standard deduction, (d) claim more exemptions.   _____ 4. _____

5. A sales tax on specific products and services is a(n) _____ tax. (a) income, (b) property, (c) consumption or use, (d) flat   _____ 5. _____

6. What type of IRS audit requires a taxpayer to appear in person and bring records? (a) correspondence, (b) office, (c) field, (d) research   _____ 6. _____

7. For people who use Form 1040EZ or 1040A, the IRS allows (a) electronic filing of tax returns, (b) electronic payment of taxes due, (c) both of these, (d) neither of these.   _____ 7. _____

8. Student loan interest and tuition can be listed as _____ on Form 1040A. (a) exemptions, (b) adjustments to gross income, (c) tax credits, (d) taxable income   _____ 8. _____

3 section:
problem solving

Activity 3.1 Form 1040EZ

Directions: Complete the Form 1040EZ below, based on this information: Georgina B. Bales, 485 West 11th Avenue, Ogden, UT 87666-6723. Her Social Security number is 999-00-8478. She does not want $3 to go to the campaign fund. She is single and claims herself (no one else can claim her). As a part-time clerk, she earned $14,500 last year, plus $200 interest on savings. Taxes withheld were $1,016. (Refer to Figure 3.5 in your textbook for the tax table.)

Department of the Treasury—Internal Revenue Service	

Form 1040EZ

Income Tax Return for Single and Joint Filers With No Dependents (99)   **20--**   OMB No. 1545-0074

Your first name and initial	Last name	Your social security number
If a joint return, spouse's first name and initial	Last name	Spouse's social security number

Home address (number and street). If you have a P.O. box, see instructions.	Apt. no.	▲ Make sure the SSN(s) above are correct.
City, town or post office, state, and ZIP code. If you have a foreign address, also complete spaces below (see instructions).		**Presidential Election Campaign** Check here if you, or your spouse if filing jointly, want $3 to go to this fund. Checking a box below will not change your tax or refund. ☐ You ☐ Spouse

Foreign country name	Foreign province/state/county	Foreign postal code

Income

Attach Form(s) W-2 here.

Enclose, but do not attach, any payment.

1   Wages, salaries, and tips. This should be shown in box 1 of your Form(s) W-2. Attach your Form(s) W-2.   **1**

2   Taxable interest. If the total is over $1,500, you cannot use Form 1040EZ.   **2**

3   Unemployment compensation and Alaska Permanent Fund dividends (see instructions).   **3**

4   Add lines 1, 2, and 3. This is your **adjusted gross income.**   **4**

5   If someone can claim you (or your spouse if a joint return) as a dependent, check the applicable box(es) below and enter the amount from the worksheet on back.
   ☐ **You**   ☐ **Spouse**
If no one can claim you (or your spouse if a joint return), enter $10,000 if **single;** $20,000 if **married filing jointly.** See back for explanation.   **5**

6   Subtract line 5 from line 4. If line 5 is larger than line 4, enter -0-. This is your **taxable income.**   ▶ **6**

Payments, Credits, and Tax

7   Federal income tax withheld from Form(s) W-2 and 1099.   **7**

8a   **Earned income credit (EIC)** (see instructions).   **8a**

b   Nontaxable combat pay election.   8b

9   Add lines 7 and 8a. These are your **total payments and credits.**   ▶ **9**

10   **Tax.** Use the amount on **line 6 above** to find your tax in the tax table in the instructions. Then, enter the tax from the table on this line.   **10**

Refund

Have it directly deposited! See instructions and fill in 11b, 11c, and 11d or Form 8888.

11a   If line 9 is larger than line 10, subtract line 10 from line 9. This is your **refund.** If Form 8888 is attached, check here ▶ ☐   **11a**

▶ b   Routing number   ▶ c Type: ☐ Checking ☐ Savings

▶ d   Account number

Amount You Owe

12   If line 10 is larger than line 9, subtract line 9 from line 10. This is the **amount you owe.** For details on how to pay, see instructions.   ▶ **12**

Third Party Designee

Do you want to allow another person to discuss this return with the IRS (see instructions)? ☐ **Yes.** Complete below. ☐ **No**

Designee's name ▶   Phone no. ▶   Personal identification number (PIN) ▶

Sign Here

Joint return? See instructions.

Keep a copy for your records.

Under penalties of perjury, I declare that I have examined this return and, to the best of my knowledge and belief, it is true, correct, and accurately lists all amounts and sources of income I received during the tax year. Declaration of preparer (other than the taxpayer) is based on all information of which the preparer has any knowledge.

Your signature	Date	Your occupation	Daytime phone number
Spouse's signature. If a joint return, **both** must sign.	Date	Spouse's occupation	If the IRS sent you an Identity Protection PIN, enter it here (see inst.)

Paid Preparer Use Only

Print/Type preparer's name	Preparer's signature	Date	Check ☐ if self-employed	PTIN
Firm's name ▶		Firm's EIN ▶		
Firm's address ▶		Phone no.		

For Disclosure, Privacy Act, and Paperwork Reduction Act Notice, see instructions.   Cat. No. 11329W   Form **1040EZ** (20--)

Activity 3.2 Taxpayer Advocate Services

Directions: Read the material below and answer the questions that follow.

The Taxpayer Advocate Service is an IRS program that provides an independent service to taxpayers. The National Taxpayer Advocate heads the program; each state has at least one taxpayer advocate. The taxpayer advocate is independent of the IRS. The goals of this service are to protect individual taxpayer rights, to improve customer service, and to reduce taxpayer burden.

The taxpayer advocate represents your interests and concerns by ensuring that taxpayer problems are resolved promptly and handled fairly. The advocate will listen to your point of view and work to address your concerns. The service is available to taxpayers suffering from hardships, including excessive professional fees (accounting and/or legal). It specializes in informing you, the taxpayer, about your rights when dealing with the IRS and helping to resolve claims. In some instances, enforcement (collection) action may be suspended while your case is being reviewed. Most cases are resolved without the need for court appearances. The National Taxpayer Advocate reports to Congress twice a year, summarizing problems and making recommendations. You can locate the Taxpayer Advocate Service online at www.irs.gov/advocate.

1. How might you use the services provided by the Taxpayer Advocate Service?

_____

_____

_____

_____

_____

_____

_____

2. What benefit is there to having such a service, even if the average taxpayer never uses it?

_____

_____

_____

_____

_____

_____

_____

_____

Chapter Project: Form 1040EZ

Directions: As part of the Chapter Project at the end of Chapter 3 in your textbook, complete the Form 1040EZ below based on this information: Ronald B. Mitchell, 218 SW 82d Avenue, Portland, OR 97262-8645. His Social Security number is 999-00-3833. He works part time while attending college but is not claimed on another person's return. He earned $12,000 in salary and $455 in tips (shown on his W-2). He is single and claims himself as an exemption. He has $200 interest from savings and $400 withheld in taxes. He does not wish to give $3 to the campaign fund. (Refer to Figure 3.5 in your textbook for the tax table.)

Form **1040EZ**	Department of the Treasury—Internal Revenue Service **Income Tax Return for Single and Joint Filers With No Dependents** (99)	**20--**	OMB No. 1545-0074

Your first name and initial | Last name | Your social security number

If a joint return, spouse's first name and initial | Last name | Spouse's social security number

Home address (number and street). If you have a P.O. box, see instructions. | Apt. no. | ▲ Make sure the SSN(s) above are correct.

City, town or post office, state, and ZIP code. If you have a foreign address, also complete spaces below (see instructions).

Presidential Election Campaign — Check here if you, or your spouse if filing jointly, want $3 to go to this fund. Checking a box below will not change your tax or refund. ☐ You ☐ Spouse

Foreign country name | Foreign province/state/county | Foreign postal code

Income — Attach Form(s) W-2 here. Enclose, but do not attach, any payment.

1. Wages, salaries, and tips. This should be shown in box 1 of your Form(s) W-2. Attach your Form(s) W-2. **1**
2. Taxable interest. If the total is over $1,500, you cannot use Form 1040EZ. **2**
3. Unemployment compensation and Alaska Permanent Fund dividends (see instructions). **3**
4. Add lines 1, 2, and 3. This is your **adjusted gross income.** **4**
5. If someone can claim you (or your spouse if a joint return) as a dependent, check the applicable box(es) below and enter the amount from the worksheet on back. ☐ You ☐ Spouse. If no one can claim you (or your spouse if a joint return), enter $10,000 if **single**; $20,000 if **married filing jointly.** See back for explanation. **5**
6. Subtract line 5 from line 4. If line 5 is larger than line 4, enter -0-. This is your **taxable income.** ▶ **6**

Payments, Credits, and Tax

7. Federal income tax withheld from Form(s) W-2 and 1099. **7**
8a. **Earned income credit (EIC)** (see instructions). **8a**
b. Nontaxable combat pay election. **8b**
9. Add lines 7 and 8a. These are your **total payments and credits.** ▶ **9**
10. **Tax.** Use the amount on **line 6 above** to find your tax in the tax table in the instructions. Then, enter the tax from the table on this line. **10**

Refund — Have it directly deposited! See instructions and fill in 11b, 11c, and 11d or Form 8888.

11a. If line 9 is larger than line 10, subtract line 10 from line 9. This is your **refund.** If Form 8888 is attached, check here ▶ ☐ **11a**
b. Routing number | ▶ c Type: ☐ Checking ☐ Savings
d. Account number

Amount You Owe

12. If line 10 is larger than line 9, subtract line 9 from line 10. This is the **amount you owe.** For details on how to pay, see instructions. ▶ **12**

Third Party Designee — Do you want to allow another person to discuss this return with the IRS (see instructions)? ☐ Yes. Complete below. ☐ No
Designee's name ▶ | Phone no. ▶ | Personal identification number (PIN) ▶

Sign Here — Under penalties of perjury, I declare that I have examined this return and, to the best of my knowledge and belief, it is true, correct, and accurately lists all amounts and sources of income I received during the tax year. Declaration of preparer (other than the taxpayer) is based on all information of which the preparer has any knowledge.
Joint return? See instructions. Keep a copy for your records.
Your signature | Date | Your occupation | Daytime phone number
Spouse's signature. If a joint return, **both** must sign. | Date | Spouse's occupation | If the IRS sent you an Identity Protection PIN, enter it here (see inst.)

Paid Preparer Use Only
Print/Type preparer's name | Preparer's signature | Date | Check ☐ if self-employed | PTIN
Firm's name ▶ | Firm's EIN ▶
Firm's address ▶ | Phone no.

For Disclosure, Privacy Act, and Paperwork Reduction Act Notice, see instructions. | Cat. No. 11329W | Form **1040EZ** (20--)

Chapter Project: Form 1040A

Directions: As part of the Chapter Project, learn how to prepare Form 1040A by downloading the Form 1040A instructions from the IRS website (www.irs.gov). Then complete Form 1040A on the following pages, based on the W-2 statement below and other information for Mr. and Mrs. O'Leary.

James P. O'Leary is a plumber; Annette L. O'Leary earned $4,000 babysitting. Her Social Security number is 999-00-3829. They both want $3 to go to the presidential campaign. They are filing jointly and have two children, Emily and Matthew, 999-00-2899 and 999-00-8988, respectively. They also had interest income of $800. Their tax-exempt interest income was $482. Annette also received $2,000 in unemployment compensation benefits. James had an IRA of $2,000. James and Annette have determined from the 1040A tax table that their total tax is $1,961. (NOTE: Do NOT use the tax table in the textbook. The Form 1040A tax table can be found in the Form 1040A instructions at the IRS website at www.irs.gov.)

22222	**a** Employee's social security number 999-00-3898	OMB No. 1545-0008		
b Employer identification number (EIN)			**1** Wages, tips, other compensation $42,000.00	**2** Federal income tax withheld $2,985.00
c Employer's name, address, and ZIP code J. T. Harris Company 40 West Century Blvd. San Diego, CA 96210-6238			**3** Social security wages $42,000.00	**4** Social security tax withheld $2,604.00
			5 Medicare wages and tips $42,000.00	**6** Medicare tax withheld $609.00
			7 Social security tips	**8** Allocated tips
d Control number			**9** Advance EIC payment	**10** Dependent care benefits
e Employee's first name and initial　　Last name　　Suff. James P. O'Leary 44 West 182nd Avenue #33 San Diego, CA 96210-6180			**11** Nonqualified plans	**12a**
			13 Statutory employee　Retirement plan　Third-party sick pay	**12b**
			14 Other	**12c**
				12d
f Employee's address and ZIP code				

15 State　Employer's state ID number CA　311-314	**16** State wages, tips, etc. $42,000.00	**17** State income tax $2,940.00	**18** Local wages, tips, etc.	**19** Local income tax	**20** Locality name

Form **W-2** Wage and Tax Statement　　**20--**　　Department of the Treasury—Internal Revenue Service

Copy 1—For State, City, or Local Tax Department

Chapter Project: Form 1040A (continued)

Form **1040A**	Department of the Treasury—Internal Revenue Service **U.S. Individual Income Tax Return** (99)	**20--**	IRS Use Only—Do not write or staple in this space.

OMB No. 1545-0074

Your first name and initial	Last name	**Your social security number**

If a joint return, spouse's first name and initial	Last name	**Spouse's social security number**

Home address (number and street). If you have a P.O. box, see instructions.	Apt. no.	▲ Make sure the SSN(s) above and on line 6c are correct.

City, town or post office, state, and ZIP code. If you have a foreign address, also complete spaces below (see instructions).

Presidential Election Campaign
Check here if you, or your spouse if filing jointly, want $3 to go to this fund. Checking a box below will not change your tax or refund. ☐ You ☐ Spouse

Foreign country name	Foreign province/state/county	Foreign postal code

Filing status
Check only one box.

1 ☐ Single
2 ☐ Married filing jointly (even if only one had income)
3 ☐ Married filing separately. Enter spouse's SSN above and full name here. ▶
4 ☐ Head of household (with qualifying person). (See instructions.) If the qualifying person is a child but not your dependent, enter this child's name here. ▶
5 ☐ Qualifying widow(er) with dependent child (see instructions)

Exemptions

If more than six dependents, see instructions.

6a ☐ **Yourself.** If someone can claim you as a dependent, **do not** check box 6a.
b ☐ **Spouse**
c **Dependents:**

(1) First name Last name	(2) Dependent's social security number	(3) Dependent's relationship to you	(4) ✓ if child under age 17 qualifying for child tax credit (see instructions)
			☐
			☐
			☐
			☐
			☐
			☐

Boxes checked on 6a and 6b ___
No. of children on 6c who:
• lived with you ___
• did not live with you due to divorce or separation (see instructions) ___
Dependents on 6c not entered above ___
Add numbers on lines above ▶ ___

d Total number of exemptions claimed.

Income

Attach Form(s) W-2 here. Also attach Form(s) 1099-R if tax was withheld.

If you did not get a W-2, see instructions.

7 Wages, salaries, tips, etc. Attach Form(s) W-2.   7
8a **Taxable** interest. Attach Schedule B if required.   8a
b **Tax-exempt** interest. **Do not** include on line 8a.   8b
9a Ordinary dividends. Attach Schedule B if required.   9a
b Qualified dividends (see instructions).   9b
10 Capital gain distributions (see instructions).   10
11a IRA distributions.   11a   11b Taxable amount (see instructions).   11b
12a Pensions and annuities.   12a   12b Taxable amount (see instructions).   12b
13 Unemployment compensation and Alaska Permanent Fund dividends.   13
14a Social security benefits.   14a   14b Taxable amount (see instructions).   14b
15 Add lines 7 through 14b (far right column). This is your **total income.** ▶   15

Adjusted gross income

16 Educator expenses (see instructions).   16
17 IRA deduction (see instructions).   17
18 Student loan interest deduction (see instructions).   18
19 Tuition and fees. Attach Form 8917.   19
20 Add lines 16 through 19. These are your **total adjustments.**   20
21 Subtract line 20 from line 15. This is your **adjusted gross income.** ▶   21

For Disclosure, Privacy Act, and Paperwork Reduction Act Notice, see separate instructions.   Cat. No. 11327A   Form **1040A** (20__)

Chapter Project: Form 1040A (continued)

Form 1040A (20__)			Page **2**
Tax, credits, and payments	**22** Enter the amount from line 21 (adjusted gross income).	**22**	
	23a Check if: ☐ **You** were born before January 2, 1949, ☐ Blind ☐ **Spouse** was born before January 2, 1949, ☐ Blind } Total boxes checked ▶ 23a ☐		
	b If you are married filing separately and your spouse itemizes deductions, check here ▶ 23b ☐		
Standard Deduction for— • People who check any box on line 23a or 23b **or** who can be claimed as a dependent, see instructions. • All others: Single or Married filing separately, $6,100 Married filing jointly or Qualifying widow(er), $12,200 Head of household, $8,950	**24** Enter your **standard deduction.**	**24**	
	25 Subtract line 24 from line 22. If line 24 is more than line 22, enter -0-.	**25**	
	26 **Exemptions.** Multiply $3,900 by the number on line 6d.	**26**	
	27 Subtract line 26 from line 25. If line 26 is more than line 25, enter -0-. This is your **taxable income.** ▶ 27	**27**	
	28 **Tax,** including any alternative minimum tax (see instructions).	**28**	
	29 Credit for child and dependent care expenses. Attach Form 2441. 29		
	30 Credit for the elderly or the disabled. Attach Schedule R. 30		
	31 Education credits from Form 8863, line 19. 31		
	32 Retirement savings contributions credit. Attach Form 8880. 32		
	33 Child tax credit. Attach Schedule 8812, if required. 33		
	34 Add lines 29 through 33. These are your **total credits.**	**34**	
	35 Subtract line 34 from line 28. If line 34 is more than line 28, enter -0-. This is your **total tax.**	**35**	
	36 Federal income tax withheld from Forms W-2 and 1000. 36		
If you have a qualifying child, attach Schedule EIC.	**37** 2013 estimated tax payments and amount applied from 2012 return. 37		
	38a **Earned income credit (EIC).** 38a		
	b Nontaxable combat pay election. 38b		
	39 Additional child tax credit. Attach Schedule 8812. 39		
	40 American opportunity credit from Form 8863, line 8. 40		
	41 Add lines 36, 37, 38a, 39, and 40. These are your **total payments.** ▶ 41		
Refund Direct deposit? See instructions and fill in 43b, 43c, and 43d or Form 8888.	**42** If line 41 is more than line 35, subtract line 35 from line 41. This is the amount you **overpaid.**	**42**	
	43a Amount of line 42 you want **refunded to you.** If Form 8888 is attached, check here ▶ ☐ 43a		
	▶ **b** Routing number ☐☐☐☐☐☐☐☐☐ ▶ **c** Type: ☐ Checking ☐ Savings		
	▶ **d** Account number ☐☐☐☐☐☐☐☐☐☐☐☐☐☐☐☐☐		
	44 Amount of line 42 you want **applied to your 2014 estimated tax.** 44		
Amount you owe	**45** **Amount you owe.** Subtract line 41 from line 35. For details on how to pay, see instructions. ▶ 45		
	46 Estimated tax penalty (see instructions). 46		
Third party designee	Do you want to allow another person to discuss this return with the IRS (see instructions)? ☐ **Yes.** Complete the following. ☐ **No** Designee's name ▶ ___ Phone no. ▶ ___ Personal identification number (PIN) ▶ ☐☐☐☐☐		
Sign here Joint return? See instructions. Keep a copy for your records.	Under penalties of perjury, I declare that I have examined this return and accompanying schedules and statements, and to the best of my knowledge and belief, they are true, correct, and accurately list all amounts and sources of income I received during the tax year. Declaration of preparer (other than the taxpayer) is based on all information of which the preparer has any knowledge.		
	Your signature Date Your occupation Daytime phone number		
	Spouse's signature. If a joint return, **both** must sign. Date Spouse's occupation If the IRS sent you an Identity Protection PIN, enter it here (see inst.)		
Paid preparer use only	Print/type preparer's name Preparer's signature Date Check ▶ ☐ if self-employed PTIN		
	Firm's name ▶ Firm's EIN ▶		
	Firm's address ▶ Phone no.		
			Form **1040A** (20__)

chapter 4

Budgets and Records

1 section:

vocabulary

Fill in the missing word(s) in the space provided at the right.

Example: All the money you receive is either _____, saved, or invested.   0. ___spent___

1. A set of goals for spending, saving, and investing the money you receive is known as a(n) _____.   1. _____

2. Money you have to spend as you wish—after all required taxes and deductions—is known as _____.   2. _____

3. A(n) _____ is an organized plan whereby you match your expected income with expenses and savings.   3. _____

4. A(n) _____ exists when estimated income exceeds estimated expenses.   4. _____

5. A(n) _____ exists when estimated expenses are greater than estimated income.   5. _____

6. Expenses that remain constant and cannot be easily changed or removed from a budget are called _____ expenses.   6. _____

7. Expenses that may change according to needs and short-term goals are called _____ expenses.   7. _____

8. A(n) _____ is a list of valuable items you own, along with their purchase prices and current values.   8. _____

9. Items of value that a person owns are called _____.   9. _____

10. Amounts of money owed to others, also known as debts, are called _____.   10. _____

11. When you subtract your debts from the total amount of things you own, the difference is known as _____.   11. _____

12. Items of value in your home, such as appliances, are called _____ property.   12. _____

13. A legally enforceable agreement between two or more parties to do or not to do something is a(n) _____.   13. _____

14. Unwritten agreements, often called _____ contracts, are created by the actions or conduct of someone.   14. _____

15. Something of value exchanged as part of a contract is called _____.   15. _____

16. _____ refers to the legal ability of persons to enter into legally binding agreements.   16. _____

17. A(n) _____ is an unconditional promise to pay money upon demand, most commonly in the form of a check.   17. _____

18. When a document is _____, the signature is verified by a notary public.   18. _____

19. The person who creates and signs a promissory note is called the _____.   19. _____

20. The person to whom a negotiable instrument is made payable is called the _____.

20. _____

21. The word _____ means legally collectible.

21. _____

22. A(n) _____ program organizes data in columns and rows and performs calculations using the data.

22. _____

2 section: review questions

After each of the following statements, circle *T* for a true statement or *F* for a false statement.

	Answers	For Scoring
1. A major reason for financial planning is to prevent careless spending.	T F	1. _____
2. To prepare your personal budget, you should first list sources of money you expect to receive, known as income.	T F	2. _____
3. Receipts and documents showing income and expenses should be kept in a safe place because they are proof or evidence to use in the event of an audit.	T F	3. _____
4. When your assets are less than your liabilities, you are said to be solvent, which is a good financial position.	T F	4. _____
5. A written agreement between two or more persons is known as an implied contract.	T F	5. _____
6. Minors are said to have limited contractual capacity to enter into an agreement.	T F	6. _____
7. A promissory note is an example of a negotiable instrument.	T F	7. _____
8. The Statute of Frauds requires that all contracts be in writing to be enforceable.	T F	8. _____
9. A cosigner is responsible for your debts only if you miss three or more payments.	T F	9. _____
10. Original documents, such as insurance policies and wills, should be kept in a safe deposit box.	T F	10. _____
11. An advantage of an electronic filing system is the ease of updating information.	T F	11. _____
12. Fixed expenses remain the same from month to month.	T F	12. _____
13. Net worth is calculated by subtracting your variable expenses from your fixed expenses.	T F	13. _____
14. An express contract can only be written (not oral).	T F	14. _____

On the line at the right of each sentence, print the letter that represents the word or group of words correctly completing the sentence or answering the question.

	Answers	**For Scoring**

1. Most financial experts agree that families should set aside at least _____ percent of their disposable income each pay period. (a) 10, (b) 15, (c) 20, (d) 25   _____ 1. _____

2. Lunches, medical bills, personal care items, and clothing are all examples of (a) income, (b) fixed expenses, (c) variable expenses, (d) investments.   _____ 2. _____

3. A house payment and utilities are examples of (a) income, (b) fixed expenses, (c) variable expenses, (d) investments.   _____ 3. _____

4. A common purpose for the net worth statement is (a) fire-loss proof, (b) damage report, (c) loan or credit application, (d) employment application.   _____ 4. _____

5. A personal property inventory is most commonly used for (a) proof of loss from fire, theft, or property damage, (b) a car loan application, (c) a credit card application, (d) an employment application.   _____ 5. _____

6. The IRS can audit your tax returns for a period of _____ year(s), except in the case of fraud, where there is no time limit. (a) one, (b) three, (c) six, (d) ten   _____ 6. _____

7. Which of these is a liability? (a) car, (b) car loan, (c) stereo, (d) savings account   _____ 7. _____

8. When a person changes the terms of an offer, she or he has made a(n) (a) agreement, (b) acceptance, (c) counteroffer, (d) exchange.   _____ 8. _____

9. The price paid, which may be in the form of money, a promise, or an action, is known as a(n) (a) offer, (b) acceptance, (c) competent party, (d) consideration.   _____ 9. _____

10. Which of these is NOT required for a legally binding agreement? (a) counteroffer, (b) agreement, (c) consideration, (d) capacity   _____ 10. _____

11. When your assets are greater than your liabilities, you are said to be (a) responsible, (b) insolvent, (c) solvent, (d) rich.   _____ 11. _____

12. An agreement entered into orally is (a) enforceable, (b) unenforceable, (c) void, (d) voidable.   _____ 12. _____

13. All products contain a(n) _____, which includes merchantability or assurance that the product will do what it was designed to do. (a) full warranty, (b) implied warranty, (c) written warranty, (d) limited warranty   _____ 13. _____

3 | section: problem solving

Activity 4.1 Simple Budget

Directions: Using Figure 4.1 (simple budget) in your textbook as an example, prepare a simple budget for yourself on the following form, listing your expected income, expenses, and savings.

Budget for _____

Income:

_____ .... $_____

_____ .... _____

_____ .... _____

Total Income .... $_____

Expenses:

_____ .... $_____

_____ .... $_____

_____ .... $_____

_____ .... $_____

_____ .... $_____

Total Expenses .... $_____

Savings:

_____ .... _____

Total expenses plus savings .... $_____

Activity 4.2 Budget for Margaret Brown

Directions: Prepare a monthly and yearly budget for Margaret Brown based on the information given. Margaret is single and lives alone in a rented apartment.

Monthly net pay totals	$1,620
Interest income on savings	400
Total income (average)	$2,020

Average monthly expenses:

Rent	$750	Cell phone	50
Utilities	100	Groceries	200
Gasoline	80	Miscellaneous	75
Insurance	125	Personal care	35
Clothing	65	Gifts and donations	10
Recreation/entertainment	100	Savings/Investments	
Car payment	220	Stocks (mutual fund)	75
Car repair/maintenance	40	Savings account	To be determined

Budget
Margaret Brown

	Monthly	Yearly
Income		
Net paychecks	$_____	$_____
Other income	_____	_____
Total income	$_____	$_____
Expenses		
Fixed expenses:		
Rent	$_____	$_____
Utilities	_____	_____
Car payment	_____	_____
Insurance	_____	_____
Total fixed expenses	$_____	$_____
Variable expenses:		
Cell phone	$_____	$_____
Gasoline	_____	_____
Car repairs and maintenance	_____	_____
Cable television/Internet	_____	_____
Groceries	_____	_____
Clothing	_____	_____
Personal care	_____	_____
Recreation and entertainment	_____	_____
Gifts and donations	_____	_____
Miscellaneous	_____	_____
Other	_____	_____
Total variable expenses	$_____	$_____
Total fixed and variable expenses	$_____	$_____
Cash surplus (total income minus total expenses)	$_____	$_____
Allocation of surplus:		
_____	$_____	$_____
_____	_____	_____

Activity 4.3 Revised Budget for Margaret Brown

Directions: Prepare a revised monthly and yearly budget for Margaret Brown. She will share an apartment with a friend; some expenses, such as rent and utilities, can be divided between the roommates. But other expenses such as the car payment, insurance, cell phone, and car maintenance will not change. Rent increases to $1,200 per month and utilities increase to $120 per month, but these expenses will be shared equally. Cable TV and Internet service will be added ($120 per month), which can be split. All the other expenses remain the same. Margaret wants to know how much more she can set aside for savings.

Budget
Margaret Brown

Income	Monthly	Yearly
Net paychecks	$_____	$_____
Other Income..	_____	_____
Total Income..	$_____	$_____
Expenses		
Fixed expenses:		
Rent..	$_____	$_____
Utilities..	_____	_____
Car payment..	_____	_____
Insurance..	_____	_____
Total fixed expenses...	$_____	$_____
Variable expenses:		
Cell phone..	$_____	$_____
Gasoline	_____	_____
Car repairs and maintenance	_____	_____
Cable television/Internet..................................	_____	_____
Groceries...	_____	_____
Clothing	_____	_____
Personal care..	_____	_____
Recreation and entertainment	_____	_____
Gifts and donations...	_____	_____
Miscellaneous	_____	_____
Other:	_____	_____
Total variable expenses	$_____	$_____
Total fixed and variable expenses	$_____	$_____
Cash surplus (total income minus total expenses)	$_____	$_____
Allocation of surplus:		
_____	$_____	$_____
_____	_____	_____

Activity 4.4 Net Worth Statement

Directions: Prepare a personal net worth statement based on what you own (assets) and what you owe (liabilities). Compute your net worth. (See Figure 4.3 in your textbook.)

Net Worth Statement

_____

_____

ASSETS		LIABILITIES	
_____ . . . . $_____		_____ . . . . . . $_____	
_____ . . . . $_____		_____ . . . . . . $_____	
_____ . . . . $_____		_____ . . . . . . $_____	
Personal property (inventory attached) _____		Total liabilities . . . . $_____	
		NET WORTH	
		Assets – liabilities . . . . $_____	
Total assets . . . . $_____		Total . . . . $_____	

Activity 4.5 Net Worth Statement for Ben Lingo

Directions: Prepare a net worth statement for Ben Lingo based on this information: He owns a car worth $2,000, but owes $1,500 on it at the bank. Ben has $150 in his savings and $82 in his checking account. His personal property inventory totals $1,200, and he also owes $80 to his credit union. (See Figure 4.3 in your textbook.)

Net Worth Statement

_____

_____

ASSETS		LIABILITIES	
_____ . . . . . . $_____		_____ . . . . . . $_____	
_____ . . . . . . $_____		_____ . . . . . . $_____	
_____ . . . . . . $_____		_____ . . . . . . $_____	
Personal property (inventory attached) _____		Total liabilities . . . . $_____	
		NET WORTH	
		Assets – liabilities . . . . $_____	
Total assets . . . . $_____		Total . . . . $_____	

Activity 4.6 Personal Property Inventory

Directions: Prepare a personal property inventory, listing items of value that you have in your room and home. Use Figure 4.4 in your textbook as an example.

Personal Property Inventory

_____

_____

Item	Purchase Date	Purchase Price	Approximate Current Value
		$_____	$_____

Total
(photographs and/or receipts attached) $_____ $_____

Activity 4.7 Personal Property Inventory for Gene Bond

Directions: Using Figure 4.4 in your textbook, prepare a personal property inventory for Gene Bond based on the following information: He has a stereo system, Model AA (SN 22D147) that he bought in 2014 for $800, still worth $500; miscellaneous clothing and jewelry, now worth $400; and a queen-size bed given to him last year as a gift, now worth $200. His alarm clock, Model 210 (SN 115C28); digital camera, Model A41 (SN 5110); iPod; and watch were bought a few years ago and now have a value of about $100. Gene has a receipt for the purchase of the stereo system.

Personal Property Inventory

_____

_____

Item	Purchase Date	Purchase Price	Approximate Current Value
		$	$
Total (photographs and/or receipts attached)		$	$

Activities 4.8–4.9 Application Forms—Credit and Car Loan

Directions: Fill out the application forms on pages 37–38, using these directions for preparing the applications.

---

1. Use a pen with dark ink that does not skip or blot.

2. Write legibly and small enough that information will fit into the space provided.

3. Fill in all blanks with the information requested; if the question does not apply to you, use one of these:

   a.   N/A (meaning information not available or not applicable).

   b.   Fill in the space with a dash (—) to indicate that you saw the question but have no answer.

4. Read the form carefully and be sure you are answering the questions properly.

5. Be truthful in your responses.

6. Read all the small print before you sign the form.

7. Be as neat as possible.

8. Have with you pertinent information, such as telephone numbers, credit card numbers, references, driver's license number, Social Security number, and so on.

9. If you make a mistake, draw one line through it and write the correct information above or below it. Do not make big scratch marks on the paper.

Activity 4.8 Credit Application

CREDIT APPLICATION

	FIRST NAME	INITIAL	LAST NAME	SPOUSE'S NAME	MARITAL STATUS
MR. MS.					

PRESENT ADDRESS (STREET AND NUMBER)	HOW LONG?

CITY	STATE	ZIPCODE	PHONE NUMBER

PREVIOUS ADDRESS (IF LESS THAN 3 YEARS)	DATE OF BIRTH

NUMBER OF DEPENDENTS: RESIDENCE (check one)   OWN ☐   RENT ☐   LIVE WITH PARENTS ☐   AMOUNT OF RENT $

CREDIT APPLICATION / **EMPLOYMENT**

HUSBAND OR SINGLE PERSON	EMPLOYED BY		POSITION	SALARY	
	ADDRESS		PHONE	HOW LONG?	
WIFE	EMPLOYED BY		POSITION	SALARY	
	ADDRESS		PHONE	HOW LONG?	

FORMER EMPLOYER	POSITION	HOW LONG?

BANK	TYPE OF ACCOUNT	BRANCH	ADDRESS (CITY, STATE)

LIST ALL STORES, FIRMS, COMPANIES THAT HAVE GIVEN YOU CREDIT

FIRM NAME	ADDRESS	ACCOUNT NUMBER

PERSONAL REFERENCE: LIST ONE OR TWO PERSONS NOT RELATED TO OR LIVING WITH YOU:

NAME	ADDRESS	PHONE NUMBER

AUTHORIZED BUYER(S)	YOUR SOCIAL SECURITY NUMBER

RETAIL INSTALLMENT CREDIT AGREEMENT (buyer acknowledges reading this agreement by his or her signature appearing at the bottom hereof).

All unpaid balances on this account will be charged 1. 75% per month on the unpaid balance, for an annual rate of 21%. Any balances paid on the due date, or before, which due date shall be the 5th of each month for purchases billed during that month, will not be assessed a finance charge. Any payments made after the 5th of each month will be assessed a finance charge. Buyer acknowledges that finance charge will accrue on all unpaid balances after the 5th of the month following the billing date of this account.

All statements made in this application are warranted by buyer to be true and accurate.

DATE _____   APPLICANT'S SIGNATURE _____

Activity 4.9 Car Loan Application

CAR LOAN APPLICATION

Date _____

I hereby apply for a loan of $_____ repayable in _____ monthly installments beginning
_____. My checking account number is_____and you

☐ may
☐ may not

charge my account for the monthly payment.

CAR LOAN APPLICATION

Mr.
Ms. _____   Date of birth _____

No. of
dependents_____

_____Print clearly_____

Home address _____   Phone number_____
_____Number and street_____

How long
there?_____

Address
mail to

☐ home
☐ work

City   State   Zip

Previous address _____
_____Street_____   City   State   Zip

Nearest relative not
living with you _____
_____Name_____   Address   Relationship

EMPLOYMENT DATA

Name of company _____

Address _____

Years there _____ Position _____

Annual salary $ _____

Supervisor's name _____

BANK REFERENCES

Checking _____
_____Name of Bank_____   Branch

Savings _____
_____Name of Bank_____   Branch

OTHER INFORMATION

Social Security number _____

Spouse's name _____

Employer _____

AUTOMOBILE

Title in
name of _____

Make _____ Model _____ Year _____

Present value _____

Driver's license number _____

Any traffic tickets? _____If yes, explain on back.

EXISTING DEBTS

List here all loans, debts, and other amounts you now owe. If none, so state.

Name and address of creditor	Account #	Original Amt.	Balance	Monthly Pmt.

Name _____

Activity 4.10 Promissory Note

Directions: Following Figure 4.6 in your textbook, fill in the blanks of the following promissory note based on this information: The note is for $500, dated today. The maker is George Miller, and the payee is Fred Williams. The interest rate is 10%; amount is to be paid back in 12 equal installments of $45.83.

PROMISSORY NOTE

$_____   _____, 20_____

I (we) _____, jointly and severally,

do agree and promise to pay to _____

the sum of _____ dollars

with interest at the rate of _____% from _____, payable in

monthly installments of $_____ beginning _____*, 20_____

and on a like day each month until paid in full, the last payment due _____*,

20_____. Said payment shall include interest. In the event of default, the maker hereof

agrees to pay attorneys' fees and court costs in collection of this note.

_____
Maker

Activity 4.11 Minors and the Law

Directions: Read the material below and then answer the questions that follow.

A minor is a person under the age of legal adulthood. In most states, a person is legally an adult at age 18. When you turn 18, you take on all the rights and responsibilities of an adult (except some privileges that are reserved for age 21).

One way you can obtain full capacity to enter into binding agreements before you reach age 18 is to become emancipated. Being *emancipated* means that you are legally responsible for yourself. In most states, you can apply to be legally emancipated if you are employed and have the maturity and the means to support yourself. In other states, you cannot be emancipated prior to age 18 without permission from your parents. Emancipation is a serious undertaking. Once you are independent, you are not entitled to receive financial support or other benefits, such as health insurance coverage, from your parents.

When you are emancipated, you have the right to make your own decisions, and you also must accept full responsibility for the consequences of your actions. For example, if you commit a crime as an emancipated youth, you will face penalties that are appropriate for an adult. When you commit a crime as a minor, the juvenile justice system is designed to reform rather than to punish. In many states, you can have your juvenile record cleared or sealed after you become an adult.

Finally, once you are emancipated, you cannot reclaim your minority status. You will remain responsible for all future actions, contracts, and obligations.

1. What are some advantages of becoming emancipated?

_____

_____

_____

_____

_____

2. What are some disadvantages of emancipation?

_____

_____

_____

_____

3. What is the age of adulthood in your state? What rights are you given when you reach that age? Are some privileges deferred until later?

_____

_____

_____

_____

_____

1 section:
vocabulary

Fill in the missing word(s) in the space provided at the right.

Example: Banks, credit unions, and savings and loan associations are
examples of _____. 0. financial institutions

1. A(n) _____ is a banking service that allows customers to deposit money
that can be transferred to individuals or businesses for payment. 1. _____

2. An account on which the depositor can withdraw money at any time is
known as a(n) _____. 2. _____

3. A(n) _____ occurs when a depositor writes a check on an account that
is insufficient to cover a check. 3. _____

4. The person to whom a check is made payable is called the _____. 4. _____

5. The person who writes checks on an account is called the _____. 5. _____

6. A(n) _____ is like a check and is used by people who do not want
to use cash or who do not have a checking account. 6. _____

7. Paper money in the form of dollar bills, fives, tens, and so on,
is called _____. 7. _____

8. A(n) _____ is the record of checking account transactions, including
checks, online payments, and deposits, kept by the depositor. 8. _____

9. A(n) _____ is provided by the bank, listing online payments, checks, and
deposits processed by the bank, as well as charges and credits to an account. 9. _____

10. A(n) _____ account is often available to bank customers who have a
small amount of activity in their accounts each month. 10. _____

11. When the payee simply signs his or her name as it appears on the front of
the check, he or she is making a(n) _____ endorsement. 11. _____

12. A(n) _____ endorsement, such as "For Deposit Only," restricts or
limits the use of a check. 12. _____

13. _____ cards provide immediate deductions from your checking
account when you make a purchase. 13. _____

14. Savings accounts at credit unions are called _____. 14. _____

15. Writing a check while hoping to deposit money to cover it before
it clears is called a(n) _____. 15. _____

16. A(n) _____ is a check guaranteed by the bank. 16. _____

17. A check drawn against the bank's own funds is a(n) _____. 17. _____

18. The process of matching your checkbook register with the bank
statement is called _____. 18. _____

19. A request to the bank not to cash a check is a(n) _____. 19. _____

20. A bank account that is opened by two or more people is called a(n) _____. 20. _____

2 section: review questions

After each of the following statements, circle *T* for a true statement or *F* for a false statement.

		Answers	For Scoring
1.	Financial institutions usually do not charge a fee for checking account services.	T F	1. _____
2.	Most financial institutions offer online and telephone banking services.	T F	2. _____
3.	Electronic funds transfer (EFT) often involves the use of ATM machines.	T F	3. _____
4.	It is important to reconcile your checkbook immediately when you receive the bank statement.	T F	4. _____
5.	When a check you have issued has been lost or stolen, you should request a stop payment order.	T F	5. _____
6.	To open an account, either checking or savings, you first must fill out and sign a signature form.	T F	6. _____
7.	When a minimum balance is not maintained in a checking account, the bank will usually waive a service charge.	T F	7. _____
8.	A debit card is the same as a credit card.	T F	8. _____
9.	A money market account is an interest-bearing checking account that pays a higher rate of interest.	T F	9. _____
10.	With online banking, you can make deposits and withdrawals.	T F	10. _____

On the line at the right of each sentence, print the letter that represents the word or group of words correctly completing the sentence or answering the question.

1. What is a check written by a bank on its own funds called? (a) certified check, (b) cashier's check, (c) money order, (d) stop payment order _____ 1. _____

2. Checks over _____ old may not be honored by a bank. (a) two weeks, (b) four weeks, (c) three months, (d) six months _____ 2. _____

3. A _____ endorsement results when the payee signs over a check to a third person. (a) blank, (b) special, (c) restrictive, (d) joint _____ 3. _____

4. A check that has cleared your bank account is said to be a(n): (a) cashier's check, (b) certified check, (c) canceled check, (d) bounced check. _____ 4. _____

5. Insurance up to _____ on each account is provided for depositors by the FDIC. (a) $20,000, (b) $50,000, (c) $100,000, (d) $250,000 _____ 5. _____

6. When payment on a check is prevented by the bank before it can be made to the payee, it is a(n) (a) overdraft, (b) stop payment order, (c) cashier's check, (d) service fee. _____ 6. _____

7. A _____ is a personal check that the bank guarantees to be good. (a) cashier's check, (b) certified check, (c) money order, (d) stop payment order _____ 7. _____

8. A _____ is a safe place to keep stocks and bonds, deeds, and other important documents. (a) home file cabinet, (b) safe at work, (c) safe deposit box, (d) hotel safe _____ 8. _____

9. A(n) _____ account charges customers fees based on the number of checks written each month; a minimum balance is usually not required. (a) share draft, (b) regular, (c) special, (d) interest-bearing _____ 9. _____

3 section:
problem solving

Activity 5.1 Signature Forms

Directions: On the following signature form, fill in the appropriate information for yourself. (Provide a fictitious Social Security number.) Assume that you are opening an individual account.

FIRST INDEPENDENT MUTUAL SAVINGS BANK
CHECKING SIGNATURE VERIFICATION

Customer Name _____   Date _____

Account No. _____   Individual _____ Joint _____

Address _____   Daytime Phone _____

City/State/ZIP _____   Evening Phone _____

Social Security No. _____   DOB _____

Occupation _____   How long? _____

Employer _____   Phone _____

Contact in case of emergency: _____   Phone _____

Relationship _____

Mother's Maiden Name or other code word _____

JOINT ACCOUNT HOLDER (if any): _____

Customer Name _____   Date _____

Account No. _____   Individual _____ Joint _____

Address _____   Daytime Phone _____

City/State/ZIP _____   Evening Phone _____

Social Security No. _____   DOB _____

Occupation _____   How long? _____

Employer _____   Phone _____

Contact in case of emergency: _____   Phone _____

Relationship _____

Mother's Maiden Name or other code word _____

SIGNATURES: _____   #1 Date _____

_____   #2 Date _____

(Use second page if more signatures are needed.)

Directions: On the following signature form, fill in the appropriate information for a joint account, for you and a friend. (Provide fictitious Social Security numbers.) Both of you must sign the form.

FIRST INDEPENDENT MUTUAL SAVINGS BANK
CHECKING SIGNATURE VERIFICATION

Customer Name _____   Date _____

Account No. _____   Individual _____ Joint _____

Address _____   Daytime Phone _____

City/State/ZIP _____   Evening Phone _____

Social Security No. _____   DOB _____

Occupation _____   How long? _____

Employer _____   Phone _____

Contact in case of emergency: _____   Phone _____

Relationship _____

Mother's Maiden Name or other code word _____

JOINT ACCOUNT HOLDER (if any): _____

Customer Name _____   Date _____

Account No. _____   Individual _____ Joint _____

Address _____   Daytime Phone _____

City/State/ZIP _____   Evening Phone _____

Social Security No. _____   DOB _____

Occupation _____   How long? _____

Employer _____   Phone _____

Contact in case of emergency: _____   Phone _____

Relationship _____

Mother's Maiden Name or other code word _____

SIGNATURES: _____   #1 Date _____

_____   #2 Date _____

(Use second page if more signatures are needed.)

Activity 5.2 Checkbook Register and Bank Reconciliation

Directions: Complete the checkbook register by computing the balances and writing them in the appropriate column. Be sure to enter the service charge shown on the bank statement. Then reconcile the checkbook register with the bank statement.

PLEASE BE SURE TO <u>DEDUCT</u> ANY PER ITEM CHARGES OR SERVICE CHARGES THAT MAY APPLY TO YOUR ACCOUNT

ITEM NO.	DATE	PAYMENT ISSUED TO OR DESCRIPTION OF DEPOSIT	AMOUNT OF PAYMENT	✓	(−) CHECK FEE (IF ANY)	AMOUNT OF DEPOSIT	BALANCE FORWARD	
165	12/17	To **Economy Gas Co.**					Payment or Deposit	
		For **Gasoline**	18 50	✓			Balance	
166	12/18	To **P & D Insurance Co.**					Payment or Deposit	
		For **Insurance for 6 mos.**	76 00	✓			Balance	
167	12/18	To **XYZ Grocery Store**					Payment or Deposit	
		For **Groceries for 2 wks.**	101 00	✓			Balance	
168	12/19	To **County Hospital**					Payment or Deposit	
		For **Medical**	16 25	✓			Balance	
	12/22	To **Deposit**					Payment or Deposit	
		For **Paycheck**		✓		285 00	Balance	
169	12/23	To **Joe's Service Station**					Payment or Deposit	
		For **Car repair**	46 24				Balance	
170	12/26	To **Universal Telephone**					Payment or Deposit	
		For **Phone bill**	11 80				Balance	
	12/26	To **Deposit**					Payment or Deposit	
		For **Refund**				50 00	Balance	
		To					Payment or Deposit	
		For					Balance	

Bank Statement

HANK A. WILLIAMS
MARY B. WILLIAMS
10 SPEARS COURT
EUGENE, OR 97405-8762

For month ended DECEMBER 31, 20--:

Checks		Deposits	Balance
	12/15		285.00
18.50	12/22		266.50
76.00	12/23		190.50
101.00	12/23		89.50
16.25	12/27		73.25
	12/29	285.00	358.25
1.00SC	12/30		357.25
Ending Balance			357.25

Other charges and deductions: NONE

Bank Reconciliation

1. Write ending balance as shown on bank statement: _____

2. Add credits or deposits made that do not appear on statement: _____

3. Total lines 1 and 2: _____

4. Write total checks outstanding (not processed): _____

Check No.	Amount

5. Subtract line 4 from line 3 and write balance (should agree with checkbook balance): _____

Apply What You Know

Directions: The following blank checks and deposit slips are for use in completing Apply What You Know problems 1 and 2 at the end of Chapter 5 in your textbook.

HANK A. WILLIAMS
MARY B. WILLIAMS
10 SPEARS COURT
EUGENE, OR 97405-8762

NO. _____

_____ 20 _____ 96-7401
3232

PAY TO THE
ORDER OF _____ $ _____

_____ DOLLARS

FOR CLASSROOM USE ONLY

HERITAGE
BANK EUGENE, OR 97405-7110

MEMO _____

⑆323274018⑆ 0103 024ꞏꞏ90759⑈

HANK A. WILLIAMS
MARY B. WILLIAMS
10 SPEARS COURT
EUGENE, OR 97405-8762

NO. _____

_____ 20 _____ 96-7401
3232

PAY TO THE
ORDER OF _____ $ _____

_____ DOLLARS

FOR CLASSROOM USE ONLY

HERITAGE
BANK EUGENE, OR 97405-7110

MEMO _____

⑆323274018⑆ 0103 024ꞏꞏ90759⑈

HANK A. WILLIAMS
MARY B. WILLIAMS
10 SPEARS COURT
EUGENE, OR 97405-8762

NO. _____

_____ 20 _____ 96-7401
3232

PAY TO THE
ORDER OF _____ $ _____

_____ DOLLARS

FOR CLASSROOM USE ONLY

HERITAGE
BANK EUGENE, OR 97405-7110

MEMO _____

⑆323274018⑆ 0103 024ꞏꞏ90759⑈

FOR DEPOSIT TO THE ACCOUNT OF

HANK A. WILLIAMS
MARY B. WILLIAMS
10 SPEARS COURT
EUGENE, OR 97405-8762

DATE _____ 20 _____

SIGN HERE FOR CASH RECEIVED

HERITAGE
BANK EUGENE, OR 97405-7110

⑈32327401⑈ 024⑈90759⑈

	DOLLARS	CENTS
CASH →		
C H E C K S		
TOTAL FROM OTHER SIDE		
TOTAL		
LESS CASH RECEIVED		
NET DEPOSIT		

96-7401
3232

BE SURE
EACH ITEM
IS PROPERLY
ENDORSED

FOR CLASSROOM USE ONLY

CHECKS AND OTHER ITEMS ARE RECEIVED FOR DEPOSIT SUBJECT TO THE TERMS AND CONDITIONS OF THIS INSTITUTION'S COLLECTION AGREEMENT.

FOR DEPOSIT TO THE ACCOUNT OF

HANK A. WILLIAMS
MARY B. WILLIAMS
10 SPEARS COURT
EUGENE, OR 97405-8762

DATE _____ 20 _____

SIGN HERE FOR CASH RECEIVED

HERITAGE
BANK EUGENE, OR 97405-7110

⑈32327401⑈ 024⑈90759⑈

	DOLLARS	CENTS
CASH →		
C H E C K S		
TOTAL FROM OTHER SIDE		
TOTAL		
LESS CASH RECEIVED		
NET DEPOSIT		

96-7401
3232

BE SURE
EACH ITEM
IS PROPERLY
ENDORSED

FOR CLASSROOM USE ONLY

CHECKS AND OTHER ITEMS ARE RECEIVED FOR DEPOSIT SUBJECT TO THE TERMS AND CONDITIONS OF THIS INSTITUTION'S COLLECTION AGREEMENT.

Chapter Project

Use the following information to complete the Chapter Project at the end of Chapter 5 in your textbook.

GENERAL INSTRUCTIONS

1. Assume the name of either Hank A. Williams or Mary B. Williams.
2. Look at the following table and list all the checks in numeric order from 101 to 105. These numbers will be used for the checks, checkbook register, and bank reconciliation as check numbers. Complete Part A by filling in the forms using the information in the table.

	DATE	CHECK TO	REASON	AMOUNT
a.	May 1	Motor Parts	Car repair	$ 52.00
b.	May 1	Landlords Incorporated	Rent	300.00
c.	May 3	Food Stores, Inc.	Groceries	33.00
d.	May 7	Deposit	Paycheck (Check No. 7401)	822.00
e.	May 18	Dr. Susan Jones	Dental bill	42.00
f.	May 21	Dandee Department Store	On account	100.00
g.	May 28	Deposit	Loan repaid (cash)	30.00

3. Process each of the items in the table in chronological order for the checkbook register in Part B. Your balance brought forward is $502.00. Keep a balance after each payment or deposit.
4. Check the bank statement (statement of account) in Part C. Compare it to the checkbook register in Part B. Check off all payments and deposits in the checkbook register.
5. Enter any service charge that the bank statement may show.
6. Prepare the bank reconciliation.

Part A: Checks and Deposit Slips

HANK A. WILLIAMS
MARY B. WILLIAMS
10 SPEARS COURT
EUGENE, OR 97405-8762

NO. _____

_____ 20_____

96-7401
3232

PAY TO THE
ORDER OF _____ $ _____

_____ DOLLARS

FOR CLASSROOM USE ONLY

HERITAGE
BANK EUGENE, OR 97405-7110

MEMO _____   _____

⑈3232740⑈8⑈ 0⑈03 024⑈90759⑈

HANK A. WILLIAMS
MARY B. WILLIAMS
10 SPEARS COURT
EUGENE, OR 97405-8762

NO. _____

_____ 20 _____ 96-7401
3232

PAY TO THE
ORDER OF _____ $ _____

_____ DOLLARS

FOR CLASSROOM USE ONLY

HERITAGE
BANK EUGENE, OR 97405-7110

MEMO _____   _____

⑈323274018⑈ 0103 024⑈90759⑈

HANK A. WILLIAMS
MARY B. WILLIAMS
10 SPEARS COURT
EUGENE, OR 97405-8762

NO. _____

_____ 20 _____ 96-7401
3232

PAY TO THE
ORDER OF _____ $ _____

_____ DOLLARS

FOR CLASSROOM USE ONLY

HERITAGE
BANK EUGENE, OR 97405-7110

MEMO _____   _____

⑈323274018⑈ 0103 024⑈90759⑈

FOR DEPOSIT TO THE ACCOUNT OF

HANK A. WILLIAMS
MARY B. WILLIAMS
10 SPEARS COURT
EUGENE, OR 97405-8762

DATE _____ 20 _____

_____
SIGN HERE FOR CASH RECEIVED

HERITAGE
BANK EUGENE, OR 97405-7110

⑈323274018⑈   024⑈90759⑈

	DOLLARS	CENTS
CASH →		
C H E C K S		
TOTAL FROM OTHER SIDE		
TOTAL		
LESS CASH RECEIVED		
NET DEPOSIT		

96-7401
3232

BE SURE
EACH ITEM
IS PROPERLY
ENDORSED

FOR CLASSROOM USE ONLY

CHECKS AND OTHER ITEMS ARE RECEIVED FOR DEPOSIT SUBJECT TO THE TERMS AND CONDITIONS OF THIS INSTITUTION'S COLLECTION AGREEMENT.

HANK A. WILLIAMS
MARY B. WILLIAMS
10 SPEARS COURT
EUGENE, OR 97405-8762

NO. _____

_____ 20 _____ 96-7401 / 3232

PAY TO THE
ORDER OF _____ $ _____

_____ DOLLARS

FOR CLASSROOM USE ONLY

HERITAGE
BANK EUGENE, OR 97405-7110

MEMO _____ _____

⑆323274018⑆ 0103 024⑈90759⑆

HANK A. WILLIAMS
MARY B. WILLIAMS
10 SPEARS COURT
EUGENE, OR 97405-8762

NO. _____

_____ 20 _____ 96-7401 / 3232

PAY TO THE
ORDER OF _____ $ _____

_____ DOLLARS

FOR CLASSROOM USE ONLY

HERITAGE
BANK EUGENE, OR 97405-7110

MEMO _____ _____

⑆323274018⑆ 0103 024⑈90759⑆

FOR DEPOSIT TO THE ACCOUNT OF

HANK A. WILLIAMS
MARY B. WILLIAMS
10 SPEARS COURT
EUGENE, OR 97405-8762

DATE _____ 20 _____

_____
SIGN HERE FOR CASH RECEIVED

HERITAGE
BANK EUGENE, OR 97405-7110

⑆323274018⑆ 024⑈90759⑆

CHECKS AND OTHER ITEMS ARE RECEIVED FOR DEPOSIT SUBJECT TO THE TERMS AND CONDITIONS OF THIS INSTITUTION'S COLLECTION AGREEMENT.

	DOLLARS	CENTS
CASH →		
C H E C K S		
TOTAL FROM OTHER SIDE		
TOTAL		
LESS CASH RECEIVED		
NET DEPOSIT		

96-7401 / 3232

BE SURE
EACH ITEM
IS PROPERLY
ENDORSED

FOR CLASSROOM USE ONLY

Name _____

Part B: Checkbook Register

PLEASE BE SURE TO <u>DEDUCT</u> ANY PER ITEM CHARGES OR SERVICE CHARGES THAT MAY APPLY TO YOUR ACCOUNT								
ITEM NO.	DATE	PAYMENT ISSUED TO OR DESCRIPTION OF DEPOSIT	AMOUNT OF PAYMENT	✓	(−) CHECK FEE (IF ANY)	AMOUNT OF DEPOSIT	BALANCE FORWARD	
		To					Payment or Deposit	
		For					**Balance**	
		To					Payment or Deposit	
		For					**Balance**	
		To					Payment or Deposit	
		For					**Balance**	
		To					Payment or Deposit	
		For					**Balance**	
		To					Payment or Deposit	
		For					**Balance**	
		To					Payment or Deposit	
		For					**Balance**	
		To					Payment or Deposit	
		For					**Balance**	
		To					Payment or Deposit	
		For					**Balance**	
		To					Payment or Deposit	
		For					**Balance**	

Part C: Bank Reconciliation

Bank Statement

HANK A. WILLIAMS
MARY B. WILLIAMS
10 SPEARS COURT
EUGENE, OR 97405-8762

For month ended MAY 31, 20--:

Checks		Deposits	Balance
	5/1		502.00
52.00	5/1		450.00
300.00	5/7		150.00
	5/13	822.00	972.00
42.00	5/24		930.00
100.00	5/27		830.00
3.00SC	5/31		827.00

| Ending Balance | | | 827.00 |

Other charges and deductions: NONE

Bank Reconciliation

1. Write ending balance as shown on bank statement: _____

2. Add credits or deposits made that do not appear on statement: _____

3. Total lines 1 and 2: _____

4. Write total checks outstanding (not processed): _____

Check No.	Amount	

5. Subtract line 4 from line 3 and write balance (should agree with checkbook balance): _____

chapter 6
Saving for the Future

1 section:
vocabulary

Fill in the missing word(s) in the space provided at the right.

Example: Needs you expect to have in the next few months or years
are said to be _____.

0. ____short-term____

1. _____ involves an employer or financial institution electronically depositing your paycheck into a bank account.

1. _____

2. Besides a scholarship or loan, another form of educational funding is a(n) _____, which is based on financial need, does not have to be repaid, and is often funded by the government.

2. _____

3. Interest drawn on the sum of the original principal plus interest is called _____ interest.

3. _____

4. Money that is paid for the use of money is called _____.

4. _____

5. A savings or checking account at a credit union is called a(n) _____ account.

5. _____

6. A(n) _____ is a type of mutual fund that invests in low-risk securities and is considered safe even though it is not FDIC insured.

6. _____

7. Deposits kept in credit unions are insured by the _____.

7. _____

8. Federal insurance for depositors in commercial banks and savings and loans is provided by the _____.

8. _____

9. _____ banks provide the widest variety of banking services of any of the financial institutions.

9. _____

10. A deposit that is set aside for a specified length of time at a specified rate is called a(n) _____.

10. _____

11. A type of savings plan that offers a more competitive interest rate than a regular savings account is called a(n) _____.

11. _____

12. The speed with which savings can be readily converted to cash is called _____.

12. _____

13. The amount of money you place in savings is called _____.

13. _____

14. Money borrowed for education, called _____, can be subsidized or unsubsidized.

14. _____

15. The day on which a certificate of deposit must be renewed or cashed in is called the _____.

15. _____

16. _____ means that you are guaranteed not to lose your savings deposit, even if the bank fails and goes out of business.

16. _____

2 section: review questions

After each of the following questions, circle *T* for a true statement or *F* for a false statement.

	Answers	For Scoring
1. Emergencies, vacations, social events, and major purchases are examples of short-term needs.	T F	1. _____
2. Cash allowances awarded to students to go to college, called scholarships, may be based on need or on high test scores.	T F	2. _____
3. A subsidized student loan has higher interest rates, and interest begins the day you receive the loan.	T F	3. _____
4. Compound interest refers to interest paid on principal and interest.	T F	4. _____
5. Work-study programs will replace your need for other sources of money for college funding.	T F	5. _____
6. When choosing a savings account, you should consider safety, liquidity, convenience, potential yield, and fees.	T F	6. _____
7. Deposits in savings and loan associations and commercial banks, but not credit unions, are insured.	T F	7. _____
8. If a depositor withdraws part or all of a certificate of deposit before its maturity date, there will be an early withdrawal penalty.	T F	8. _____
9. Financial institutions can offer interest compounded in many ways, including daily, quarterly, and yearly.	T F	9. _____
10. Some ways to make saving easier include direct deposit and automatic deductions.	T F	10. _____

On the line at the right of each sentence, print the letter that represents the word or group of words correctly completing the sentence or answering the question.

1. Which of the following is not an example of a long-term savings goal?
(a) home ownership, (b) college education, (c) retirement,
(d) automobile purchase _____ 1. _____

2. Which of the following items is the most liquid? (a) home,
(b) regular savings, (c) certificate of deposit, (d) automobile _____ 2. _____

3. A type of savings plan whereby you set aside money at a financial
institution for a set period is a (a) regular account, (b) share draft
account, (c) certificate of deposit, (d) money market account. _____ 3. _____

4. Which of the following is not a benefit of direct deposit? (a) Your
money is available in your account faster. (b) You do not have to make
a special trip to the bank. (c) You can have part or all of your deposit
put into your savings account. (d) Your money earns more interest than
in any other type of savings plan. _____ 4. _____

5. Which of the following do banks usually offer? (a) ATMs, (b) numerous
locations, (c) drive-up windows, (d) all of these _____ 5. _____

6. The FDIC insures a depositor's money up to (a) $10,000, (b) $20,000,
(c) $100,000, (d) $250,000. _____ 6. _____

7. Money will earn more interest if it is (a) compounded quarterly,
(b) compounded daily, (c) compounded yearly, (d) compounded monthly _____ 7. _____

3 section:
problem solving

Activity 6.1 Short-Term Savings Plan

Directions: Complete this worksheet, entering your short-term needs on the left and your savings plan to meet those needs on the right.

Short-Term Needs

List some of your daily needs and their cost (e.g., food).

_____ $ _____

_____ _____

_____ _____

_____ _____

_____ _____

_____ _____

List some of your weekly expenses and their cost (e.g., entertainment).

_____ $ _____

_____ _____

_____ _____

_____ _____

_____ _____

List some monthly expenses that you expect to have and their cost (e.g., haircut, club dues).

_____ $ _____

_____ _____

_____ _____

_____ _____

_____ _____

List some expenses that you expect to have in the next year or two (e.g., car, prom, vacation).

_____ $ _____

_____ _____

_____ _____

_____ _____

_____ _____

_____ _____

Savings Plans

How much money do you have to meet these daily needs?

_____

_____

Do you have money left over for weekly, monthly, and next year's goals?

_____

_____

How much could you save from your daily, weekly, or monthly income?

_____

_____

Of what you can save, how much will you designate for

short-term needs: _____

long-term needs: _____

Do you think you could save more money than you do now?

_____

_____

In order to save money, what items have you purchased because you could not afford to buy the items you really wanted?

_____

_____

_____

What percentage of your total income do you save?

_____

When you spend more than you should, how do you make up for it? (Withdraw from savings?)

_____

_____

_____

Activity 6.2 Long-Term Goal Plan

Directions: Complete this worksheet based on your personal goals and plans to meet those goals.

Long-Term Goals

List at least three goals that you expect to achieve by the time you are age 25 (e.g., college education, marriage, trips).

1. _____

    _____

2. _____

    _____

3. _____

    _____

List at least three goals that you expect to achieve by the time you have reached age 40 (e.g., family, home purchase, career).

1. _____

    _____

2. _____

    _____

3. _____

    _____

List at least three goals that you expect to achieve by the time you reach age 65, or achievements that you expect to accomplish by the time you retire.

1. _____

    _____

2. _____

    _____

3. _____

    _____

Savings Plans

How much money do you anticipate saving to meet the goals you hope to accomplish by age 25?

_____

_____

If you are going to college, how do you expect to pay for it?

_____

_____

_____

Do you have other sources of money besides savings to meet these goals? If so, what?

_____

_____

How much money do you expect to have set aside when you reach age 40?

_____

How much money do you expect to have set aside when you reach age 65?

_____

Do you think you will need some retirement plan in addition to Social Security?

_____

How much income a month do you think you will need for retirement?

_____

Which types of savings plans do you expect to use to meet your long-term goals (e.g., CDs, bonds)?

_____

_____

In order to be financially secure at retirement, how much money do you believe you need to have in savings or investments?

_____

Do you know any persons who are presently retired? If so, how do they meet their financial needs (e.g., savings, Social Security)?

_____

_____

Activity 6.3 Advantages and Disadvantages of Savings Options

Directions: List one advantage and one disadvantage for each of these savings options.

Item	Advantage	Disadvantage
1. Regular savings account	_____	_____
2. Certificate of deposit	_____	_____
3. Money market fund	_____	_____

Activity 6.4 Compounding Interest Annually and Semiannually

Directions: Fill in the following charts by calculating interest compounded annually. The principal (beginning balance) is multiplied by the interest rate (decimal format) to get the amount of interest paid. Then the interest is added to the beginning balance to get the ending balance. The ending balance becomes the beginning balance for the next year. Interest rates shown are annual (yearly) rates.

Year	Beginning Balance	8% Interest	Ending Balance
1	$1,000.00	_____	_____
2	_____	_____	_____
3	_____	_____	_____
4	_____	_____	_____
5	_____	_____	_____
Total amount of interest		$ _____	

Year	Beginning Balance	7% Interest	Ending Balance
1	$1,000.00	_____	_____
2	_____	_____	_____
3	_____	_____	_____
4	_____	_____	_____
5	_____	_____	_____
Total amount of interest		$ _____	

Directions: Fill in the following chart by calculating interest compounded semiannually. The principal is multiplied by one-half the interest rate to get the amount of interest paid. Then the amounts of interest are added together, and this total is added to the beginning balance to get the ending balance. The ending balance becomes the beginning balance for the next year. The annual interest rate is 8.25 percent.

Year	Beginning Balance	First-Half Interest		Second-Half Interest		Total Interest	Ending Balance
1	$1,000.00	_____	+	_____	=	_____	_____
2	_____	_____	+	_____	=	_____	_____
3	_____	_____	+	_____	=	_____	_____
4	_____	_____	+	_____	=	_____	_____
5	_____	_____	+	_____	=	_____	_____

Activity 6.5 Compounding Interest Quarterly and Monthly

Directions: Fill in the following chart by calculating interest compounded quarterly. The principal (beginning balance) is multiplied by one-fourth the interest rate to get the amount of interest paid. Then the four quarters of interest are added together, and this total is added to the beginning balance to get the ending balance. The ending balance becomes the beginning balance for the next year. The annual percentage yield is 8 percent.

Year	Beginning Balance	First Quarter	Second Quarter	Third Quarter	Fourth Quarter	Total Interest	Ending Balance
1	$500.00	_____	_____	_____	_____	_____	_____
2	_____	_____	_____	_____	_____	_____	_____
3	_____	_____	_____	_____	_____	_____	_____
4	_____	_____	_____	_____	_____	_____	_____
5	_____	_____	_____	_____	_____	_____	_____

Directions: Fill in the following chart by calculating interest compounded monthly. The principal is added to the monthly deposits to compute interest for the month. Assume that all deposits are made on the first day of each month and are entitled to interest for the entire month. Be sure to use one month's interest rate (divide the total annual percentage yield [APY] by 12). The APY is 6 percent.

Month	Beginning Balance	Deposit	Total	6% Interest	Ending Balance
1	$ 0.00	$50.00	$ 50.00	_____	_____
2	_____	50.00	_____	_____	_____
3	_____	50.00	_____	_____	_____
4	_____	50.00	_____	_____	_____
5	_____	50.00	_____	_____	_____
6	_____	50.00	_____	_____	_____
7	_____	50.00	_____	_____	_____
8	_____	50.00	_____	_____	_____
9	_____	50.00	_____	_____	_____
10	_____	50.00	_____	_____	_____
11	_____	50.00	_____	_____	_____
12	_____	50.00	_____	_____	_____

Total interest earned during the year $ _____

Project 1
Assessing Your Financial Health

WORKSHEET 1
Rate Your Job

Directions: Rate each of the following characteristics on a 1- to 5-point scale. A score of 5 means *always*; a score of 4 means *usually*; a score of 3 means *as often as needed*; a score of 2 means *sometimes*; a score of 1 means *never*; and a score of 0 means *not applicable*. If you do not have a job, complete this worksheet after doing research about your desired future job.

Your Score
1. You enjoy the work you do, and you look forward to going to work each day. _____
2. You are willing to get extra training, education, or skills in order to be challenged. _____
3. You seek additional responsibility and can do the job well. _____
4. You like the work environment, and others recognize you as someone who will help and be a team player. _____
5. You receive regular pay raises large enough to keep you ahead of inflation and support your desired lifestyle. _____

Your total _____

Job Score
1. The product or service is in demand and prospects look good for the future. _____
2. The industry is growing as a whole, with opportunities for advancement in other companies similar to yours. _____
3. The product or service is economy-resistant (rising prices or economic downturns don't greatly affect sales). _____
4. Turnover among employees is generally low. _____
5. Pay scale and fringe benefits compare well with other companies in the same field. _____

Job total _____

Employer's Score
1. Your boss calls on you to handle tough assignments and gives you credit for your accomplishments. _____
2. The boss regularly solicits your suggestions and follows them. _____
3. The company promotes from within. _____
4. The company has a large number of customers rather than just a few big ones. _____
5. The company is well established and still growing. _____

Employer's total _____
Total of all points _____

WORKSHEET 2
Cash Flow Statement

Directions: Keep a record of income and expenses for a month. (You might want to do this for a year to build a budget base for the following year.) In the first column, list each item you receive or spend in a month. In the second column, project your annual income or expense for each item. In the third column, check any items that need attention. In the fourth column, indicate how much (increase or decrease) each item should change monthly. Add a plus sign (increase) or minus sign (decrease) to each entry. In the fifth column, indicate how much additional money you would save or spend annually by making the changes in the fourth column. Use a plus sign (save) or minus sign (spend) for each entry. See the example below.

Example:	THIS MONTH	YEARLY TOTAL	NEED CHANGE	MONTHLY CHANGE	YEARLY EFFECT
Entertainment expense	$38.00	$456.00	✔	+$12.00	−$144.00

ITEM	1 THIS MONTH	2 YEARLY TOTAL	3 NEED CHANGE	4 MONTHLY CHANGE	5 YEARLY EFFECT
Income:					
Take-home pay	_____	_____	_____	_____	_____
Bonuses/gifts	_____	_____	_____	_____	_____
Interest income	_____	_____	_____	_____	_____
Other _____	_____	_____	_____	_____	_____
Totals	_____	_____	_____	_____	_____
Outgo:					
_____	_____	_____	_____	_____	_____
_____	_____	_____	_____	_____	_____
_____	_____	_____	_____	_____	_____
_____	_____	_____	_____	_____	_____
_____	_____	_____	_____	_____	_____
_____	_____	_____	_____	_____	_____
_____	_____	_____	_____	_____	_____
_____	_____	_____	_____	_____	_____
_____	_____	_____	_____	_____	_____
_____	_____	_____	_____	_____	_____
_____	_____	_____	_____	_____	_____
_____	_____	_____	_____	_____	_____
_____	_____	_____	_____	_____	_____
Savings	_____	_____	_____	_____	_____
Totals	_____	_____	_____	_____	_____

Analysis:
List ways you can cut expenses or increase income (such as by substituting activities, buying cheaper products, or working odd jobs in the summer).

_____

_____

_____

_____

WORKSHEET 3
Net Worth Analysis

Directions: Fill in the blanks below. In column 1, write in the market value of each item you possess or debt you owe. See Chapter 4 for definitions of terms (assets, liabilities, and net worth). In column 2, write in what each item will be worth in one year. In column 3, indicate the value of each item in five years. You can assume an item will increase if it gains in value over time (through interest or inflation) or if you add to or purchase an item from that category.

ITEM	1 TODAY'S BALANCE	2 ONE-YEAR PROJECTION	3 FIVE-YEAR PROJECTION
Assets:			
_____	$ _____	$ _____	$ _____
_____	_____	_____	_____
_____	_____	_____	_____
_____	_____	_____	_____
_____	_____	_____	_____
_____	_____	_____	_____
_____	_____	_____	_____
_____	_____	_____	_____
_____	_____	_____	_____
_____	_____	_____	_____
Total assets	_____	_____	_____
Liabilities:			
_____	_____	_____	_____
_____	_____	_____	_____
_____	_____	_____	_____
_____	_____	_____	_____
_____	_____	_____	_____
_____	_____	_____	_____
_____	_____	_____	_____
Total liabilities	_____	_____	_____
Net Worth	_____	_____	_____

Analysis:
List major purchases that you wish to make and how you plan to pay for them.

_____

_____

_____

_____

_____

WORKSHEET 4
Tax Liability

Directions: To complete this worksheet, first list your gross income, adjusted gross income, taxable income, tax before credits, and total tax for the last three years you have filed tax returns and paid income taxes. If you have not yet filed a tax return, use the projected gross income that you would receive in the entry-level position of your choice (used for Worksheet 1). Compute taxes owed on that amount (see Chapter 3). Then compute how much you could save in income taxes if you made changes as shown. Finally, list some of the tax deductions and credits available on the Form 1040 provided that you might use to decrease your tax liability.

YEAR	GROSS INCOME	ADJUSTED GROSS INCOME	TAXABLE INCOME	TAX (BEFORE CREDITS)	TOTAL TAX (AFTER CREDITS)
1. _____	_____	_____	_____	_____	_____
2. _____	_____	_____	_____	_____	_____
3. _____	_____	_____	_____	_____	_____

How would each of the above years' tax liabilities have changed *if* you could have had the following changes:

YEAR	CHANGE	TAX DECREASE
1	IRA deduction of $2,000	$ _____
2	Child care credit of $500	$ _____
3	One more exemption	$ _____

Analysis:
Examine Schedule A of Form 1040 (itemized deductions), as shown on page 65. Identify some deductions you might wish to take advantage of to reduce your tax liability.

_____

_____

_____

_____

_____

Examine Form 1040 on pages 63–64 and list additional types of income, deductions, and credits that are required and/or permitted when this form is used.

_____

_____

_____

_____

_____

Name _____

Form **1040**

Department of the Treasury—Internal Revenue Service (99)

U.S. Individual Income Tax Return 20--

OMB No. 1545-0074 | IRS Use Only—Do not write or staple in this space.

For the year Jan. 1–Dec. 31, 20--, or other tax year beginning _____ , 2013, ending _____ , 20 ____

See separate instructions.

| Your first name and initial | Last name | | Your social security number |

| If a joint return, spouse's first name and initial | Last name | | Spouse's social security number |

Home address (number and street). If you have a P.O. box, see instructions. | Apt. no.

▲ Make sure the SSN(s) above and on line 6c are correct.

City, town or post office, state, and ZIP code. If you have a foreign address, also complete spaces below (see instructions).

Presidential Election Campaign
Check here if you, or your spouse if filing jointly, want $3 to go to this fund. Checking a box below will not change your tax or refund. ☐ You ☐ Spouse

| Foreign country name | Foreign province/state/county | Foreign postal code |

Filing Status

Check only one box.

1. ☐ Single
2. ☐ Married filing jointly (even if only one had income)
3. ☐ Married filing separately. Enter spouse's SSN above and full name here. ▶
4. ☐ Head of household (with qualifying person). (See instructions.) If the qualifying person is a child but not your dependent, enter this child's name here. ▶
5. ☐ Qualifying widow(er) with dependent child

Exemptions

6a ☐ **Yourself.** If someone can claim you as a dependent, **do not** check box 6a . . . . .

b ☐ **Spouse** . . . .

c **Dependents:**		(2) Dependent's social security number	(3) Dependent's relationship to you	(4) ✓ if child under age 17 qualifying for child tax credit (see instructions)
(1) First name	Last name			☐
				☐
				☐
				☐

If more than four dependents, see instructions and check here ▶ ☐

d Total number of exemptions claimed . . . .

Boxes checked on 6a and 6b _____
No. of children on 6c who:
• lived with you _____
• did not live with you due to divorce or separation (see instructions) _____
Dependents on 6c not entered above _____
Add numbers on lines above ▶ ☐

Income

Attach Form(s) W-2 here. Also attach Forms W-2G and 1099-R if tax was withheld.

If you did not get a W-2, see instructions.

7	Wages, salaries, tips, etc. Attach Form(s) W-2	7	
8a	**Taxable** interest. Attach Schedule B if required	8a	
b	**Tax-exempt** interest. **Do not** include on line 8a . . .	8b		
9a	Ordinary dividends. Attach Schedule B if required	9a	
b	Qualified dividends	9b		
10	Taxable refunds, credits, or offsets of state and local income taxes	10	
11	Alimony received	11	
12	Business income or (loss). Attach Schedule C or C-EZ	12	
13	Capital gain or (loss). Attach Schedule D if required. If not required, check here ▶ ☐	13	
14	Other gains or (losses). Attach Form 4797	14	
15a	IRA distributions .	15a		b Taxable amount . . .	15b	
16a	Pensions and annuities	16a		b Taxable amount . . .	16b	
17	Rental real estate, royalties, partnerships, S corporations, trusts, etc. Attach Schedule E	17	
18	Farm income or (loss). Attach Schedule F	18	
19	Unemployment compensation	19	
20a	Social security benefits	20a		b Taxable amount . . .	20b	
21	Other income. List type and amount _____	21	
22	Combine the amounts in the far right column for lines 7 through 21. This is your **total income** ▶	22	

Adjusted Gross Income

23	Educator expenses	23		
24	Certain business expenses of reservists, performing artists, and fee-basis government officials. Attach Form 2106 or 2106-EZ	24		
25	Health savings account deduction. Attach Form 8889 .	25		
26	Moving expenses. Attach Form 3903	26		
27	Deductible part of self-employment tax. Attach Schedule SE .	27		
28	Self-employed SEP, SIMPLE, and qualified plans . .	28		
29	Self-employed health insurance deduction . . .	29		
30	Penalty on early withdrawal of savings	30		
31a	Alimony paid **b** Recipient's SSN ▶ _____	31a		
32	IRA deduction	32		
33	Student loan interest deduction	33		
34	Tuition and fees. Attach Form 8917	34		
35	Domestic production activities deduction. Attach Form 8903	35		
36	Add lines 23 through 35	36	
37	Subtract line 36 from line 22. This is your **adjusted gross income** . . . . . ▶	37	

For Disclosure, Privacy Act, and Paperwork Reduction Act Notice, see separate instructions.

Cat. No. 11320B

Form **1040** (20--)

Form 1040 (20--)   Page **2**

Tax and Credits

38	Amount from line 37 (adjusted gross income)	38
39a	Check if: ☐ **You** were born before January 2, 1949, ☐ Blind. ☐ **Spouse** was born before January 2, 1949, ☐ Blind. } **Total boxes checked ▶ 39a**	
b	If your spouse itemizes on a separate return or you were a dual-status alien, check here ▶ 39b ☐	

Standard Deduction for—

- People who check any box on line 39a or 39b **or** who can be claimed as a dependent, see instructions.
- All others:

Single or Married filing separately, $6,100

Married filing jointly or Qualifying widow(er), $12,200

Head of household, $8,950

40	**Itemized deductions** (from Schedule A) **or** your **standard deduction** (see left margin) . .	40
41	Subtract line 40 from line 38	41
42	**Exemptions.** If line 38 is $150,000 or less, multiply $3,900 by the number on line 6d. Otherwise, see instructions	42
43	**Taxable income.** Subtract line 42 from line 41. If line 42 is more than line 41, enter -0- . .	43
44	**Tax** (see instructions). Check if any from: **a** ☐ Form(s) 8814 **b** ☐ Form 4972 **c** ☐ _____	44
45	**Alternative minimum tax** (see instructions). Attach Form 6251	45
46	Add lines 44 and 45 . . . . ▶	46

		47	
47	Foreign tax credit. Attach Form 1116 if required	47	
48	Credit for child and dependent care expenses. Attach Form 2441	48	
49	Education credits from Form 8863, line 19	49	
50	Retirement savings contributions credit. Attach Form 8880	50	
51	Child tax credit. Attach Schedule 8812, if required . . .	51	
52	Residential energy credits. Attach Form 5695	52	
53	Other credits from Form: **a** ☐ 3800 **b** ☐ 8801 **c** ☐ _____	53	

54	Add lines 47 through 53. These are your **total credits** . . . . ▶	54
55	Subtract line 54 from line 46. If line 54 is more than line 46, enter -0- . . . . ▶	55

Other Taxes

56	Self-employment tax. Attach Schedule SE	56
57	Unreported social security and Medicare tax from Form: **a** ☐ 4137 **b** ☐ 8919 . . .	57
58	Additional tax on IRAs, other qualified retirement plans, etc. Attach Form 5329 if required . .	58
59a	Household employment taxes from Schedule H	59a
b	First-time homebuyer credit repayment. Attach Form 5405 if required	59b
60	Taxes from: **a** ☐ Form 8959 **b** ☐ Form 8960 **c** ☐ Instructions; enter code(s) _____	60
61	Add lines 55 through 60. This is your **total tax** . . . . ▶	61

Payments

If you have a qualifying child, attach Schedule EIC.

62	Federal income tax withheld from Forms W-2 and 1099 . .	62
63	2013 estimated tax payments and amount applied from 2012 return	63
64a	**Earned income credit (EIC)**	64a
b	Nontaxable combat pay election **64b**	
65	Additional child tax credit. Attach Schedule 8812	65
66	American opportunity credit from Form 8863, line 8 . . .	66
67	Reserved	67
68	Amount paid with request for extension to file	68
69	Excess social security and tier 1 RRTA tax withheld . . .	69
70	Credit for federal tax on fuels. Attach Form 4136 . . .	70
71	Credits from Form: **a** ☐ 2439 **b** ☐ Reserved **c** ☐ 8885 **d** ☐	71

72	Add lines 62, 63, 64a, and 65 through 71. These are your **total payments** . . . . . ▶	72

Refund

Direct deposit? See instructions.

73	If line 72 is more than line 61, subtract line 61 from line 72. This is the amount you **overpaid**	73
74a	Amount of line 73 you want **refunded to you.** If Form 8888 is attached, check here . ▶ ☐	74a
▶ b	Routing number ▶ c Type: ☐ Checking ☐ Savings	
▶ d	Account number	
75	Amount of line 73 you want **applied to your 2014 estimated tax** ▶ 75	

Amount You Owe

76	**Amount you owe.** Subtract line 72 from line 61. For details on how to pay, see instructions ▶	76
77	Estimated tax penalty (see instructions) 77	

Third Party Designee

Do you want to allow another person to discuss this return with the IRS (see instructions)? ☐ **Yes.** Complete below.   ☐ **No**

Designee's name ▶   Phone no. ▶   Personal identification number (PIN) ▶

Sign Here

Joint return? See instructions. Keep a copy for your records.

Under penalties of perjury, I declare that I have examined this return and accompanying schedules and statements, and to the best of my knowledge and belief, they are true, correct, and complete. Declaration of preparer (other than taxpayer) is based on all information of which preparer has any knowledge.

Your signature	Date	Your occupation	Daytime phone number
Spouse's signature. If a joint return, **both** must sign.	Date	Spouse's occupation	If the IRS sent you an Identity Protection PIN, enter it here (see inst.)

Paid Preparer Use Only

Print/Type preparer's name	Preparer's signature	Date	Check ☐ if self-employed	PTIN
Firm's name ▶			Firm's EIN ▶	
Firm's address ▶			Phone no.	

Form **1040** (20--)

SCHEDULE A (Form 1040)	Itemized Deductions	OMB No. 1545-0074

Department of the Treasury
Internal Revenue Service (99)

▶ Information about Schedule A and its separate instructions is at www.irs.gov/schedulea.
▶ Attach to Form 1040.

20--

Attachment Sequence No. 07

Name(s) shown on Form 1040 | Your social security number

Medical and Dental Expenses

Caution. Do not include expenses reimbursed or paid by others.

1 Medical and dental expenses (see instructions) . . . . . | 1
2 Enter amount from Form 1040, line 38 | 2 |
3 Multiply line 2 by 10% (.10). But if either you or your spouse was born before January 2, 1949, multiply line 2 by 7.5% (.075) instead | 3
4 Subtract line 3 from line 1. If line 3 is more than line 1, enter -0- . . . . | 4

Taxes You Paid

5 State and local (check only one box):
   a ☐ Income taxes, or
   b ☐ General sales taxes } . . . . | 5
6 Real estate taxes (see instructions) . . . . | 6
7 Personal property taxes . . . . | 7
8 Other taxes. List type and amount ▶ _____
_____ | 8
9 Add lines 5 through 8 . . . . | 9

Interest You Paid

Note. Your mortgage interest deduction may be limited (see instructions).

10 Home mortgage interest and points reported to you on Form 1098 | 10
11 Home mortgage interest not reported to you on Form 1098. If paid to the person from whom you bought the home, see instructions and show that person's name, identifying no., and address ▶
_____
_____ | 11
12 Points not reported to you on Form 1098. See instructions for special rules . . . . | 12
13 Mortgage insurance premiums (see instructions) . . . . . | 13
14 Investment interest. Attach Form 4952 if required. (See instructions.) | 14
15 Add lines 10 through 14 . . . . | 15

Gifts to Charity

If you made a gift and got a benefit for it, see instructions.

16 Gifts by cash or check. If you made any gift of $250 or more, see instructions . . . . | 16
17 Other than by cash or check. If any gift of $250 or more, see instructions. You must attach Form 8283 if over $500 . . . | 17
18 Carryover from prior year . . . . | 18
19 Add lines 16 through 18 . . . . | 19

Casualty and Theft Losses

20 Casualty or theft loss(es). Attach Form 4684. (See instructions.) . . . . | 20

Job Expenses and Certain Miscellaneous Deductions

21 Unreimbursed employee expenses—job travel, union dues, job education, etc. Attach Form 2106 or 2106-EZ if required. (See instructions.) ▶ _____ | 21
22 Tax preparation fees . . . . | 22
23 Other expenses—investment, safe deposit box, etc. List type and amount ▶ _____
_____ | 23
24 Add lines 21 through 23 . . . . | 24
25 Enter amount from Form 1040, line 38 | 25 |
26 Multiply line 25 by 2% (.02) . . . . | 26
27 Subtract line 26 from line 24. If line 26 is more than line 24, enter -0- . . . . | 27

Other Miscellaneous Deductions

28 Other—from list in instructions. List type and amount ▶
_____
_____ | 28

Total Itemized Deductions

29 Is Form 1040, line 38, over $150,000?
☐ No. Your deduction is not limited. Add the amounts in the far right column for lines 4 through 28. Also, enter this amount on Form 1040, line 40.
☐ Yes. Your deduction may be limited. See the Itemized Deductions Worksheet in the instructions to figure the amount to enter. } . . | 29

30 If you elect to itemize deductions even though they are less than your standard deduction, check here . . . . ▶ ☐

For Paperwork Reduction Act Notice, see Form 1040 instructions.   Cat. No. 17145C   Schedule A (Form 1040) 20--

SCHEDULE B (Form 1040A or 1040) Department of the Treasury Internal Revenue Service (99)	**Interest and Ordinary Dividends** ▶ Attach to Form 1040A or 1040. ▶ Information about Schedule B (Form 1040A or 1040) and its instructions is at *www.irs.gov/scheduleb*.	OMB No. 1545-0074 20-- Attachment Sequence No. 08

Name(s) shown on return | Your social security number

Part I **Interest** (See instructions on back and the instructions for Form 1040A, or Form 1040, line 8a.) **Note.** If you received a Form 1099-INT, Form 1099-OID, or substitute statement from a brokerage firm, list the firm's name as the payer and enter the total interest shown on that form.	**1** List name of payer. If any interest is from a seller-financed mortgage and the buyer used the property as a personal residence, see instructions on back and list this interest first. Also, show that buyer's social security number and address ▶	**Amount**

	---	**1**

	---	
	2 Add the amounts on line 1	**2**
	3 Excludable interest on series EE and I U.S. savings bonds issued after 1989. Attach Form 8815 . . .	**3**
	4 Subtract line 3 from line 2. Enter the result here and on Form 1040A, or Form 1040, line 8a . . . . ▶	**4**

Note. If line 4 is over $1,500, you must complete Part III.

Part II **Ordinary Dividends** (See instructions on back and the instructions for Form 1040A, or Form 1040, line 9a.) **Note.** If you received a Form 1099-DIV or substitute statement from a brokerage firm, list the firm's name as the payer and enter the ordinary dividends shown on that form.	**5** List name of payer ▶	**Amount**

	---	**5**

	---	
	6 Add the amounts on line 5. Enter the total here and on Form 1040A, or Form 1040, line 9a . . . . ▶	**6**

Note. If line 6 is over $1,500, you must complete Part III.

Part III **Foreign Accounts and Trusts** (See instructions on back.)	You must complete this part if you **(a)** had over $1,500 of taxable interest or ordinary dividends; **(b)** had a foreign account; or **(c)** received a distribution from, or were a grantor of, or a transferor to, a foreign trust.	Yes	No
	7a At any time during 2013, did you have a financial interest in or signature authority over a financial account (such as a bank account, securities account, or brokerage account) located in a foreign country? See instructions		
	If "Yes," are you required to file FinCEN Form 114, Report of Foreign Bank and Financial Accounts (FBAR), formerly TD F 90-22.1, to report that financial interest or signature authority? See FinCEN Form 114 and its instructions for filing requirements and exceptions to those requirements		
	b If you are required to file FinCEN Form 114, enter the name of the foreign country where the financial account is located ▶		
	8 During 2013, did you receive a distribution from, or were you the grantor of, or transferor to, a foreign trust? If "Yes," you may have to file Form 3520. See instructions on back		

For Paperwork Reduction Act Notice, see your tax return instructions.   Cat. No. 17146N   Schedule B (Form 1040A or 1040) 20--

chapter

7 Credit in America

section: 1 vocabulary

Fill in the missing word(s) in the space provided at the right.

Example: One of the earliest forms of credit was the _____ at the local general store.

0. __charge account__

1. The free period, also called _____, allows you to avoid a finance charge if you pay in full before the due date.

1. _____

2. One who lends money or the use of goods and services in return for payment at a later date is known as a(n) _____.

2. _____

3. The use of someone else's money with the agreement to pay it back later is called _____.

3. _____

4. A(n) _____ is a pre-established amount that can be borrowed on demand.

4. _____

5. A loan on which the goods purchased with the loan serve as _____ is a type of secured loan.

5. _____

6. _____ is credit whereby you can add purchases up to a set credit limit.

6. _____

7. A loan for a specific amount that must be repaid in full, including finance charges, by a stated due date is called _____ credit.

7. _____

8. A(n) _____ is money borrowed against the credit card limit.

8. _____

9. A manufacturer-related company, called a(n) _____, makes loans through authorized representatives.

9. _____

10. _____ are unlicensed lenders who charge illegal interest rates.

10. _____

11. A service to customers called _____ allows them to charge now and not be billed for several months.

11. _____

12. The interest you pay for the use of credit is called a(n) _____.

12. _____

13. Almost everyone uses _____ credit, which involves having work performed and paying for it later.

13. _____

14. Businesses called _____ stores offer goods and services directly to consumers and include department stores, drugstores, and clothing stores.

14. _____

15. Small loan companies, also called _____, charge higher interest rates because they take more risk.

15. _____

16. In some states, maximum interest rates are set by _____ laws.

16. _____

17. A(n) _____ is a legal business where loans are made based on the value of merchandise used as collateral.

17. _____

18. _____ is the value of property you possess, such as bank accounts, investments, and other assets, after deducting your debts.

18. _____

section:
2 review questions

After each of the following statements, circle *T* for a true statement or *F* for a false statement.

	Answers	For Scoring
1. Most disadvantages of credit can be eliminated by wise use of credit.	T F	1. _____
2. Department stores, drug stores, and finance companies are all examples of retail outlets.	T F	2. _____
3. Interest rates on loans are usually higher at credit unions than they are at banks.	T F	3. _____
4. Where no usury laws exist, financial institutions may charge whatever rate of interest is agreed upon.	T F	4. _____
5. In an installment purchase agreement, the item you are purchasing will serve as the collateral.	T F	5. _____
6. Affinity cards are issued and serviced by specific organizations, such as professional organizations and college alumni associations.	T F	6. _____
7. Credit has helped the American economy to grow at a healthy pace.	T F	7. _____
8. A line of credit is a pre-established amount you can borrow without a new loan application.	T F	8. _____
9. The Truth in Lending Act requires all lenders to calculate APR the same way.	T F	9. _____
10. A debtor is a person who borrows money from others.	T F	10. _____

On the line at the right of each sentence, print the letter that represents the word or group of words correctly completing the sentence or answering the question.

1. Credit cards such as Visa and MasterCard are examples of (a) 30-day credit agreements, (b) revolving credit agreements, (c) APRs, (d) installment loans.   _____ 1. _____

2. Which of the following is an example of service credit? (a) telephone bill, (b) bank credit card, (c) gasoline purchase, (d) retail store agreement   _____ 2. _____

3. Finance companies charge higher rates of interest on loans because (a) they are small and have less money to lend, (b) they have lenient loan policies, (c) they take more risk, (d) they compete with banks and savings and loans for business.   _____ 3. _____

4. Pawnbrokers sell merchandise you have pawned, called _____, if you do not repay the loan plus interest by a specified date. (a) note, (b) security, (c) capital, (d) collateral   _____ 4. _____

5. Which statement about an installment purchase agreement is not true? (a) Interest is included in each monthly payment. (b) New purchases may be added on. (c) New purchases may not be added on. (d) This type of account generally has a maximum loan amount.   _____ 5. _____

6. GM Financial is an example of a (a) retail store, (b) credit union, (c) sales finance company, (d) loan shark.   _____ 6. _____

3 | section:
problem solving

Activity 7.1 Advantages and Disadvantages of Using Credit

Directions: From memory, list four advantages and three disadvantages of using credit. Apply them to your personal life or as listed in the textbook.

1. List four advantages of credit:

   a. _____

   _____

   b. _____

   _____

   c. _____

   _____

   d. _____

   _____

2. List three disadvantages of credit:

   a. _____

   _____

   b. _____

   _____

   c. _____

   _____

3. Answer the following questions as to your beliefs.

   a. Do the advantages of credit outweigh the disadvantages of credit? Why or why not?

   _____

   _____

   b. Could a person survive in our economy without using credit at all? Explain your answer.

   _____

   _____

   c. What are some ways that all people must use some form of credit?

   _____

   _____

   _____

   _____

   d. How will you use credit this year?

   _____

   _____

   _____

Activity 7.2 The Great Depression

Directions: Interview a person who lived through the Great Depression (1930s). Ask the person the following questions and record his or her answers.

Person's name _____ Age during Great Depression _____

Where did person live (city, state)? _____

What major things do you remember about the Depression?

_____

_____

_____

_____

_____

_____

What things do you do today (or not do) because of your experiences during the Depression?

_____

_____

_____

_____

_____

Do you think we could have another Great Depression? Why or why not?

_____

_____

_____

_____

_____

_____

_____

The Great Recession of 2007–2009 deeply affected many people. Ask two or three adults how they were affected and what they have done differently to avoid such financial pain in the future.

_____

_____

_____

_____

_____

_____

_____

Activity 7.3 Retail Stores

Directions: For four retail stores in your area, supply the following information. Most of it you will know because you shop there; for some items, you will need to ask parents or friends or go to the stores.

1. List four retail stores in your area. Include a department, drug, grocery, clothing, or specialty (e.g., jewelry) store. In the right columns, put an X on the line indicating which type of credit card is honored at each store.

Retail Stores	Accepts Store Credit Cards	Accepts Bank Credit Cards
a. _____	_____	_____
b. _____	_____	_____
c. _____	_____	_____
d. _____	_____	_____

2. Of the above stores listed, how many offer regular charge account credit? _____ installment credit? _____

3. Choose one major chain store or national or regional store (e.g., JCPenney, Sears, Walmart). Describe the types of credit plans that are available.

   a. Regular charge account credit: _____

   _____

   _____

   _____

   b. Installment purchase agreement: _____

   _____

   _____

   _____

4. List two retail stores in your area that accept cash only.

   _____

   _____

5. What kind of discount is given at these retail stores because cash is paid?

   _____

   _____

   _____

   _____

   _____

   _____

Activity 7.4 Credit Questionnaire

Directions: Answer the following questions in the space provided.

1. Do you use credit in any form? If so, how?

   _____

   _____

2. Do you feel credit has increased your standard of living? Explain.

   _____

   _____

   _____

3. Do you think Americans in general rely on credit too much? Explain your answer.

   _____

   _____

4. In relation to credit, what advice can you give to people beginning to work for the first time and starting out on their own?

   _____

   _____

   _____

5. Do you know anyone with credit problems? What did they do wrong?

   _____

   _____

   _____

6. How many credit cards do you carry in your wallet?

   _____ None   _____ 1–5   _____ 6–10   _____ 11–15   _____ More

7. What major purchases do you have planned for the next five years?

   _____

   _____

   _____

8. If you needed to borrow a large sum of money, what three places, in order of preference, would you go to apply for a loan?

   a. _____

   b. _____

   c. _____

9. If you found that you were in financial trouble because of credit and had great difficulty paying your monthly bills, what would you do?

   _____

   _____

   _____

   _____

   _____

Activity 7.5 Your Credit Card Means Freedom

Directions: Read the information below and then answer the questions that follow.

Some people believe that credit cards are evil—that they lead to overspending, to debt problems, and to moral decline. But credit cards can also mean the difference between having a good vacation and staying at home. Consider the following:

1. In order to rent a car, you will need a credit card. The card must have a limit high enough to allow for charges of $150 or greater. Most rental companies will not accept cash or debit cards because they want assurance that there is a source of payment if you incur other charges, such as by keeping the car longer or by damaging it.

2. Motels and hotels usually also require a credit card. Once you have checked out and are ready to leave, they may allow you to use a debit card or cash, but in order to secure a reservation and in order to stay at the facility, you will need a valid credit card with available credit for charging.

3. While on the road, you may also need a credit card to buy gasoline. Many stations do not accept cash after dark. The only way to obtain self-service gasoline may be to use your credit card at the pump. If you have an emergency, such as needing a tow truck, the credit card provides a way to pay for it on the spot. When you're out of town, most merchants will not accept checks, so the credit card allows you the instant ability to buy necessities.

4. A credit card is a safer way to carry money when you travel. If the card is lost or stolen, you can get it replaced and can get cash advances from the card. If your cash is stolen, however, you cannot get it replaced.

5. If you are traveling in a foreign country, using your credit card will enable you to get the up-to-the-minute exchange rate, thus preventing merchants from giving you less than your fair dollar's worth. Both debit and credit cards can be used to get foreign currency from ATM machines abroad as well, also giving you the best exchange rate possible.

Credit cards are not evil. They're tools that can be used wisely to make your travel plans flow much more smoothly.

1. Have you been in a situation where a credit card would have been very useful? Describe what happened.

_____

_____

_____

_____

_____

2. Explain why cash is not always the best thing to have in order to pay for your vacation expenses.

_____

_____

_____

_____

_____

Activity 7.6 Comparing Credit Card Choices

Directions: Websites such as Bankrate (www.bankrate.com) help you compare credit cards and give you descriptions of features such as interest rates, rewards programs, qualification requirements, and other information. Visit Bankrate's website and answer the following questions:

1. What are two of the top-rated credit cards? Why are they considered the best choices for many consumers?

_____

_____

_____

_____

_____

2. What is the lowest interest rate (or range of rates) being charged on the cards that are listed? Do you consider these rates to be reasonable? On what factors did you base your answer?

_____

_____

_____

_____

_____

3. Of the features being compared, which one is the most important to you? Why?

_____

_____

_____

_____

_____

4. Is your bank or credit card (or a family member's credit card) listed among the best? If so, why do you think it is a good credit card?

_____

_____

_____

_____

_____

5. If your bank or credit card (or a family member's credit card) is not listed among the best, would you consider changing credit cards? Which one would you choose and why?

_____

_____

_____

_____

8 Credit Records and Laws

1 section: vocabulary

Fill in the missing word(s) in the space provided at the right.

Answers

Example: Before potential creditors will grant credit to you, they must determine whether you are a good risk—that you are _____.

0. ____creditworthy____

1. A responsible attitude toward paying bills and honoring obligations on time is called _____.

1. _____

2. Your _____ is the complete record of your borrowing and repayment performance.

2. _____

3. A credit bureau issues a written statement called a(n) _____, which contains accumulated information about a person through subscribers and public records.

3. _____

4. _____ are businesses that pay a monthly fee to the credit bureau for access to consumer credit information.

4. _____

5. _____ scores are the most common credit scores lenders use to determine credit risk.

5. _____

6. _____ is the ability to repay a loan or make payments on a debt out of current income.

6. _____

7. A(n) _____ is a consumer request that requires the credit bureaus to deny all access to a consumer's credit information or files.

7. _____

8. A(n) _____ is a business that gathers, stores, and sells credit information to members.

8. _____

9. A(n) _____ system is used by credit bureaus in determining a person's credit score.

9. _____

10. A(n) _____ credit rating is earned when you don't miss payments and pay off debts early.

10. _____

11. A(n) _____ credit rating is earned when you pay your bills on time and often pay more than the minimum payment due.

11. _____

12. A(n) _____ credit rating is likely to result in denial of new credit.

12. _____

13. A(n) _____ credit rating is given to a person who pays all bills during the grace period, but occasionally takes longer.

13. _____

14. A(n) _____ is a company hired by a creditor to collect an overdue account balance.

14. _____

15. The act of treating people differently based on prejudice rather than individual merit is called _____.

15. _____

section:
2 review questions

After each of the following statements, circle *T* for a true statement or *F* for a false statement.

	Answers	For Scoring

1. Your credit history is an important record of your past experiences with credit, and you have rights and responsibilities for its accuracy.   T F   1. _____

2. A credit bureau is a nonprofit company established by members for the benefit of members.   T F   2. _____

3. A person is entitled to one free credit report every 12 months from each of the three major credit bureaus.   T F   3. _____

4. Businesses can make an inquiry to check your credit without your permission.   T F   4. _____

5. A debt collector is allowed to make telephone calls at any time in order to collect overdue balances.   T F   5. _____

6. The Consumer Credit Protection Act prevents discrimination in the evaluation of creditworthiness.   T F   6. _____

7. Information gathered for credit reports may come from credit applications when you apply for credit.   T F   7. _____

8. In a point system, the credit bureau assigns points based on factors such as amount of income, amount of current debt, and number of late payments.   T F   8. _____

9. An excellent credit rating results when you pay your bills on the due date every month and never miss a payment.   T F   9. _____

10. Most lenders utilize some variation of the five "C's" of credit to determine whether or not a person is considered a good credit risk.   T F   10. _____

11. It is lawful for creditors to ask you for personal information, such as employment and residence history, in order to determine your creditworthiness.   T F   11. _____

12. If you believe your bill contains an error, there usually is no hurry in resolving the problem.   T F   12. _____

On the line at the right of each sentence, print the letter that represents the word or group of words correctly completing the sentence or answering the question.

1. A person with a credit score of 700 would have a credit rating of (a) A, (b) B, (c) C, (d) D.   _____   1. _____

2. The _____ provides that you may see your credit report at no charge within 60 days of a credit denial. (a) Fair Credit Billing Act, (b) Truth in Lending Act, (c) Fair Credit Reporting Act, (d) Equal Credit Opportunity Act.   _____   2. _____

3. If you believe there is an error in your billing statement, your complaint must be in writing and mailed within _____ days after you receive the statement. (a) 10, (b) 30, (c) 60, (d) 90   _____   3. _____

4. Your letter of complaint must be acknowledged by the creditor within _____ days. (a) 10, (b) 30, (c) 60, (d) 90   _____   4. _____

5. Within _____ days of receiving your complaint, the creditor must
either correct the error or explain why the bill is correct. (a) 10,
(b) 30, (c) 60, (d) 90   _____ 5. _____

6. Which is not one of the five "C's" of credit? (a) challenge, (b) capacity,
(c) character, (d) collateral   _____ 6. _____

7. The Truth in Lending Act limits the consumer's liability to _____
after the consumer reports a credit card lost or stolen. (a) $10, (b) $25,
(c) $50, (d) $100   _____ 7. _____

8. Paying your bills on time and paying more than the minimum payment
due earns you a(n) _____ credit rating. (a) excellent, (b) good,
(c) fair, (d) poor   _____ 8. _____

9. Which of the following questions could a creditor legally ask you?
(a) "Do you plan to have children?" (b) "What is your ethnic origin?"
(c) "Where do you work?" (d) "What church do you attend?"   _____ 9. _____

10. Which of the following would probably not be included in your credit
report? (a) monthly balances of your accounts, (b) a listing of your
credit accounts, (c) your medical history, (d) your salary   _____ 10. _____

11. Credit reports are issued by (a) credit unions, (b) subscribers,
(c) creditors, (d) credit bureaus.   _____ 11. _____

12. Bankruptcy information stays on a credit report for _____ years.
(a) three, (b) five, (c) seven, (d) ten   _____ 12. _____

13. Which of the following would be a good first step in getting started
with credit? (a) applying for a credit card, (b) getting a small loan,
(c) opening a savings account, (d) opening a store credit account   _____ 13. _____

14. Which of the following could become part of your credit record?
(a) a lawsuit, (b) a divorce, (c) bankruptcy, (d) all of these   _____ 14. _____

15. The act known for its provisions requiring full disclosure of all costs
in a credit transaction is called the (a) Fair Credit Reporting Act,
(b) Fair Credit Billing Act, (c) Consumer Credit Protection Act,
(d) Equal Credit Opportunity Act   _____ 15. _____

16. Which of the following categories constitutes the largest percentage of
your FICO score? (a) length of credit history, (b) payment history,
(c) types of credit, (d) amounts owed   _____ 16. _____

17. In many cases, people with poor credit ratings have (a) missed some
monthly payments, (b) failed to pay back debts, (c) filed for bankruptcy,
(d) all of these.   _____ 17. _____

18. Debt collectors are required to (a) use any means available to collect
debts, (b) give consumers the chance to clarify and dispute their bills,
(c) be licensed, (d) all of these.   _____ 18. _____

3 | section:
problem solving

Activity 8.1 Credit Report

Directions: A sample credit report is shown below. Examine it and use the legend of symbols to orally describe the information given.

CREDIT REPORT

Date: 12/1/20—

** AHZOCHAR, BENJAMIN B, CAROLINE A
   WEST SHORE DR, CHICAGO, IL 60601, FROM 3/1/—, RENTING
   PA 456 MILL STREET, CHICAGO, IL 60613, 12/— TO 2/1/—, RENTING
   AKA BB AHZOCHAR, BUD AHZOCHAR
   M, 3 DEP, BD 3/11/—, SS1 999-00-1101, SS2 999-00-4939

   E1 AUTO MECHANIC, WILLIAM'S REPR SVC, CHICAGO, EMP 11/1/—, VER 3/11/—, $1800
   E2 INSTRUCTOR, SMITH COLLEGE, CHICAGO, EMP 6/30/—, VER 3/11/—, $2032

** SUM CR DATA
   OA 5
   CS TWO ONES, TWO TWOS, ONE THREE
   LIF

** PR AND OA

   3/2/— JUDG LIEN $2100, JJ BLDRS, CHICAGO, IL

** INQS

   10/15/— INQ. BY WILLIAM'S REPAIR SERVICE, CHICAGO
   11/1/— INQ. BY LACY'S DEPT. STORE, CHICAGO
   1/8/— INQ. BY CHASE MANHATTAN BANK, N.Y.

** CS RATINGS

FIRM NAME	RPTD	OPND	H/C	BAL	CS	ACCOUNT NUMBER
JCPENNEY	2/—	1/—	500	80	I-1	505-393-292-1 (REV)
AVCO FIN. SERV.	4/—	2/—	1,000	932	J-3	LN 444-22-A
ORB & CO.	3/—	2/—	750	0	J-2	488-3-212 (REV)
AMEXPRESS	9/—	8/—	3000	1100	J-2	481-3-333-214-2 (OPEN)
EXXON	8/—	3/—	300	0	I-1	483-333-234-44-3

END OF REPORT

LEGEND OF SYMBOLS:

PA past address
AKA also known as
M married
DEP dependents
BD date of birth
SS1 Social Security number first person
SS2 Social Security number second person
E1 employment first person
E2 employment second person
EMP employment date

VER date employment verified
SUM CR Summary credit data
OA open accounts as of report date
CD current date
LIF letter in file
PR public records
OA other information
INQS inquiries into file
RPTD date information reported
OPND date account opened
H/C high credit amount
BAL balance reported

CS current status ratings:
  I individual account
  J joint account
  1 current
  2 pays in grace period
  3 payments 30 days late
  4 payments more than 30 days late
  5 under collection
  REV revolving account
  OPEN open account

Activity 8.2 Loan Application

Directions: Complete the following loan application. Assume you need $1,000 to buy a car. Also assume that you are working at a part-time job of your choice and have checking and savings accounts (make up the information). List other sources of credit you have established (for example, department stores). As you answer each question, consider why the creditor would want to have that kind of information.

PURPOSE OF LOAN _____ AMOUNT _____ TERM OF REPAYMENT _____					
Name of Applicant (last, middle, first)			Phone Number ( )		Maiden Name
Mailing Address	City	State	Zip	How long?	Rent, lease, own
Previous Address (if above is less than three years)				How long?	Rent, lease, own
Date of Birth	Social Security Number	Ages of Dependents (including yourself)			
Year your home purchased	Name of Mortgagor		Account No.	Monthly Payments/Balance	
Present Employer (Name and Address)				Your Position	
How long?	Monthly Salary	Supervisor's Name		Business Phone	
Previous Employer (if less than three years)				How long?	
Name and Address of Nearest Relative Not Living with You				Relationship	
Name of Bank	Branch		Accounts (ckg., svg.)	Account Numbers	
Names and Addresses of Creditors 1.			Account Numbers	Monthly Payments/Balance	
2.					
3.					
4.					
5.					
Name of Joint Applicant (last, middle, first)			Phone Number ( )		Maiden Name
Mailing Address	City	State	Zip	How long?	Rent, lease, own
Date of Birth	Social Security Number	Relationship to Applicant			
Employer (Name and Address)				Your Position	
How long?	Monthly Salary	Supervisor's Name		Business Phone	
Names and Addresses of Creditors 1.			Account Numbers	Monthly Payments/Balance	
2.					

Activity 8.3 Credit Bureau Counselor Interview

Directions: Call and make an appointment to talk with a credit bureau counselor. Explain your purpose as an educational project (you may wish to work in groups). Ask the following questions and record your responses.

1. Name of Credit Bureau _____

   Name of Person Interviewed _____ Position _____

   Date Interviewed _____ Address of Bureau _____

2. About how many subscribers do you have? _____

   About how many reports do you issue each year? _____

   What is the fee for your services to subscribers? _____

   To nonsubscribers? _____

3. What type of system do you use in gathering information?

   _____

   _____

   _____

4. How are credit ratings determined—by the bureau or by subscribers? What type of rating system is used? Explain. _____

   _____

   _____

   _____

   _____

5. What kinds of information are found in a typical credit file?

   _____

   _____

   _____

   _____

6. What advice can you give to a person beginning a credit file?

   _____

   _____

   _____

7. When credit is denied, what is the basis for the denial?

   _____

   _____

   _____

8. How do bankruptcy and/or bad debts affect creditworthiness?

   _____

   _____

   _____

   _____

Activity 8.4 Credit Terminology

Directions: Answer the following questions about credit in the space that is provided.

1. What are the five "C's" of credit?

C_____

C_____

C_____

C_____

C_____

2. List the credit bureaus in your area by looking in the *Yellow Pages* or doing an online search. Include their addresses and telephone numbers.

_____

_____

_____

_____

_____

_____

_____

_____

3. Define what each of these credit ratings means:

a. excellent: _____

_____

_____

_____

b. good:_____

_____

_____

_____

c. fair:_____

_____

_____

_____

d. poor: _____

_____

_____

_____

Activity 8.5 Credit Laws

Directions: Answer the following questions about credit laws in the space that is provided.

1. What are the major provisions of the Fair Credit Reporting Act?

_____

_____

_____

_____

_____

_____

_____

2. What are the major provisions of the Fair Credit Billing Act?

_____

_____

_____

_____

_____

_____

_____

3. What are the major provisions of the Consumer Credit Protection Act?

_____

_____

_____

_____

_____

_____

_____

4. What are the major provisions of the Equal Credit Opportunity Act?

_____

_____

_____

_____

_____

_____

_____

chapter 9
Costs of Credit

1 section: vocabulary

Fill in the missing word(s) in the space provided at the right.

Answers

Example: A(n) _____ is a court order that will allow creditors to collect the debts you have agreed to pay.

0. ____judgment____

1. The total amount that is financed or borrowed, on which interest is computed, is called _____.

1. _____

2. The _____ rate of interest is charged by banks to their best business customers.

2. _____

3. The true rate of interest you are paying when you make installment loan payments and spread interest over the life of that loan is called the _____.

3. _____

4. With a(n) _____, you get back a portion of what you spent in credit purchases over the year.

4. _____

5. _____ is the remaining credit available to you on current accounts.

5. _____

6. When computations to determine interest involve the formula $I = P \times R \times T$, this is said to be _____ interest.

6. _____

7. With a(n) _____ loan, the interest rate goes up and down with inflation and other economic conditions.

7. _____

8. The _____ that you will pay on a loan is always expressed as a percentage in the simple interest equation.

8. _____

9. _____ is expressed as a fraction of a year in the formula for simple interest.

9. _____

10. A deposit, or _____, is often made when purchasing a large or expensive item to ensure that you will continue to make payments.

10. _____

11. The legal process that allows part of your paycheck to be withheld for payment of a debt is known as _____.

11. _____

12. A(n) _____ code protects your account name, number, and other information by making it unreadable to others.

12. _____

13. _____ is a scam that uses online pop-up or e-mail messages to deceive you into disclosing personal information.

13. _____

14. _____ occurs when you buy something without thinking about it and making a conscious decision.

14. _____

2 section:
review questions

After each of the following statements, circle *T* for a true statement or *F* for a false statement.

	Answers	For Scoring
1. Interest rates tend to increase when the economy is growing.	T F	1. _____
2. The rate of interest that banks offer to their very best individual customers is called the prime rate.	T F	2. _____
3. The time of repayment of a loan is expressed as a fraction of one year: 12 months, 52 weeks, or 360 days.	T F	3. _____
4. To determine simple interest, multiply the number of payments by the amount of each payment and then subtract the principal.	T F	4. _____
5. The average daily balance method often results in a lower finance charge than does the previous balance method.	T F	5. _____
6. It is your responsibility to your creditors to limit spending to amounts that can be repaid according to the credit agreement.	T F	6. _____
7. Rebates often serve to increase the cost of credit.	T F	7. _____
8. An installment plan may require a down payment up front	T F	8. _____
9. Secured loans typically have higher interest rates than unsecured loans.	T F	9. _____

On the line at the right of each sentence, print the letter that represents the word or group of words correctly completing the sentence or answering the question.

1. To minimize the cost of credit, you should (a) keep the number of credit accounts to a minimum, (b) carry more credit than you need, (c) make minimum payments, (d) avoid credit incentive programs. _____ 1. _____

2. When creditors use the _____, they apply the finance charge only to the amount owed after you've paid your bill each month. (a) previous balance method, (b) adjusted balance method, (c) average daily balance method, (d) adjusted daily balance method _____ 2. _____

3. A good rule of thumb is that purchases under _____ should not be charged but should be paid in cash. (a) $5, (b) $10, (c) $25, (d) $50 _____ 3. _____

4. The formula $I = P \times R \times T$ is for computing (a) annual percentage rate, (b) compounded interest, (c) simple interest, (d) costs of loans. _____ 4. _____

5. The difference between the total price paid and the cash price is the (a) principal, (b) down payment, (c) annual percentage rate (APR), (d) finance charge. _____ 5. _____

6. A trade-in is _____ the purchase price of merchandise to determine the principal of a loan. (a) added to, (b) subtracted from, (c) not considered in, (d) computed as a percentage of _____ 6. _____

7. Your credit limit minus the amount you already owe is called (a) principal, (b) interest, (c) deferred credit, (d) unused credit. _____ 7. _____

Name _____

3 section:
problem solving

Activity 9.1 Simple Interest

Directions: Calculate the following simple interest problems. Write your answers in the space provided; show your work. Use the formula $I = P \times R \times T$ and round your answers to the nearest cent or the nearest tenth of a percent. Use four decimal places for fractions of time.

1. (a) I = ? P = $500 R = 8% T = 3 months (3/12)	(b) I = ? P = $50 R = 12% T = 1 month (1/12)	(c) I = ? P = $1,000 R = 18% T = 24 months (24/12)	(d) I = ? P = $600 R = 15% T = 60 days (60/360)
2. (a) I = $6 P = ? R = 12% T = 3 months (3/12)	(b) I = $15 P = ? R = 15% T = 90 days (90/360)	(c) I = $300 P = ? R = 12% T = 6 months (6/12)	(d) I = 90¢ P = ? R = 6% T = 60 days (60/360)
3. (a) I = $12 P = $200 R = ? T = 6 months (6/12)	(b) I = $390 P = $2,000 R = ? T = 18 months (18/12)	(c) I = 50¢ P = $25 R = ? T = 6 weeks (42/360)	(d) I = $3 P = $50 R = ? T − 180 days (180/360)
4. (a) You have agreed to borrow $50 and after six months pay back $58. How much interest are you paying? What is the annual interest rate?		(b) If you borrow $800 at 18% for 11 months, how much total interest will you pay?	

Activity 9.2 Installment Interest

Directions: For the following problems, compute (a) total installment price, (b) amount of finance charge, and (c) annual percentage rate. Use the Math Minute and Figure 9.4 in your textbook as examples.

1. Cash price is $500. After making a down payment of $100, the payments are $50 a month for nine months.

   a.

   b.

   c.

2. Cash price is $6,000. A down payment of 10% is required. Monthly payments will be $120 a month for 52 months.

   a.

   b.

   c.

3. Cash price is $910, with a down payment of $100. Balance is due in 24 equal payments of $40.

   a.

   b.

   c.

4. Cash price is $85, with a down payment of $10, and 8 monthly payments of $11.

   a.

   b.

   c.

5. Cash price is $811.35, with a down payment of $83. Balance is due in 18 equal payments of $48.46.

   a.

   b.

   c.

Name _____

Activity 9.3 Adjusted Balance Method

Directions: Using the adjusted balance method of computing the finance charge, complete the following charts by inserting the appropriate amounts. Then compute the total finance charge. For the first chart, use an annual percentage rate (APR) of 18%. You will make monthly payments. Round your answers to the nearest cent.

Payment Number	Beginning Balance	Payment Amount	Adjusted Balance	Finance Charge	New Balance
1	$800.00	$80.00			
2		80.00			
3		80.00			
4		80.00			
5		80.00			
6		80.00			
Total finance charge paid in six payments			$_____		

For this chart, use an APR of 15%. You will make monthly payments. Round your answers to the nearest cent.

Payment Number	Beginning Balance	Payment Amount	Adjusted Balance	Finance Charge	New Balance
1	$1,000.00	$100.00			
2		100.00			
3		100.00			
4		100.00			
5		100.00			
6		100.00			
7		100.00			
8		100.00			
Total finance charge paid in eight payments			$_____		

An APR of 21.6% would yield what monthly rate? _____%

If you paid 1.75% a month on the unpaid balance, what would the APR be? _____%

Activity 9.4 Previous Balance Method

Directions: Using the previous balance method of computing the finance charge, complete the following charts by inserting the appropriate amounts. Then compute the total finance charge. For the first chart, use an annual percentage rate (APR) of 18%. You will make monthly payments. Round your answers to the nearest cent.

Payment Number	Beginning Balance	Finance Charge	Adjusted Balance	Payment Amount	New Balance
1	$800.00			$80.00	
2				80.00	
3				80.00	
4				80.00	
5				80.00	
6				80.00	
Total finance charge paid in six payments			$_____		

For this chart, use an APR of 15%. You will make monthly payments. Round your answers to the nearest cent.

Payment Number	Beginning Balance	Finance Charge	Adjusted Balance	Payment Amount	New Balance
1	$1,000.00			$100.00	
2				100.00	
3				100.00	
4				100.00	
5				100.00	
6				100.00	
7				100.00	
8				100.00	
Total finance charge paid in eight payments			$_____		

Name

Activity 9.5 Average Daily Balance Method

Directions: The average daily balance is calculated as follows: The sum of the daily balances of a customer's account is divided by the number of days in the billing cycle:

Daily Balance	=	Previous Balance	+	Debits	+	Purchases	−	Payments and Credits

$$\text{Average Daily Balance} = \frac{\text{Sum of Daily Balances}}{\text{Number of Days in Billing Cycle}}$$

Example: 31-day billing cycle; account shows the following activity during the billing period:

Date	Item	Debit	Credit	Balance
8/20	Previous Balance			$200.00
8/22	Payment		$50.00	
8/26	Credit (return)		20.00	
8/30	Charge	$60.00		
9/05	Payment		20.00	
9/10	Debit (cash adv.)	25.00		

The calculation is as follows: Number of days is multiplied times the balance for those days. For example, between 8/20 and 8/22 there are two days, and the balance was $200 for those two days (2 × $200 = $400).

Number of Days		Daily Balance	Extension
(20–22)	2	$200	$ 400
(22–26)	4	150	600
(26–30)	4	130	520
(30–05)	6	190	1,140
(05–10)	5	170	850
	21 days		
	10 left in cycle	195	1,950
	31		$5,460

$$\frac{\$5,460}{31} = \$176.13 \text{ average daily balance}$$

The average daily balance is then multiplied by the monthly percentage rate. For example, an annual percentage rate (APR) of 18 percent is 1½ percent per month.

$176.13 × .015 = $2.64 finance charge assessed for the month

1. Compute the daily balances and the average daily balance (30-day billing cycle). Then compute the monthly finance charge based on an APR of 15%. Round answers to the nearest cent.

Date	Item	Debit	Credit	Balance	No. of Days	Extension
6/5	Balance			$350	_____	_____
6/10	Charge	$50		_____	_____	_____
6/15	Payment		$30	_____	_____	_____
6/18	Credit		20	_____	_____	_____
6/20	Charge	10		_____	_____	_____
6/25	Payment		30	_____	_____	_____

Average daily balance $ _____

Monthly finance charge $ _____

2. Compute the daily balances and the average daily balance (25-day billing cycle). Then compute the monthly finance charge based on an APR of 15%. Round answers to the nearest cent.

Date	Item	Debit	Credit	Balance	No. of Days	Extension
3/1	Balance			$500	_____	_____
3/3	Payment		$50	_____	_____	_____
3/6	Charge	$65		_____	_____	_____
3/8	Charge	30		_____	_____	_____
3/10	Credit		11	_____	_____	_____
3/14	Charge	30		_____	_____	_____
3/18	Payment		20	_____	_____	_____

Average daily balance $ _____

Monthly finance charge $ _____

3. Compute the daily balances and the average daily balance (31-day billing cycle). Then compute the monthly finance charge based on an APR of 15%. Round answers to the nearest cent.

Date	Item	Debit	Credit	Balance	No. of Days	Extension
11/18	Balance			$180	_____	_____
11/26	Charge	$30		_____	_____	_____
11/28	Charge	16		_____	_____	_____
12/1	Payment		$35	_____	_____	_____
12/8	Charge	28		_____	_____	_____
12/12	Credit		10	_____	_____	_____
12/15	Charge	30		_____	_____	_____

Average daily balance $ _____

Monthly finance charge $ _____

chapter

10 Problems with Credit

1 section:
vocabulary

Fill in the missing word(s) in the space provided at the right.

Answers

Example: _____ is a loan backed by specific assets that the debtor pledged as collateral to assure repayment.

0. __Secured debt__

1. Exercising good _____ means following an individual plan for using credit wisely.

1. _____

2. With _____, a finance company loans you money to pay off your debt.

2. _____

3. _____ services will help you develop a personalized budget plan.

3. _____

4. If a person agrees to pay back a debt after it has been discharged by bankruptcy, the agreement is called _____.

4. _____

5. With _____ bankruptcy, the debtor works out a court-enforced repayment plan whereby he or she makes a single monthly payment to the court and the court distributes the funds to creditors.

5. _____

6. _____, often called straight bankruptcy, allows some assets that are considered necessary for survival to be retained.

6. _____

7. _____ includes assets that a debtor is allowed to keep after bankruptcy because they are considered necessary for survival.

7. _____

8. _____ occurs when a debtor files a petition with the court asking to be declared bankrupt.

8. _____

9. _____ occurs when creditors file a petition with the court asking that a debtor be declared bankrupt.

9. _____

10. _____ is a legal process that relieves debtors of the responsibility of paying their debts or protects them while they try to repay.

10. _____

11. The _____ suggests that consumers limit the use of credit to no more than 20 percent of yearly take-home pay, with payments of no more than 10 percent of monthly take-home pay.

11. _____

12. _____ refers to debt that does not have to be paid.

12. _____

13. A(n) _____ is a cash advance from your next payroll check.

13. _____

14. _____ is a form of bankruptcy for businesses that attempts to reorganize the debt structure rather than liquidate the business.

14. _____

15. _____ is the process of reestablishing a good credit rating.

15. _____

2 section:
review questions

After each of the following statements, circle *T* for a true statement or *F* for a false statement.

	Answers	For Scoring
1. Credit problems often arise after months and years of poor planning.	T F	1. _____
2. The 20/10 Rule suggests that you limit the use of credit to no more than 20 percent of your yearly gross pay, with payments of no more than 10 percent of your monthly gross pay.	T F	2. _____
3. A credit repair plan is a record of your debts and a strategy for repaying them off.	T F	3. _____
4. Credit counseling services are typically free.	T F	4. _____
5. To qualify for a debt consolidation loan, you must have some type of collateral that secures the payment of the debt.	T F	5. _____
6. When you declare bankruptcy, you are said to be insolvent.	T F	6. _____
7. When you declare bankruptcy, all of your debts are erased and you get a fresh start without carrying forward previous obligations.	T F	7. _____
8. Discharged debts are debts that a person declaring bankruptcy no longer has to pay.	T F	8. _____
9. Chapter 7 is a liquidation form of bankruptcy that wipes out most debts in exchange for giving up most assets.	T F	9. _____
10. The purpose of Chapter 11 bankruptcy is to liquidate the company and pay off its creditors.	T F	10. _____
11. Involuntary bankruptcy is the most common kind of bankruptcy.	T F	11. _____
12. In many cases, persons declaring bankruptcy must give up most of their property to be sold to pay debts.	T F	12. _____
13. Income taxes, child support, and alimony are examples of debts that are not discharged by bankruptcy.	T F	13. _____
14. If you file for Chapter 7 bankruptcy, any cosigners you have are no longer obligated to repay the loans they cosigned.	T F	14. _____
15. It is a good idea to get legal advice when considering filing for bankruptcy.	T F	15. _____

On the line at the right of each sentence, print the letter that represents the word or group of words correctly completing the sentence or answering the question.

1. Which of the following is commonly known as straight bankruptcy? (a) involuntary bankruptcy, (b) voluntary bankruptcy, (c) Chapter 7 bankruptcy, (d) Chapter 13 bankruptcy _____ 1. _____

2. The 20/10 Rule does not apply to (a) credit cards, (b) open-end credit, (c) mortgage loans for housing, (d) closed-end credit. _____ 2. _____

3. If you file for Chapter 13 bankruptcy, the judgment remains on your
credit record for _____ years. (a) two, (b) three, (c) six, (d) seven   _____ 3. _____

4. When a debtor has reaffirmed a debt after a bankruptcy judgment,
he or she has _____ days to change his or her mind about promising
to repay. (a) 30, (b) 60, (c) 90, (d) 120   _____ 4. _____

5. To repair a poor credit rating, you can (a) declare bankruptcy,
(b) obtain more credit cards, (c) challenge incorrect information,
(d) threaten to sue.   _____ 5. _____

6. Which of the following debts is not discharged by bankruptcy?
(a) credit card purchases, (b) medical bills, (c) car loans,
(d) student loans   _____ 6. _____

7. The biggest cause of bankruptcy is (a) job loss, (b) medical expenses,
(c) divorce, (d) poor financial planning.   _____ 7. _____

8. Under _____, debtors may keep most of their property but must submit
a payment plan to the court. (a) liquidation, (b) reaffirmation,
(c) exemption, (d) reorganization   _____ 8. _____

9. Credit problems can arise from (a) emergencies, (b) impulse buying,
(c) careless budgeting, (d) all of these.   _____ 9. _____

10. When designing a credit payment plan, accounts with the _____
should be first priority. (a) lowest minimum monthly payment,
(b) lowest credit limit, (c) highest credit balance, (d) highest interest rate   _____ 10. _____

11. To be insolvent means that you are (a) unable to get more credit,
(b) unable to finance your car, (c) unable to pay your bills,
(d) unwilling to meet your financial responsibilities.   _____ 11. _____

12. Which of the following is one of the goals of bankruptcy laws in the
United States? (a) to give relief to creditors who cannot pay their bills,
(b) to give fair treatment to creditors competing for debtors' assets
(c) to make it very easy for people to get out of paying back their debts,
(d) all of these   _____ 12. _____

13. When a creditor asks the court to declare a debtor bankrupt, this action
is known as _____ bankruptcy. (a) involuntary, (b) voluntary,
(c) Chapter 7, (d) Chapter 13   _____ 13. _____

14. Which of the following is a debt that would be discharged by bankruptcy?
(a) alimony, (b) child support, (c) income taxes, (d) loan payment   _____ 14. _____

15. Under _____, the court sells the debtor's assets and uses the proceeds to
pay the debts. (a) liquidation, (b) reaffirmation, (c) reorganization,
(d) exemption   _____ 15. _____

16. Which of the following forms of bankruptcy is used for businesses?
(a) Chapter 13, (b) Chapter 7, (c) Chapter 11, (d) all of these   _____ 16. _____

3 | section:
problem solving

Activity 10.1 The 20/10 Rule

Directions: Credit counselors often suggest the use of the 20/10 Rule to people who use credit: Your total borrowing should never exceed 20 percent of your yearly take-home pay, and you should never take on monthly payments that total more than 10 percent of your monthly take-home pay.

1. If your yearly take-home pay is $27,000, your total borrowing should not exceed _____. If your monthly take-home pay is $2,250, your monthly credit payments should not be more than _____.

2. If your yearly take-home pay is $18,000, your total borrowing should not exceed _____. If your monthly take-home pay is $1,500, your monthly credit payments should not be more than _____.

3. If your yearly take-home pay is $36,000, your total borrowing should not exceed _____. If your monthly take-home pay is $3,000, your monthly credit payments should not be more than _____.

Activity 10.2 Bankruptcy Notices

Directions: Bankruptcy notices are public records, and when filed they are published in the newspaper. Read the following legal notices of bankruptcies, and answer the questions shown.

Barton County Bankruptcies

June 29, 20—

Paula L. Buckner, bus driver, of 112 Taylor St., Monroe. Brenda D. Laslo, attorney. Liabilities, $9,413.52; assets, $275; property claimed as exempt, $397.

June 30, 20—

Claudette Haldane, doing business as Halco Co., of 2710 First St., Monroe. Ryan Edwards, attorney. Liabilities, $12,070.45; assets, $2,040; property claimed as exempt, $1,357.

Sheila L. Trent, teacher, of 374 Gardner, Monroe, and P.O. Box 2715, Monroe. Angela Ramirez, attorney. Liabilities, $182,325.84; assets, $165,221; property claimed as exempt, $21,755.

David Collier, fry cook, and Dorinne Collier, baker, of 594 Sawyer St., Monroe. Ben T. Shepherd, attorney. Liabilities, $16,054.27; assets, $6,400; property claimed as exempt, $8,225.

Lewis M. Anders, millwright, and Annette C. Anders, cashier, of 663 Cherrywood Ave., Camden. Ben T. Shepherd, attorney. Liabilities, $14,884.20; assets, $2,899; property claimed as exempt, $5,970.

July 1, 20—

Leo D. Yancy, millwright, and Gloria J. Yancy, housewife, of 3114 Burgess Road, Burlington. Lydia Holbrook, attorney. Liabilities $20,221; assets, $6,280; property claimed as exempt, $9,940.

Darrell and Claudia McKinney, no occupations available, of 138 Harper Ave., Monroe. Brenda D. Laslo, attorney. Liabilities, $8,123; assets, $4,561; property claimed as exempt, $8,470.

Lawrence D. North, cabinet maker, and Natalie Y. North, homemaker, of 1040 Cooper Street, Burlington. Lydia Holbrook, attorney. Liabilities, $48,125; assets, $52,374; property claimed as exempt, $29,540.

Adrian and Olivia Mendoza, carpet installers, of 8174 Forrest Road, Monroe. Angela Ramirez, attorney. Liabilities, $65,022; assets, $61,718; property claimed as exempt, $14,570.

July 2, 20—

Marcus P. and Ingrid E. Davis, no occupations available, of 708 Trenton St., Monroe. Represented by self. Liabilities, $71,967; assets, $53,440; property claimed as exempt, $19,360.

Eric V. Crenshaw, insurance salesperson, and Mirium L. Crenshaw, no occupation available, of 519 Spring Hill Dr., Monroe. Ryan Edwards, attorney. Liabilities, $57,832; assets, $54,725; property claimed as exempt, $25,675.

Craig Henderson, truck driver, of 840 Southland Ave., Apt. 9, Camden. Ben T. Shepherd, attorney. Liabilities, $15,276; assets, $2,114; property claimed as exempt, $2,500.

1. In what county are these bankruptcy notices?

_____

2. How many days of reported bankruptcies are included in this clipping?

_____

3. How many single persons filed on the days shown?

_____

4. How many couples filed jointly on the days shown?

_____

5. List the occupations of the persons claiming bankruptcy during the time shown in this clipping.

_____

_____

_____

_____

6. How many persons used the services of an attorney?

_____

7. How many persons are represented by themselves?

_____

Activity 10.3 Bankruptcy Review

Directions: Answer the following questions in the space that is provided.

1. Contrast the following:

Chapter 7 Bankruptcy	Chapter 11 Bankruptcy	Chapter 13 Bankruptcy

2. List four advantages of bankruptcy.

    a. _____

    b. _____

    c. _____

    d. _____

3. List four disadvantages of bankruptcy.

    a. _____

    b. _____

    c. _____

    d. _____

4. List items exempted by bankruptcy (and their values).

    _____

    _____

    _____

    _____

5. List debts not discharged by bankruptcy.

    _____

    _____

    _____

    _____

    _____

Activity 10.4 An Abuse of Bankruptcy Protection

Directions: Read the information below and then answer the questions in the space that is provided.

A dishonest person can use bankruptcy for personal advantage, as the following story will indicate.

John Smith (not his real name) was well established in credit when he lost his job. At that time, he held over ten charge cards from retailers and four bank credit cards.

He maintained his lifestyle during his unemployment (which lasted over two years), as though nothing had happened. He charged merchandise on his accounts to the maximum available and was careful to make all minimum monthly payments in a timely manner. As the months rolled by, he stretched every credit card to its absolute maximum credit limit, taking cash advances against the bank cards and buying all sorts of luxuries from watches to trips.

He sold his house, bought a smaller house with less than $22,975 equity, and hid away the profits from the sale in foreign bank accounts. He sold his expensive car and purchased one with a value of less than $3,675. He made sure all property in his name fell within the "exempt" category of bankruptcy law in his state. Meanwhile, he continued to use credit and make expensive purchases.

Finally, his credit ran out, and he could charge no more. He had amassed over $50,000 in debt. With no job and no assets remaining that could be used for collateral, he declared bankruptcy.

1. Do you see any ethical problems in this story? If so, what?

_____

_____

_____

_____

2. Were the bankruptcy laws designed to protect someone like John?

_____

_____

_____

_____

_____

3. What lessons can be learned from this story?

_____

_____

_____

_____

Activity 10.5 Credit Scams

Directions: After reading the information below, conduct online research to learn more about RFID credit card scams. Then answer the questions that follow.

Today's consumers face many types of credit scams. A relatively new scam is known as wireless identity theft (or contactless identity theft), which uses Radio Frequency Identification (RFID) technology. Basically, RFID is able to identify an object using a radio frequency transmission. It can identify, track, sort and detect a variety of types and sources of encrypted information. RFID card readers, which are relatively inexpensive, can be used by thieves to identify and capture information found on debit and credit cards, drivers' licenses, passports, and other types of electronically encoded data. Someone can bump into you or get close to your purse or wallet and capture all of the electronic information in your possession. To protect yourself from this form of electronic pickpocketing, you can take measures such as using RFID blocking products. Wallets, card and passport sleeve protectors, and other products are available to help protect you.

1. How does RFID work?

_____

_____

_____

_____

2. How do credit cards with built-in RFID chips differ from traditional credit cards?

_____

_____

_____

_____

3. Do you think RFID credit cards are safer than traditional magnetic strip credit cards? Why or why not?

_____

_____

_____

_____

4. What can be done to protect yourself from wireless identity theft? Give examples. Do you think these extra precautions are necessary? Why or why not?

_____

_____

_____

_____

Project 2
Managing Credit and Debt

Directions: Following the instructions in the student text, complete Worksheets 1–5.

WORKSHEET 1
Credit Analysis

Directions: List each type of credit you have and its features. Then complete the analysis to determine what action can and should be taken.

	Monthly Payment	No. of Payments Left	Outstanding Balance	APR	Special Features	Ranking
Installment credit:	_____ ×	_____ =	_____	____	_____	_____
Personal loans:						
Automobile	_____ ×	_____ =	_____	____	_____	_____
Home improvement	_____ ×	_____ =	_____	____	_____	_____
Other:	_____ ×	_____ =	_____	____	_____	_____
_____	_____ ×	_____ =	_____	____	_____	_____
Charge accounts:						
1. _____	_____ ×	_____ =	_____	____	_____	_____
2. _____	_____ ×	_____ =	_____	____	_____	_____
3. _____	_____ ×	_____ =	_____	____	_____	_____

Total debt outstanding.............................. $_____

Average APR.. _____

How long will it take to pay off the outstanding debt? (Total outstanding debt divided by total monthly payments)_____

Which debts do you feel comfortable with?_____

Which debts will you pay off first (those with the highest rates/priority ranking)?

_____

What are some anticipated future debt needs?_____

_____

Which credit sources will you use for future debt (those with lowest rates)?

_____

WORKSHEET 2
Credit Card Comparison Chart

Directions: Conduct an online search for a credit card comparison website. Select two different credit cards and then complete the table below that compares their features.

	Credit Card #1	Credit Card #2
Name of credit card		
Type of credit card (charge card or revolving account)		
Annual percentage rate		
Introductory rate		
Annual fee		
Transaction fees (cash advances, balance transfers, etc.)		
Penalty fees (late fees, over-the-limit fees, etc.)		
Grace period		
Rewards program/Rebate plan		
Other features (credit guard, travel accident insurance, extended warranty, etc.)		

WORKSHEET 3
Guarding Your Credit

Directions: Use the Federal Reserve System's website or other credible sites, such as the Federal Trade Commission's website or the website of one of the three major credit bureaus (Equifax, Experian, and TransUnion), to answer the following questions.

1. Why is a credit report important to me, both now and in the future?

_____
_____
_____
_____

2. How can I get a free copy of my credit report?

_____
_____
_____
_____

3. Who else can see my credit report?

_____
_____
_____
_____

4. How long does negative information, such as late payments, stay on my credit report? Is there anything I can do to speed up the process?

_____
_____
_____
_____

5. What can cause my credit score to change? What is my role in that process?

_____
_____
_____
_____

6. How can I correct errors on my credit report? What is the cost?

_____
_____
_____
_____

7. What other suggestions about guarding and managing your credit does the website offer?

_____
_____
_____

WORKSHEET 4
Your Debt Load

Directions: Answer the following statements with a "Yes" or "No." Then read the information following the statements to make an assessment of your debt load.

1. You pay only the minimum amount due each month on charge and credit accounts.	YES	NO
2. You make so many credit purchases that your debt load (total debts outstanding) never shrinks.	YES	NO
3. You are usually not able to make it until the end of the month and must borrow from savings.	YES	NO
4. You have borrowed from parents or others and do not have plans to repay the debt.	YES	NO
5. You are behind on one or more of your payments.	YES	NO
6. You worry about money often and are discouraged.	YES	NO
7. Money is a source of arguments and disagreements in your family.	YES	NO
8. You often juggle payments, paying one creditor while giving excuses to another.	YES	NO
9. You really don't know how much money you owe.	YES	NO
10. Your savings are slowly disappearing, and you are unable to save regularly.	YES	NO
11. You've taken out loans to pay off debts or have debt consolidation loans.	YES	NO
12. You are at or near the limit of your credit lines on credit and charge accounts.	YES	NO
13. You worry more about the amount of the payment than the amount of interest (interest rate) you are paying on loans.	YES	NO

ASSESSMENT: Total number of "Yes" answers _____

If you answered:

- "Yes" to 8 or more statements, you need to take immediate action to correct your debt load.
- "Yes" to 4–7 statements, you should seek to remedy the defects in your debt load soon.
- "Yes" to 1–3 statements, you are in pretty good shape and can solve your debt problems.
- "No" to all of the statements, congratulations—keep up the good work!

WORKSHEET 5
Situational Analysis

Directions: For each situation described below, explain how you would respond and why. What are the ethical issues involved in each decision?

1. You walk by an ATM in a mall. You see a bank debit card that was left there by a previous user. You look around and there is no one nearby to claim the card. If you leave it there, someone else may find it. What would you do?

   _____

   _____

   _____

   _____

2. You make a payment on your credit account at a customer service center. The worker, who is new and in training, accidentally credits your account for more than you paid. For example, you gave her $25 and she credited your account twice, totaling $50. What would you do?

   _____

   _____

   _____

   _____

3. Someone you know returns merchandise to a store and gets a credit on his charge account, knowing that he purchased the merchandise elsewhere. What would you do?

   _____

   _____

   _____

   _____

4. Your friend frequently buys clothing on credit, wears it to a special event, and returns it to the store before the account is due, claiming the garment is damaged or dirty. She then receives a credit or a refund for the merchandise. What would you do?

   _____

   _____

   _____

   _____

5. Your friend Tonya wants to borrow money, but you have none to give her. You have loaned money to her in the past, but she has not repaid it. Your other friend Sally has some extra money from a side job. If you vouch for your friend Tonya, then Sally will lend her the money based on your word. What would you do?

   _____

   _____

   _____

   _____

6. Another customer at the credit union where you belong has the same last name as you. Last month, the customer made her car payment of $350, but the credit union accidentally posted her payment to your savings account. It has been a month and nothing has happened; the credit union has not reversed the entry. What would you do?

   _____

   _____

   _____

   _____

chapter 11

Personal Decision Making

1 section: vocabulary

Fill in the missing word(s) in the space provided at the right.

Answers

Example: New ideas, products, or services that bring about changes in the way we live are known as _____.

0. ___innovations___

1. Money left over after expenses are paid, called _____, can be spent as you wish.

1. _____

2. _____ are the principles by which a person lives.

2. _____

3. Getting something in return for giving up something else is called a(n) _____.

3. _____

4. A(n) _____ is not relevant for a future decision; it happened in the past and cannot be recovered.

4. _____

5. A tradeoff results in a(n) _____, which is the value of your next best choice—what you are giving up.

5. _____

6. Advertising intended to convince consumers to buy a specific good or service is called _____.

6. _____

7. Advertising intended to promote the image of a store, company, or retail chain is called _____.

7. _____

8. A(n) _____ is a specific consumer group to which products in advertising are designed to appeal.

8. _____

9. Advertising intended to promote a general product group without regard to where the product is purchased is called _____.

9. _____

10. Marking an item to sell for $5.99 instead of $6.00 is an example of _____.

10. _____

11. A(n) _____ is an item of merchandise marked down to an unusually low price, sometimes below the store's cost.

11. _____

12. A(n) _____ is a long-established practice that takes on the force of an unwritten law.

12. _____

13. The items necessary for maintaining physical life are called _____.

13. _____

14. Ideals and values that are important to society as a whole are called _____.

14. _____

15. Goods and services provided by government to its citizens are known as _____.

15. _____

16. _____ is a marketing strategy designed to target specific people who are likely to buy certain products.

16. _____

17. _____ are tastes that reflect your likes and dislikes.

17. _____

18. The _____ refers to all activities related to production and distribution of goods and services in a geographic area.

18. _____

19. _____ tells you how much it costs per ounce or other unit of measure.

19. _____

2 | section:
review questions

After each of the following statements, circle *T* for a true statement or *F* for a false statement.

	Answers	For Scoring

1. You identify the need for a product or service in the first step of the decision-making process.   T   F   1. _____
2. Your friends, relatives, and coworkers rarely influence your buying decisions.   T   F   2. _____
3. You should keep a written record of the information you collect on choices of products and services.   T   F   3. _____
4. Spending patterns vary according to age and gender as well as within different stages of one's life.   T   F   4. _____
5. Values and goals are intrinsic and change often.   T   F   5. _____
6. Until basic needs are met, there is little need for other enhancements.   T   F   6. _____
7. Natural resources are of great value and concern because they are limited—some cannot be replaced.   T   F   7. _____
8. Selecting the best choice is the last step in the decision-making process.   T   F   8. _____
9. The primary goal of advertising is to motivate consumers to purchase a product or service.   T   F   9. _____
10. With company advertising, specific products or prices are not emphasized; the purpose is to convince you to retain loyalty to a store or to a company.   T   F   10. _____

On the line at the right of each sentence, print the letter that represents the word or group of words correctly completing the sentence or answering the question.

1. A billboard advertisement promoting the nutritional value of milk is an example of (a) product advertising, (b) company advertising, (c) industry advertising, (d) micromarketing.   _____ 1. _____
2. In order to attract customers into stores, retailers may use which of the following promotional techniques? (a) displays, (b) contests and sweepstakes, (c) frequent-buyer cards, (d) all of these   _____ 2. _____
3. Which of the following statements is true about coupons? (a) They are offered only by manufacturers. (b) They offer instantly redeemable savings. (c) They are used to reach a limited market. (d) They must be mailed in to be redeemed.   _____ 3. _____
4. The second step of the decision-making process is to (a) define the problem or goal, (b) compare choices, (c) obtain accurate information, (d) take action.   _____ 4. _____
5. Which of the following items is not a personal factor that influences buying decisions? (a) the economy, (b) personal resources, (c) goals, (d) customs   _____ 5. _____
6. Basic needs include all of the following except (a) shelter, (b) clothing, (c) education to achieve personal goals, and (d) safety and security.   _____ 6. _____
7. Which of the following is (are) not considered an external factor that influences consumer spending? (a) values and goals, (b) economy, (c) environment, (d) technological advances   _____ 7. _____
8. A product name repeated several times during commercials is an example of (a) company advertising, (b) product advertising, (c) target marketing, (d) micromarketing.   _____ 8. _____

Name _____

3 section: problem solving

Activity 11.1 Decision-Making Process

Directions: Choose a personal decision or problem to be solved and follow the six-step plan on this page. Write the information in the appropriate spaces. If you can't think of a personal decision to make, use the following information and provide a solution. Use another piece of paper if more space is needed for your responses.

It is 90 days until Christmas. You have exactly $50. You are not working, but you receive an allowance of $50 a month. From your allowance, you must buy your lunches (about $25) and pay your miscellaneous expenses. There are 10 people on your Christmas list. You would like to spend an average of $50 on each of them.

1. Define the Problem or Goal

_____

_____

_____

_____

2. Obtain Accurate Information

_____

_____

_____

_____

3. Compare Choices

_____

_____

_____

_____

4. Make a Decision

_____

_____

_____

_____

5. Take Action

_____

_____

_____

_____

6. Reevaluate Your Choice

_____

_____

_____

_____

Activity 11.2 Needs and Wants

Directions: Fill in the answers to the questions in the space provided.

1. Following are basic needs for survival. Explain the type, quality, and amount of each that is provided for you by your parents or family.
   a. Food and water (e.g., three balanced meals a day, unlimited water)

   _____

   _____

   b. Shelter (e.g., large secure apartment building, small bedroom for privacy)

   _____

   _____

   c. Clothing (e.g., one pair of comfortable walking shoes, one warm coat)

   _____

   _____

2. Explain life-enhancing wants for yourself with regard to:
   a. Food, clothing, and shelter

   _____

   _____

   _____

   b. Medical/dental care

   _____

   _____

   _____

   c. Education

   _____

   _____

   _____

   d. Travel, vacation, recreation, entertainment

   _____

   _____

   _____

   e. Gadgets, luxuries

   _____

   _____

   _____

3. How much money do you think it costs your parents or family to provide your basic needs in Question 1? How much money do you or your parents or family expect to spend on your life-enhancing wants in Question 2?

   _____

   _____

   _____

   _____

Activity 11.3 Individual and Collective Goals

Directions: Answer the questions below on individual needs and wants and collective values based on your own feelings and perceptions. There are no right or wrong answers, but you should carefully consider the reasons for your answers.

1. Personal needs and wants depend on the following individual goals and values. After each question, describe yourself—who you are, what you want, and what you expect to be.

   a. Personal style: Describe your tastes (preferences). (Are they formal or informal? Flashy? Dominating? Easygoing? etc.)

   _____

   _____

   _____

   _____

   b. Income: How much money do you expect or want to earn each year in your final occupation choice?

   _____

   _____

   c. Education: How much formal education do you expect to achieve?

   _____

   _____

   d. Security level: Do you feel secure from harm, physical or otherwise? Explain.

   _____

   _____

   _____

   _____

   e. Leisure time: What are some activities you enjoy doing in your spare time, and how much time do you expect to spend on them?

   _____

   _____

   _____

   _____

2. Society makes decisions (choices) based on collective needs and wants. Beside the collective values listed below, place an X on the line indicating the importance of each value in your thinking and that of society.

	YOUR THINKING			SOCIETY'S THINKING		
	Very Important	Somewhat Important	Not Important	Very Important	Somewhat Important	Not Important
a. Legal protection	_____	_____	_____	_____	_____	_____
b. Employment	_____	_____	_____	_____	_____	_____
c. Progress	_____	_____	_____	_____	_____	_____
d. Quality of environment	_____	_____	_____	_____	_____	_____
e. Public goods	_____	_____	_____	_____	_____	_____

Activity 11.4 Marketing Factors

Directions: Complete the following items on marketing factors that affect your buying decisions. You will need to use newspapers, magazines, or other sources (e.g., advertising brochures, leaflets, inserts, online advertising) to complete this activity.

1. Describe a billboard advertisement that you see frequently. Where is the billboard located?

_____

_____

2. Name the radio station that you listen to most frequently and note what type of station it is:
   (a) country, (b) rock, (c) rap, (d) religious, or (e) other. (If other, specify type.)

_____

_____

3. How would you describe the target market of the radio station in Question 2?

_____

_____

4. What types of commercials do you hear most frequently on your favorite radio station?

_____

_____

5. Which types of advertisements appear most frequently in the following magazines?

   a. *Time, Forbes, USA TODAY*

   _____

   b. *Sports Illustrated, Runner's World, Tennis*

   _____

   c. *Seventeen, Better Homes and Gardens, Martha Stewart Living*

   _____

   d. *Reader's Digest, People, Ebony*

   _____

6. Cut two coupons each from magazines and newspapers and attach them below. Circle the expiration dates on the coupons or note on the coupon that an expiration date does not apply.

Activity 11.5 Personal Factors Affecting Buying Decisions

Directions: Complete the following worksheet. Answer all parts of each question or statement.

PERSONAL FACTORS AND COMMENTS

1. a. Rate how well you manage your personal resources by placing an *X* on the appropriate line.

	Excellent	Good	Fair	Poor
(1) Time	_____	_____	_____	_____
(2) Money	_____	_____	_____	_____
(3) Energy	_____	_____	_____	_____
(4) Skills and abilities	_____	_____	_____	_____
(5) Credit	_____	_____	_____	_____

   b. What can you do to improve in one or more of the above areas?

_____

_____

2. a. Specifically describe your position in life as to:

   (1) What you are doing now

_____

   (2) What you would like to do now

_____

   (3) Who or what has influenced your goals

_____

   b. Generally describe your position in life as to:

   (1) Where you will be in three years

_____

_____

   (2) What your career goals are

_____

_____

   c. Briefly state how happy you are as to:

   (1) Where you are now

_____

_____

   (2) Where you plan to be in three years

_____

_____

   (3) What your career goals are

_____

_____

3. a. Describe your background; childhood experiences; and events, organizations, and activities that have influenced you.

   _____

   _____

   _____

   _____

   _____

   b. List the experiences that have cost you money (e.g., uniforms, dues, time). Note whether the experience was worth the cost.

   _____

   _____

   _____

   _____

   _____

4. a. List your goals and values.

   (1) Short-term goals: _____

   _____

   (2) Long-term goals: _____

   _____

   (3) Lifelong values: _____

   _____

   b. What are some costs that you have incurred or that you will incur to meet your goals?

   _____

   _____

   c. What are some costs that you will pay because of lifelong values?

   _____

   _____

5. a. List the luxuries that you enjoy each week.

   _____

   b. How much money do you spend each week for your luxuries?

   _____

   c. Are you satisfied with the amount of money spent for your luxuries? Explain.

   _____

   _____

   d. How can you improve your spending habits?

   _____

   _____

   _____

Activity 11.6 External Factors

Directions: Analyze how you are affected by and concerned with the following external factors that influence your decisions and purchases. Then answer the questions on the next page.

Societal Factors	How I Am Affected	How I Feel About Them

The Economy
    High interest rates
    High prices (inflation)		

Technological Advances
    New inventions
    Fashion, industrial, and/or
        scientific changes		

Environmental Concerns
    Air quality
    Energy conservation
        (alternative fuel sources)		

Social Pressures
    Social status
    Attractive appearance		

1. Name some products that appeal mostly to your sense of being a part of a group and conforming to what everybody wants to wear, be, or do.

   _____

   _____

   _____

   _____

2. What items are on your want list? Do you want the latest items? Why?

   _____

   _____

   _____

   _____

   _____

   _____

   _____

3. What product or service does your family purchase or participate in because it is the thing to do, or because it is something that you or others expect your family to do?

   _____

   _____

   _____

   _____

4. List items that you wear or possess that you do not really care for or rarely use; that is, you believe that you must have these items because other people have them or because of your family's need to have what everybody else has.

   _____

   _____

   _____

   _____

5. What are your concerns for the environment? Do you believe enough is being done by lawmakers to protect your rights to clean air, water, and a safe life?

   _____

   _____

   _____

   _____

   _____

chapter 12 Renting a Residence

1 section: vocabulary

Fill in the missing word(s) in the space provided at the right.

Answers

Example: A(n) _____ is a social organization of female students who share a residence.

0. ____sorority____

1. _____ is combining telephone, Internet, and cable TV into one package.

1. _____

2. A(n) _____ is a nonrefundable charge for a service.

2. _____

3. The person who rents property is called the _____.

3. _____

4. A(n) _____ is an individually owned unit in an apartment-style complex with shared ownership of common areas.

4. _____

5. A(n) _____ is a refundable amount paid in advance to protect the owner against damage or nonpayment.

5. _____

6. _____ is the process of using another's property for a fee.

6. _____

7. A(n) _____ rental contains basic furniture, such as a bed, dresser, sofa, chairs, and dining table and chairs.

7. _____

8. A(n) _____ is a building with two separate living units that share a common central wall.

8. _____

9. The _____ is the owner of the property that is rented or leased.

9. _____

10. A rental _____ is a detailed list of current property conditions.

10. _____

11. Buildings that contain many small rooms for on-campus student housing are called _____.

11. _____

12. A(n) _____ is a written agreement to rent property at a certain price for a specified time period.

12. _____

13. A studio apartment, or a(n) _____, has one large room that serves as the living room, dining area, and bedroom.

13. _____

14. _____ is the legal process of removing a tenant from rental property.

14. _____

15. _____ is the process by which students join fraternities and sororities.

15. _____

16. The landlord is also known as the _____ when signing a lease.

16. _____

17. In a housing _____, students share in cooking, cleaning, and maintaining the building.

17. _____

18. With a(n) _____ option, you rent furniture with the option to buy.

18. _____

2 section:
review questions

After each of the following statements, circle *T* for a true statement or *F* for a false statement.

		Answers	For Scoring
1. Unfurnished rentals are usually lower in rent than furnished rentals.		T F	1. _____
2. Renting a moving truck for a local move is just as expensive as moving across the state.		T F	2. _____
3. Utility companies often require new customers to pay a deposit, which is usually refundable when their credit has been established.		T F	3. _____
4. Both a lease and a month-to-month rental agreement are legally binding when signed.		T F	4. _____
5. It is necessary to give at least 30 days' notice if you intend to move out of your rented residence; otherwise, you may lose all or part of your deposit.		T F	5. _____
6. Most people begin their independent lives as homeowners.		T F	6. _____
7. A major disadvantage of apartment living is the lack of privacy.		T F	7. _____
8. Most apartments have more space than the average duplex or house.		T F	8. _____
9. It is important to determine if potential roommates have compatible personalities and living habits.		T F	9. _____
10. Generally, the larger the apartment, the more rent you will pay.		T F	10. _____
11. A rental application is used to screen an applicant's ability to pay rent.		T F	11. _____
12. A lease move-in special is always advantageous to the renter, even if he or she has to move out early.		T F	12. _____
13. An inventory should be taken when you first move into any rental unit.		T F	13. _____

On the line at the right of each sentence, print the letter that represents the word or group of words correctly completing the sentence or answering the question.

1. College students usually find _____ to be the most economical housing choice.
   (a) duplexes, (b) dormitories, (c) rental houses, (d) condominiums _____ 1. _____

2. An expense that would probably be shared equally by roommates is
   (a) entertainment, (b) laundry, (c) utilities, (d) clothing. _____ 2. _____

3. You should begin to plan the actual move to a residence _____ in advance.
   (a) several days, (b) two weeks, (c) one month, (d) several months _____ 3. _____

4. A(n) _____ often has all or part of the utilities included in the rent.
   (a) co-op, (b) apartment, (c) condominium, (d) rental house _____ 4. _____

5. Which of the following item(s) would not likely be provided in a furnished apartment? (a) dining table, (b) towels and sheets, (c) sofa and chairs, (d) bed and dresser _____ 5. _____

6. Some schools permit only _____ to live in on-campus apartments.
   (a) students with families, (b) married students, (c) graduate students, (d) all of these _____ 6. _____

7. When deciding where to live, all of the following are factors to consider except
   (a) installation charges, (b) distance from school or work, (c) safety, (d) repairs and maintenance. _____ 7. _____

8. Which of the following situations might require an additional security deposit or fee for a tenant? (a) having a pet, (b) using the on-site laundry facilities, (c) using the on-site recreational facilities, (d) on-street parking   _____ 8. _____

9. To live in a sorority or fraternity, new members must go through (a) hazing, (b) pledging, (c) credit checks, (d) all of these.   _____ 9. _____

10. Which of the following statements is true regarding dormitories? (a) Most rooms have their own bathrooms. (b) Rooms usually come furnished. (c) Most rooms are intended for single occupancy. (d) Meals at the college cafeteria are usually not included with the cost of the room.   _____ 10. _____

11. A landlord cannot refuse to rent you property based on (a) your past rental history, (b) your credit rating, (c) your employment history, (d) whether you are divorced or have children.   _____ 11. _____

12. Which of the following is not an advantage to renting? (a) lower cost, (b) fewer responsibilities, (c) tax benefits, (d) all of these   _____ 12. _____

3 section: problem solving

Activity 12.1 Classified Ads

Directions: In the space provided, attach a classified ad from your local newspaper to illustrate each of the following situations.

1. A furnished one- or two-bedroom apartment

5. An unfurnished house for rent that has two or more bedrooms

2. An unfurnished one- or two-bedroom apartment

6. A house for rent that is located in an outlying or undesirable area

3. An unfurnished duplex for rent that has two or more bedrooms

7. A house for sale that has two or more bedrooms

4. A condominium or a townhouse for rent

8. A house for sale in an exclusive area, or one featuring many extras

Activity 12.2 Apartments for Rent

Directions: Below is an excerpt of the classified ads for furnished and unfurnished apartments from a local newspaper. Answer the following questions and statements using these ads.

Apartments, Furnished 610

LOOK!

— FURNISHED
— FREE UTILITIES
— CLEAN & CARPETED
STUDIOS, $600–$750

Near Shopping & Business
Call Brian 555-8567 or 555-5876.
FARMDALE MANOR

1455 BAILEY HILL ROAD
1 BEDROOM $700
2 BEDROOM $950
Attractive complex offers the feeling
of country living with the convenience of shopping, bus line &
schools nearby. Call 555-6785,
555-9432, 555-2273.

SILVER LACE

A beautiful place, in one of
Eugene's finest neighborhoods,
2222 Willamette. 1-2 bedrooms.
Have everything you would want in
your home, including pool and
sauna. Adults, no pets. Very quiet.
555-8906 or 555-9704.

MARLATT
1/2 BLOCK TO CAMPUS
749 East 17th — Spacious 1 bedroom. Carpet, drapes, appliances.
Quiet area. $795. Call—555-0123.
—IPM Co.—   Realtor
1065 HIGH ST.   555-8040.

WILLOW TREE APTS
Single Adult Living. Modern Studio
Quints. Furnished private bath &
refrigerator. Kitchen with washer
& dryer.

ALL UTILITIES PAID
$650–$795 a month. Inquire 1560
Lincoln, #1 or Call 555-8890.

U OF O

Modern 2 bedroom, carpeted, dishwasher, private patio overlooks
courtyard with summer pool.
Congenial neighbors, 5 blocks to
Taylors. Only 1 left. Gary, 555-
1032 or 1255 Mill St., #5.

November Special
Call & ask about special. Close to
campus & town. Quiet, modern
studios & lofts. Furnished or
unfurnished. Covered parking.
Adult living. Bus at door. 95 West
15th. Debbie 555-6209 eves.
Riverside Realty

APARTMENTS FOR RENT
Carpet, electric heat
Eugene: 1 Bedroom, 15th &
Willamette, $600; Studio, 5th &
Madison, $595; Studio, near
Bailey Hill, $700. 1 Bedroom, 4th
& Adams, $695 (1/2 off 2nd & 6th
month). 555-9200; 555-9696.

WEST SIDE

Quiet & clean, 1 & 2 bedroom nicely
furnished, well managed and maintained. Walking distance to: post
office, shopping, bank, church,
parks—on bus. Adults, no pets.
555-5544 or 555-5353.

Apartments, Furnished 610

LARGE & QUIET
1 & 2 Bedroom. Reasonable price.
South Eugene. 555-6060.

SPRINGFIELD, LARGE
Studio (or unfurnished). Spotless.
$579. Bus line. 555-7446.

Large 1 Bedroom, $650-775
Eugene, 2 locations. Christian
Owner. 555-4424, 555-7773.

SPRINGFIELD Mall, 1 bedroom,
furnished/unfurnished. $650 up.
1813 "M" St., 555-4090.

ATTRACTIVE Studio, all electric,
no pets. $700. Utilities paid for 6
months. 432 West 6th. 555-6654.

STUDIO, clean, all utilities paid.
Near shopping & bus. $600.
Newly painted. Call 555-9988.

BARGAIN RATE large 1 bedroom,
carpeted, Springfield, $625 plus
deposit. Adults, no pets. 555-4704.

2833 WILLAMETTE, air conditioned, 1 bedroom, garbage &
water paid. $650. 555-3205.

DOWNTOWN 1 Bedroom $625, 2
Bedroom $660 plus deposit. For
appointment call 555-2500.

"THIS OLD HOUSE" has 1
BEDROOM rental, SOON! 695 W.
11th. $650 monthly. 555-8890.

LARGE 2 BEDROOM $799; 1
Bedroom $759; No children, no
pets. 555-5876, 555-3602 eves. best.

1-2 BEDROOM Motel apartments.
Linens, Cable TV, utilities. Clean.
Reasonable. 555-3764.

NEAR MALL - 2 bedroom laundry
facilities. Cats O.K. $775 month.
555-2273 or 555-5483.

Apartments, Unfurnished 615

Riviera Village
130 RIVER AVE.

Belt Line to River Road, south on
River Road, then first left turn.
THE CHOICE IS YOURS!
Choose from 1 and 2 bedroom,
ranch-style and townhouse units
with or without fireplaces.
Choose from family, adult only, or
senior citizen areas.
Enjoy the spacious grounds, ample
parking, convenient laundry facilities, children's play areas, and rest-
ful, country-like atmosphere.

—1 bedroom townhouse $800
—2 bedroom, $775
—2 bedroom - fireplace, $800
—2 bedroom townhouse $875
Manager, 130 River Avenue,
No. 63. 555-8998.
—IPM Co.—   Realtor
1065 HIGH ST.   555-8040.

HANDY LOCATION
2933 Willamette - Spacious 1 bedroom, dishwasher, disposal, water-
garbage paid. $650 555-9704.

Apartments, Unfurnished 615

CHURCHILL VILLAGE
1700 BAILEY HILL RD.
Enjoy Quiet, Comfort,
Space & Convenience.

QUIET—
—No neighbors above you.
COMFORT—
—Modern kitchens.
—Private patios.
—Off-street parking.
—Swimming pool.
SPACE—
—13 acre park-like atmosphere.
CONVENIENCE—
—Schools & shopping nearby.
—On the bus line.
2 Bedroom, $800.
3 Bedroom (with washer/dryer
hookups), $1,100.
Children & pets welcome. Senior
Citizen discounts available.
Call 555-2003 for showing appoint-
ment or drop by between 10 a.m.
and 6 p.m.
—IPM Co.—   Realtor
1065 HIGH ST.   555-8040.

OAK PARK Townhouses

3 Bedrooms
—1400 sq. ft.
—2 1/2 baths
—2 car carports
—Storage
—Central heat & air
—Fireplace
—Sunken Living Room
—Complete Kitchen
—Balconies & Patios
—$1,050 month

Others from $800

1500 Norkenzie Road
555-5353

$695-$825
1 BEDROOM

COUNTRY STYLE LIVING
WITH CITY CONVENIENCE

Appliances, drapes, carpeting
HANDICAPPED ACCESSIBLE
Studios $550
BUS, CLOSE TO SCHOOLS
Rec Room & RV Parking
CHILDREN & SMALL PETS OK
SENIOR Discount on 2 Bedrooms

Redwood Park Apartments
555-7800 4103 W. 18th

1. How do the furnished apartments compare with the unfurnished apartments in terms of
   size and facilities?

   _____

   _____

   _____

   _____

2. What is the most expensive
   one-bedroom apartment listed?

   _____

   _____

3. What is the least expensive
   apartment listed?

   _____

   _____

4. List some of the features available at various apartments.

   _____

   _____

   _____

   _____

   _____

5. How many apartments do not
   accept pets?

   _____

   _____

6. List the number of apartments
   with washer and dryer hookups.

   _____

   _____

7. Name special features that
   would be good for families with
   children.

   _____

   _____

   _____

   _____

Activity 12.3 Houses, Duplexes, Multiplexes for Rent

Directions: Below is a clipping representing a portion of the classified ads in a local newspaper. Represented are houses, duplexes, and multiplexes. After examining this clipping, answer the questions and statements that follow.

Houses, Unfurnished　　605

SECLUDED COUNTRY—New three bedroom, fireplace. Cheshire. Two children ok. References. $1,050. Call 555-5876.

VENETA AREA, available December 10. 3 bedroom, 2 bath, fireplace, appliances, double garage. $1,100 month. 555-6785.

NICE 2 PLUS BEDROOM Home with private yard, fireplace. $1,075. Drive by 761 Polk, 555-3764 6-10 p.m. or weekends.

NORTHWEST EUGENE Newer 1600 sq. ft. 3 Bedroom, 2 bath, family room, fireplace, appliances. $1,400 + deposit. 555-2273.

2 BEDROOM home on west side. Fireplace with wood, front porch, garage. $1,100 + deposit. Eves. & weekends, 555-6654.

LEASE 1 YEAR, 2 Bedroom, Westside, quiet, bike path, garden, carport. 1880 W 15th. $1,000 + deposits. 555-9696.

LARGE 3 BEDROOM, quiet area. 2 bath, all carpeted, appliances, clean, RV parking. $1,150 plus deposit. 2249 Willona. 555-5353.

SANTA CLARA—$1,195
Clean 3 bedroom, appliances, fireplace, fenced, garage. 555-7800.

3736 PEPPERTREE
3 bedroom, 1 1/2 bath, kids & pet okay. Fenced. $1,250. 555-8040.

3717 PEPPERTREE
3 bedroom, 2 baths, kids & pet okay. $1,095 555-7446.

2 BEDROOM
South Hills Springfield. Seclusion. $995. 555-4424.

Houses, Unfurnished　　605

SPRINGFIELD clean 2 bedroom, stove, refrigerator, utility hookup. Adults. $1,000. 555-2983.

OLDER 3 bedroom mobile home, on 1/2 acre, Prairie Road area. $900 plus deposit. 555-6654.

THURSTON 3 bedroom, carpet, appliances, fireplace, garage, $1,100 plus deposit. 555-9988.

THURSTON older 2 bedroom, carpet, appliances, storage, $1,025 plus deposit. 555-3205.

VENETA, modern 1 bedroom, paneled walls, storage, electric heat. $910. 555-7446; 555-7856.

4 Bedrooms, $1,300/offer. Bus line. Close-in. Appliances. First, deposit, references. 555-4090.

3 BEDROOM, 1 bath, large fenced yard. 775 N. 54th, Springfield. $1,100, $350 deposit. 555-2003.

3 BEDROOM, 1 1/2 bath, fireplace, double garage, 3553 South E, Springfield. 555-6060; 555-6209.

1, 2 & 3 BEDROOM MOBILE HOMES, $750 & Up, Thurston area park. Call 555-7773.

2 BEDROOM MOBILE
555-3205 or 555-2983.

Duplexes, Multiplexes, Furnished　　607

EASTSIDE EUGENE, 1 bedroom Duplex. Electric heat, water & garbage paid. $895.
　　　　Call 555-3764.

QUIET & PRIVATE
large 1 bedroom, new carpet (or unfurnished). $850. 555-3602.

Duplexes, Multiplexes, Furnished　　607

Proudly Offered
—SHASTA PARK—
BELTLINE & BARGER DR.
555-4424
RENTS FROM $895.

Resident managers will show your choice of duplexes, townhouses or single family homes, including 4 bedroom homes. Enjoy full lawn care, a responsive maintenance program & garbage service. Amenities include garages, fireplaces, laundry hook-ups & play areas.

Garden space available
Senior citizens discount
Children & Small pets welcome!

Follow signs to office Monday thru Saturday, 9 to 5; OR—

Call for showing appointment.
—IPM Co.—　　　　　　Realtor
1065 HIGH ST.　　　　　555-8040.

SPECIAL
MOVE-IN BONUSES
Pacific Park
Duplexes

2220 Shady Ln., Springfield
IDEAL LOCATION
2 BEDROOM Duplexes & Townhouses with garages. $1,000-$1,150. 2 Children. Large playground. 555-9200.

All Weatherized Units

Duplexes, Multiplexes, Furnished　　607

FREE RENT
1st 1/2 month FREE, new luxury duplex on bus line. 3 bedroom unit with stone heatilator fireplace. Earthtone carpeting & draperies. Fully applianced with dishwasher, disposal, & laundry hookup. Large, fenced yard & covered parking. Kids & small pets OK. $995 monthly + deposits. 392 Mira Ct. Call, 555-8898.

JUNCTION CITY

2 bedroom 440 East 5th　　$800
2 bedroom 420 East 5th　　$825
2 bedroom 400 East 6th　　$850
2 bedroom 915 W. 7th Place　$875

NORTHWEST COLLECTIONS
& Property Management, Inc.
795 Hiway 99N　　555-2500.
Monday-Friday 9 a.m.-6 p.m.

LARGE DUPLEXES
Air conditioning, fireplaces, patios with barbecue, 1 1/2 baths, 2 and 3 bedroom units. Excellent location next to schools and shopping, off Coburg Road. Quiet park-like setting, fully maintained. Garage, utility room. $900 to $1,125. L. G. Campbell Co., 555-5483.

ECHO HOLLOW WEST
New Management!
Special Discount Rent
2 Bedroom...$900
3 Bedroom...$1,100
Large Units with Garages.
$450 deposit—$275 pet fee.
555-9988.

1. How many houses that have one or two bedrooms are listed?

_____

2. Are mobile homes listed under "Houses" or under "Duplexes, Multiplexes"?

_____

3. Name some extra features advertised to lure customers to rent some of the houses, duplexes, and multiplexes.

_____

_____

4. List the ads that most appeal to you.

_____

_____

_____

5. How many ads specifically state that children and pets are accepted?

_____

6. Identify the least expensive unit and the most expensive unit in the clipping.

_____

Activity 12.4 Moving Costs and New Installation Charges

Directions: As a group project, using local sources of information, check the costs of moving and installation fees in your area.

1. One-Way Truck Rental
   a. Give your source of information.

   _____

   b. Provide a description of the truck, van, or pickup to be rented.

   _____

   _____

   c. List amounts for the (1) required refundable deposit, (2) daily fee, (3) mileage fee, and
      (4) approximate gasoline cost (gallons used).

   _____

   _____

   _____

   _____

   d. Name the amount of insurance required and the type of coverage. Also, note if the insurance
      deposit must be made in cash and, if not, how else it can be handled.

   _____

   _____

   _____

2. Water, Sewage, and Garbage Services
   a. Give your sources of information.

   _____

   _____

   b. Note on which bill water is paid for in your local area (e.g., part of the electric bill, water bill, and
      so on).

   _____

   c. Who pays for garbage collection in your local area (e.g., private individuals, the city, and so on)?

   _____

   d. Note on which bill sewage service is handled in your local area (e.g., part of another bill, sewage
      bill, and so on).

   _____

   e. List any deposits or fees for water, sewage, and garbage services. Also, provide the typical
      monthly rates for (1) water, (2) sewage, and (3) garbage services.

   _____

   _____

   _____

   _____

3. TV, Phone, and Internet Services
    a. Give your sources of information.

   _____

   _____

      (1) Are there different types of TV plans offered? If so, what are they? (List the features and cost
          of each plan.)

      _____

      _____

      _____

      _____

      _____

      (2) Are there different types of phone plans offered? If so, what are they? (List the features and
          cost of each plan.)

      _____

      _____

      _____

      _____

      _____

      (3) Are there different types of Internet plans offered? If so, what are they? (List the features and
          cost of each plan.)

      _____

      _____

      _____

      _____

      _____

    b. Is bundling available? If so, what types of packages are offered?

   _____

   _____

   _____

   _____

   _____

    c. List (1) the fees and/or deposits required for a person to obtain TV, phone, and/or Internet ser-
       vices and (2) installation costs.

   _____

   _____

   _____

   _____

    d. Is there a required contract? If so, what is it and what is the cost to terminate the contract early?

   _____

   _____

   _____

Activity 12.5 Cell Phone Costs and Services

Directions: As a group activity, contact a cell phone provider or visit a sales center or a retail location where cell phones and service can be purchased. Fill in the following information.

1. What is the least expensive cell phone you can purchase? Describe its features.

   _____

   _____

   _____

   _____

2. What is the most expensive cell phone you can purchase? Describe its features.

   _____

   _____

   _____

   _____

3. a. What types of individual plans are offered? (List the features and cost of each plan.)

   _____

   _____

   _____

   _____

   _____

   _____

   _____

   _____

   _____

   b. What is the cost per minute if you go over your plan minutes? If the rate varies, explain how.

   _____

   _____

   _____

   _____

   c. Is there a family plan or shared minutes plan that could save you money? Describe it.

   _____

   _____

   _____

   _____

4. What is the one-time activation charge?

   _____

   _____

   _____

5. Is there a security deposit for a person without established credit? If so, how much is it and how long must it remain on deposit?

_____

_____

6. Is a contract required? If so, what is the cost to terminate service before the contract is over?

_____

_____

_____

7. List other cell phone services and options (such as Internet access and Bluetooth).

_____

_____

_____

_____

_____

_____

_____

_____

_____

_____

_____

_____

_____

8. a. What is the cost to replace your phone if it is lost or stolen? _____

_____

    b. Can you buy insurance to protect yourself from such loss? If so, how much does it cost?

_____

Activity 12.6 Affordable Housing

Directions: Read the information below and answer the questions that follow.

The availability of affordable housing for low-income families is a problem in the United States. Several organizations mobilize citizens to help. One such group, Habitat for Humanity, is a nonprofit, nondenominational Christian organization that builds affordable houses for low-income families in the United States and around the world. Volunteers work side-by-side with those in need to build these houses. Through volunteer labor and tax-deductible donations, Habitat builds and rehabilitates simple, decent houses and sells them at no profit and with no-interest loans to families who would not otherwise be able to buy a home. To learn more about the group's efforts and ways you can participate, visit its website.

Another group, Volunteers of America, is a faith-based nonprofit organization that provides affordable housing to low-income and homeless people throughout the United States. The organization also provides assistance services to help the formerly homeless return to self-sufficiency. Its website contains more information about the organization and how you can volunteer.

Homelessness is a social problem in this country that joint efforts of citizens should be able to solve. Many people believe that a safe and comfortable place to live is a requirement for human dignity and that people must be given every opportunity to participate fully in society. Having a place to live is just the beginning, but it helps people make that first step toward self-reliance and responsibility.

You can make a difference. Consider volunteering in an activity of your choice to help others in your community or elsewhere. If you volunteer with a group, you could gain valuable skills as well as the satisfaction of helping people in need and working with others to accomplish a goal. Communities offer many opportunities to get involved in helping others, from serving meals at a homeless shelter to gathering donations for a local free-food store.

1. What programs are available in your community to help alleviate homelessness?

   _____

   _____

   _____

   _____

   _____

   _____

   _____

2. What other services do volunteer organizations provide in your community? Which of these activities most interest you? Why?

   _____

   _____

   _____

   _____

   _____

   _____

   _____

   _____

chapter 13 — Buying a Home

section 1: vocabulary

Fill in the missing word(s) in the space provided at the right.

Answers

Example: A loan to purchase real estate is called a(n) _____.   0. ___mortgage___

1. _____ are the expenses incurred in transferring ownership from buyer to seller in a real estate transaction.   1. _____

2. A rejection of an original offer with a listing of what terms would be acceptable is called a(n) _____.   2. _____

3. The difference between the market value of property and the amount owed on it is called _____.   3. _____

4. The _____ is a real estate marketing service in which agents pool their home listings and agree to share commissions on the sales.   4. _____

5. A(n) _____ is a formal document that expresses interest in entering into a real estate contract with someone else.   5. _____

6. The value given a home by a real estate appraiser is called its _____ value.   6. _____

7. The _____ value is used for purposes of computing property taxes owed against a home.   7. _____

8. A(n) _____ loan is a mortgage agreement offered through a commercial bank or mortgage broker that does not have government backing.   8. _____

9. A(n) _____ is the process of searching public records to check for ownership and claims to a piece of property.   9. _____

10. _____ are conditions that limit a buyer's liability in case one or more of them are not met.   10. _____

11. Real estate agents earn _____ for their work, which is a percentage of the home sale price.   11. _____

12. A(n) _____ mortgage is one whereby the interest rate does not change during the term of the loan.   12. _____

13. The _____ value of a home is the highest price that the property will bring on the market.   13. _____

14. A(n) _____ is a formal agreement to the terms of the buyer's offer.   14. _____

15. A(n) _____ is a financial claim against property.   15. _____

16. _____ protects the buyer from any claims arising from a defective title.   16. _____

17. A(n) _____ mortgage is one whereby the interest rate changes in response to the movement of interest rates in the economy.   17. _____

18. A(n) _____ is the legal document that transfers title of real property.   18. _____

2 | section:
review questions

After each of the following statements, circle *T* for a true statement or *F* for a false statement.

	Answers	For Scoring

1. The interest you pay on your home loan, along with the property taxes, are tax deductible.　　　T　F　1. _____

2. Renting or owning real estate is a type of tax shelter.　　　T　F　2. _____

3. The most common source for down payment money is a bank.　　　T　F　3. _____

4. Each loan payment you make decreases your debt and increases your equity.　　T　F　4. _____

5. A lien is a right or privilege one person has to use the land of another person.　　　T　F　5. _____

6. The Multiple Listing Service (MLS) gives people wanting to buy a home a greater exposure to available homes.　　　T　F　6. _____

7. When a seller accepts an offer exactly as stated, this is called a counteroffer.　　T　F　7. _____

8. The seller pays the real estate agent's commission.　　　T　F　8. _____

9. Most lenders require that the borrower buy title insurance.　　　T　F　9. _____

10. If you and the seller have agreed on the transaction, the house will be taken off the market until the deal is completed.　　　T　F　10.

On the line at the right of each sentence, print the letter that represents the word or group of words correctly completing the sentence or answering the question.

1. Home ownership offers (a) financial advantages, (b) quality-of-life advantages, (c) tax savings, (d) all of these.　　_____ 1. _____

2. A legal document that establishes ownership is a(n) (a) lien, (b) counteroffer, (c) title, (d) escrow.　　_____ 2. _____

3. The cost of home ownership is lowered through (a) property insurance, (b) tax deductions, (c) home maintenance, (d) all of these.　　_____ 3. _____

4. Real estate agents earn commissions that are usually between _____ percent of the home sale price. (a) 3 and 5, (b) 6 and 8, (c) 10 and 12, (d) 12 and 15　　_____ 4. _____

5. Earnest money protects the (a) buyer, (b) seller, (c) real estate agent, (d) lender.　　_____ 5. _____

6. When you apply for a mortgage, which of the following will be checked? (a) your references, (b) your credit history, (c) your income, (d) all of these　　_____ 6. _____

7. To qualify for a conventional loan to purchase a home, a borrower must (a) be a low-income buyer, (b) be a first-time homebuyer, (c) have a good credit score, (d) have collateral to secure the loan.　　_____ 7. _____

8. To finance your purchase of a house, you must (a) have funds for the down payment, (b) meet certain lending requirements, (c) select the type of mortgage you want, (d) all of these.　　_____ 8. _____

9. Who conducts a title search and issues a report? (a) an attorney, (b) a real estate agent, (c) a title insurance company, (d) the buyer of real estate　　_____ 9. _____

10. Real estate agents use comps to get a general idea of a property's _____ value, which helps sellers establish a list price for their home. (a) appraised, (b) assessed, (c) estimated, (d) market　　_____ 10. _____

3 section:
problem solving

Activity 13.1 Homes for Sale

Directions: Examine the partial listing of homes and answer the questions below.

HUGE HOUSE VIEW LOW PRICE

($150,000)

2455 WILSON DR.
(Drive up City View)
Call JOY at 555-7856 or 555-8567.
Countryman Realty Assoc. Inc.

VERY NICE 2 bedroom, 1 1/2 bath condo. Beautifully decorated, fireplace, pool and lots of extras. 5 3/4% (annual percentage rate) to a qualified buyer. Only $199,000. Please call Enid Delaney, 555-9704.

"Where the Action Is!"
Gordon Brunton
EBL, Inc. REALTY
1601 Willamette 555-4704.

HERE IT IS!
—3 Bedroom, 2 bath
—Kitchen eating area
—Fireplace
—Many More Extras
—Priced to sell - $219,000
McPHEETERS
REAL ESTATE, INC.
642 Charnelton 555-8890, 555-8906.

OPEN TODAY NEW HOMES
By Krumdieck
Priced From $149,950.
Low Interest, Long Term
SEE OUR AD IN CLASS 405
Robert Belknap Realtor
895 Country Club Road 555-4653.

EDGEWOOD WEST—4 bedroom, 3 bath, tri-level home. 2200+ sq. ft. EXCELLENT BUY at $174,500 with low down, also, 5.4% annual percentage rate. Underlying ODVA loan. WINNIE, 555-2983.

"Where the Action Is!"
Gordon Brunton
EBL, Inc. REALTY
1601 Willamette 555-7404.

CUSTOM BUILD
HIGH QUALITY HOMES
27 LOTS TO CHOOSE FROM

A dip in interest rates plus a discount on lot and competitive construction costs may make this the time for a new home.

JACK ADKINS
Construction Inc., 555-9988.

---

3 bedroom charmer, family room, wet bar, 2 fireplaces, new carpets, 1700 square feet, YOU WILL LOVE IT for $205,000. Call Fritz, 555-3205.

"Where the Action Is!"
Gordon Brunton
EBL, Inc. REALTY
1601 Willamette 555-7404.

Santa Clara Homes 417

VAULTED CEDAR CEILING
Adds warmth to this exceptional 3-bedroom, 1 1/2-bath home on an extra large lot with irrigation well. Priced at just $169,900, an extra good buy. Call TOM YATES, 555-2358, or MARK BEEMAN, 555-9696 or 555-7800.

SPECIAL HOME
It is one of those RARE properties that shows pride of ownership and is priced to sell TODAY! Three-bedroom, 2 baths and well decorated living area. Great landscaping and fenced yard. Only $174,500. Call CHUCK COY, 555-4090 or 555-7856, or DON MOGENSON, 555-2003.

IRVING
CURTIS IRVING REALTY

NEW LOW PRICE
This custom 1 level home has 3 bedrooms, 2 1/2 baths, 1780 sq. ft. Traffic-free living room, formal dining room, family room with fireplace. Schrader insert, inside utility. Enjoy the master Bedroom suite with access to private courtyard, walk-in closet & master bath. Ideal Oregon Vet financing, now $199,900.

Call Al or Evelyn
AL MOORE REALTY
642 Polk 555-4424.

OPEN HOUSE 1 to 4
$3,500 cash down. Attractive home, front living room with hot wood-burning fireplace, 2 bedrooms (king-sized master), kitchen with built-in range/dishwasher, large bathroom, dining room overlooks private grass & fir treed yard. Oversized 2-car garage. Room for RV parking. Take over broker-owner's loan balance of $126,000. 7.8% annual percentage rate. $665 monthly for 25 years, + taxes. 555-7446. 2481 Canterbury (off Irving Road)

OPEN 1-4
2848 Country Lane
Brand new listing, 3-bedroom, 1 1/2-bath, 2 fireplaces, one in kitchen, screened-in patio, nicely landscaped fenced yard. Nice, well-cared-for neighborhood. $192,000. Directions: Coburg Road to Oakmont, right on Oakmont to Rustic, right on Rustic to Country Lane. Hostess; AMY PINEGAR, 555-6060 or 555-5353.

PLUS
This 3-bedroom, 2-bath home is a possible 4-bedroom with rock fireplace in family, hardwood floor in kitchen, formal dining and pool in fenced backyard. Only 3 years old and $191,900. Call TOM YATES, 555-2358, or MARK BEEMAN, 555-9696 or 555-7800.

2290 Square Feet
FOR $204,000
Lovely spacious home in a terrific area with 4 bedrooms and 2 baths, large yard, deck, nice carpeting, formal dining, and enough elbow room at an affordable price. Contract with low down possible. Call: RUSS ROYER, 555-4653, or SCARLET LEE, 555-8898 or 555-9200.

IRVING
CURTIS IRVING REALTY

FAIR OAKS
LOVELY custom home on golf course with over 3000 square feet of luxury all on one level, including:
• 4 Bedrooms
• 3 1/2 Baths
• Formal Dining
• Separate Family Room
• Den (with private bath & entry)
• Spacious kitchen
• Large eating area off kitchen
• 3 Fireplaces
• Abundant storage & closets

All tastefully decorated with color coordinated wallpapers, select tiles, draperies and floor coverings. This is a very exciting home to view—offered at $315,000 with EXCELLENT TERMS. For an appointment to view this SPECIAL PROPERTY, please call Edna Johnson 555-2500 eves & weekends or the office anytime.

Countryman Realty Assoc. Inc.
1234 High 555-3602.

BY OWNER, Lovely 6 year old 3 bedroom, 2 1/2 bathroom house. Formal dining room, large living room, landscaped yard. 1 Block from elementary school. $184,000. Owner will carry 2nd with little down to qualified buyer. Please call 555-5483 for appointment. You may drop by to see house at 3771 Keeler.

DRIVE BY
549 Panda Loop (Garden Way to Kodiak). Super quality in this 3 bedroom, 2 1/2 bath house. Ready to move into, small equity. Owner will carry 2nd too! Call Pam Hysmith, 555-6209.

JEAN TATE
REAL ESTATE, Inc. 555-5544.

SPYGLASS!
Cozy cottage for small family, with skylights. Oak, French doors to private deck. Assumable loan and owner will consider a second. Only $257,900. To view, call Sue, 555-7773 eves.

RAMS REALTY
315 W. Broadway 555-8040

LOWEST PRICE
We believe. Over 1300 feet of living space. 3 bedrooms, 1 1/2 bath with large open beam family room and wood stove. Low down and easy payments. $149,900. Eddie, 555-2222.

BOB CARLILE Realty, Inc.
1473 Willamette 555-2358

1565 BOND LANE
3 bedroom, 3 bath home. $161,000. Your car or camper for down. Call 555-4090 anytime.

HARLOW REALTY

8 3/4%
BY OWNER. 3 Bedroom, 1 1/2 bath, inside utility, 2-car garage, shop, large fenced yard, $181,900. 555-2003.

FULLY WEATHERIZED. 3 bedrooms, 1 1/2 bath, fireplace, large fenced backyard in nice neighborhood, close to park. $169,000. Principals only. 555-8898.

---

1. What is the highest home price listed?

_____

2. How many of the homes are open for someone to see?

_____

3. How many houses are offered for sale by the owner?

_____

4. What descriptive words are used to make houses sound attractive?

_____

_____

Activity 13.2 The Listing Agreement

Directions: Based on the information supplied, fill out the listing agreement as though you were the owner of the property being listed for sale. Owner: John L. and Patricia C. Smith; Property Address: 616 Oak Street, Oakland, California 94601; Time of Listing: 120 days; Listing Price of Home: $199,000; Date: April 1, current year; Name of Real Estate Company: J. B. Adams Realty; Real Estate Agent: Carmen Kreitz; Real Estate Broker: J. B. Adams

---

REAL ESTATE LISTING AGREEMENT
Exclusive Right to Sell

In consideration of the agreements expressed herein, the real estate agency listed below hereby agrees to produce best efforts to secure a buyer for the property described as:

The undersigned, hereinafter called Owner, does hereby employ said agency listed above for a period of _____ days and grants said agency sole authority to offer for sale, including advertise and place "for sale" signs thereon, said property for a price of $_____.

THE OWNER AGREES:

1. To pay the customary real estate commission in the amount equal to 7 percent for which said property is sold.

2. To cooperate with the real estate agent and broker in every way possible to bring about a sale.

3. In the event this agreement is revoked or the property withdrawn from sale during the period of this agreement, Owner shall pay reasonable costs and damages.

THE AGENT AGREES:

1. To make a careful inspection of said property and make an earnest and continued effort to sell said property at the terms set forth in this agreement.

2. To promote and advertise such property in a professional manner; to prepare a brochure and list property with the Multiple Listing Service.

3. To show said property at reasonable times, maintain signs and lock boxes, and inform the Owner of progress as this agreement continues.

Date: _____

Owner: _____

Owner: _____

Date: _____

Broker: _____

Agent: _____

Activity 13.3 The Earnest Money Offer

Directions: Based on the information given below, prepare the earnest money agreement shown on the next page.

Buyers: Viet L. and Sue M. Nygen
1246 Eastwood Avenue, Apt. #226, Brentwood, CA 94513
Phone: (213) 555-0168

Sellers: Marge B. and George M. Hensen
235 Crestwood Drive
Anaheim, CA 92808

Property: Located in the city of Anaheim, Orange County, California
described as 339 West Lake Drive, Anaheim, California

Price: $289,000

Earnest money: $35,000

Down payment: $50,000

Balance: $204,000 to be paid by buyers qualifying for a loan
from FarWest Mortgage Bank at a fixed rate not to
exceed 5.5%.

Deed: Warranty

Title insurance: FarWest Title Insurance Company

No liens, encumbrances, etc., except those conveyed for public utilities purposes.

Closing date: April 15, 20—
Proration date: April 15, 20—

Offer is subject to a satisfactory pest control and damage report.

Time: Until 5 p.m. on January 18, 20— to accept offer

Escrow agent: Eric Fontova
Broker: R. K. Henry
Sales commission: 7% of the purchase price

Date of buyers' signatures: January 15, 20—

REAL ESTATE EARNEST MONEY OFFER

City of _____, County of _____, State of _____,
_____, hereafter called Buyer(s), agrees to purchase the following
described property:

for a total purchase price of .... $_____
as follows: Earnest money .... $_____
            Down payment of .... $_____
            Balance of .... $_____ $_____
payable in the following manner: _____
_____
_____
Seller will deliver to Buyer a _____ deed to said property, furnish a policy of title insurance
from _____
showing title vested in buyer free of liens, encumbrances, easements, rights, and conditions,
except as follows:_____
Escrow agent for closing shall be _____
and closing date shall be _____, 20___; taxes, property insurance, mortgage interest, and
other items shall be prorated as of _____, 20___.
All attached floor coverings, storm windows and doors, lighting fixtures, landscaping, built-in
appliances, and fences now on the premises shall be included in this sale, except: _____
_____

This offer is subject to: _____
_____
If this agreement is not completed by reason of the Buyer's default, Seller is released from any
obligation and shall retain the deposit money as liquidated damages. The buyer has until _____
(a.m. or p.m.) on _____, 20___ to indicate acceptance by signing at the bottom of this offer.

_____   _____
Real Estate Broker   Buyer

_____, 20_____   _____
                                  Buyer

_____   _____
Phone number of Buyer   Address

ACCEPTANCE

    The undersigned accepts the foregoing offer and agrees to sell the property described above
on the terms and conditions set forth.
    The undersigned agrees to pay _____ the sales commission of
$_____ upon recording of the deed and completion of this sale.

                                  _____
                                  Seller

_____   _____
Date   Seller

Activity 13.4 Real Estate for Sale

Directions: Using the Sunday newspaper in your area or online resources, obtain the following types of ads and attach them to this activity sheet.

1. A house for sale by owner

2. A house for sale in your neighborhood or close area

3. A house for sale with more than four bedrooms

4. A house for sale on more than one acre

5. Property for sale by a lake, river, ocean, or other recreation site

6. The lowest-priced house ad you can find

7. The most expensive house ad you can find

8. A house with the most special features

9. Attach a picture of a house that is featured in the paper, online, or in a special advertisement or brochure published by a real estate company.

Activity 13.5 Finding the Right Real Estate Agent

Directions: Read the text below and then answer the questions that follow.

If you decide to list your home with a real estate agent, first ask your friends and relatives for recommendations. They may offer names of agents who did a good job for them. Then contact agents from several companies for a listing presentation. You want to find an agent that you feel comfortable with and that knows the market in your area well. Here are some questions to ask:

1. Are you licensed?
2. How long have you been working as a real estate agent?
3. How long have you worked in this area?
4. About how many homes have you sold recently?
5. For about how many of these sales did you find the buyers?
6. What services will you provide for me as your client?
7. Do you subscribe to the Multiple Listing Service?
8. How will you market my home? Will you hold open houses? How many?
9. At what price should I list my home? Please show me the prices for which comparable homes actually sold recently to support your assessment.
10. What commission percentage will you charge?

Keep in mind that an agent's commission is negotiable. The agent will not likely tell you so, but he or she may be willing to come down on the commission in order to make the sale. As part of negotiating with a prospective buyer, consider negotiating the agent's commission as well.

Reject any agent who is not licensed. Also reject any agent whose company is not a member of the local Multiple Listing Service (MLS). A listing in the MLS is a major benefit that a real estate agent can provide that you cannot get on your own. The MLS exposes your home listing to many buyers, increasing your chances for making the sale.

1. Ask a real estate agent to explain an agent's responsibilities to buyers and sellers in a real estate transaction.

_____

_____

_____

_____

_____

_____

_____

_____

2. Why is it important for your agent to know the market in your area?

_____

_____

_____

_____

_____

_____

_____

_____

14 Buying and Owning a Vehicle

Name _____

1 section: vocabulary

Fill in the missing word(s) in the space provided at the right.

Answers

Example: A(n) _____ service allows you to choose the vehicle features you want and have a professional car buyer handle the price negotiation for you.

0. ____car-buying____

1. _____ is the process of getting a new- or used-car loan prearranged through your bank or credit union.

1. _____

2. The _____ is the price shown on the tag in the car's window; it is the manufacturer's suggested retail price.

2. _____

3. A(n) _____ is a simple road test where you drive the car for several miles in typical traffic and road conditions.

3. _____

4. A(n) _____ assures that a car meets minimum clean-air standards.

4. _____

5. A car's _____ is an alphanumeric number that identifies it.

5. _____

6. _____ are high-priced, high-profit dealer services that add little or no value to a car.

6. _____

7. A(n) _____ test can tell you whether to expect serious engine trouble ahead.

7. _____

8. The decline in value of a vehicle due to normal wear and tear is called _____.

8. _____

9. Rare cars and very old vehicles in excellent condition may experience_____, or an increase in value.

9. _____

10. A(n) _____ lists the legal owner and the registered owner of a vehicle.

10. _____

11. When car paint begins to _____, it permanently loses its color and shine.

11. _____

12. A(n) _____ is a large parking lot where car owners can park and advertise their cars.

12. _____

13. The car's interior _____, or seat-covering material, must be maintained to preserve it.

13. _____

14. A(n) _____ is a written statement about a product or service's qualities or performance that the seller assures are true.

14. _____

15. _____ protect consumers from the consequences of buying a defective car.

15. _____

16. A(n) _____ can be used to smooth out car surface scratches, scuffs, and stains.

16. _____

17. A(n) _____ is a type of vehicle that uses alternate energy sources.

17. _____

18. The Federal Trade Commission requires dealers to place a sticker, called the _____, on all used cars they offer for sale.

18. _____

19. A(n) _____ is a service provided by specialists who clean and polish the exterior, along with treating and cleaning the interior.

19. _____

2 section:
review questions

After each of the following statements, circle *T* for a true statement or *F* for a false statement.

	Answers	For Scoring

1. The first step in buying a car is deciding what type of car you both need and want. — T F — 1. _____

2. It is important to get a credit preapproval after you have selected the car of your choice. — T F — 2. _____

3. It is almost impossible to determine a fair price for a new car. — T F — 3. _____

4. Special features can usually be added on to a car at a lesser cost by the car dealership than by a specialty shop. — T F — 4. _____

5. Vehicle emission tests are required by all states. — T F — 5. _____

6. Preapproval adds to the total costs of buying a car. — T F — 6. _____

7. Private sellers are not covered under the FTC Used Car Rule. — T F — 7. _____

8. Most car dealerships offer financing options for car purchases. — T F — 8. _____

9. Lemon laws generally require you to have good documentation of your car's problems. — T F — 9. _____

10. Generally, vinyl upholstery is more durable than cloth. — T F — 10. _____

On the line at the right of each sentence, print the letter that represents the word or group of words correctly completing the sentence or answering the question.

1. When is the best time to get credit preapproval for a car loan? (a) before visiting car dealers, (b) during price negotiations, (c) after determining which car you would like to purchase, (d) after the purchase _____ 1. _____

2. Which of the following is not a dealer add-on? (a) tune-up, (b) protective wax or polish, (c) rust proofing, (d) window tinting _____ 2. _____

3. The single greatest cost of owning a new car is (a) the car payment, (b) depreciation, (c) fuel, (d) insurance. _____ 3. _____

4. When your vehicle is new, you should (a) drive at a constant speed rather than at varying speeds, (b) shift gears rapidly to help break in your transmission, (c) avoid long trips, (d) all of these. _____ 4. _____

5. As a general rule, most experts advise having your oil changed every _____ miles. (a) 1,000 to 3,000, (b) 3,000 to 5,000, (c) 10,000, (d) 25,000 to 30,000 _____ 5. _____

6. Which of the following would not be considered as part of performing routine maintenance on a car? (a) rotating the tires, (b) changing the oil, (c) replacing the spark plugs, (d) replacing the transmission _____ 6. _____

7. If the sticker price for a new car is $20,250 and the invoice price is $18,000, what would a fair price be for the car? (a) $16,500, (b) $19,000, (c) $21,000, (d) none of these _____ 7. _____

8. Which of the following would not be covered by warranty? (a) tune-up, (b) transmission, (c) engine, (d) drivetrain _____ 8. _____

9. If you are uncomfortable with price negotiations, you may want to (a) buy a used car, (b) hire a car-buying service, (c) buy a new car, (d) buy a car from a private seller. _____ 9. _____

3 section:
problem solving

Activity 14.1 Car-Buying Checklist

Directions: When buying a used car, you should look for a number of things. Read through the list below and see if there is anything you can add to it. You and your mechanic should look for cracks, leaks, breaks, abnormal noises, and missing or inoperable parts, as follows:

_____ Frame and body. Is it straight and solid?

_____ Engine. Does it run smoothly? Is there evidence of oil leaking? Are the belts in place? Is the exhaust working properly?

_____ Differential. Is the differential fluid clear and clean?

_____ Transmission. Is the transmission fluid level proper? Is the fluid clear and clean?

_____ Cooling system. Does the air conditioning and heating system work properly? Is the water pump leaking?

_____ Electrical system. Is there evidence of battery leakage? Does the vehicle start promptly, even when cold?

_____ Fuel system. Is there a gas smell? Is there evidence of leaking around the fuel door or lid?

_____ Warning system. Do the gauges and warning devices work?

_____ Brakes. Do the brake lights work? Is the brake pedal firm under pressure? Does the vehicle stop in a straight line?

_____ Steering system. Does the car go straight when the wheel is left open for a few seconds?

_____ Suspension. Do the springs and shocks work properly? Does the car ride smoothly even over small bumps and holes?

_____ Tires. Do you see visible cracks, damage, or wear?

_____ Exhaust system. Does the engine emit smoke when running? Has the car been tested for emission standards?

What additional items would you check?

_____

_____

_____

Interview a mechanic or adult who has worked on vehicles and write a short report about his or her recommendations when buying a used car.

Activity 14.2 All About Tires

Directions: The U.S. Department of Transportation requires that tire manufacturers provide considerable information about a tire on the sidewall so that the buyer can clearly read its codes and markings. Based on the code explanations below, write out the same information that you can find on a tire.

SAMPLE:	YOUR CAR:
P185/70R14 P stands for passenger tire. 185 is the nominal width of the tire (in millimeters). 70 is the aspect ratio (the ratio of the sidewall's height to the width). In other words, this tire is 70% of 185 mm (or about 135 mm) tall. R stands for radial ply. 14 stands for the diameter of the wheel.	
Treadwear 420 Traction A Temperature B * Treadwear index: this tire lasts 4.2 times as long as a tire graded "100." * The highest grade of traction is "A"; "C" is the lowest. * Index of a tire's ability to tolerate high temperatures. "A" is the highest grade; "C" is the lowest.	
DOT Y7J6 CCD 032 Serial number, identity in case of recall.	
MAX LOAD 545 KG (1201 LBS) 240 KPA 35 (PSI) MAX PRESS The tire can support up to 1,201 pounds, including the car and its occupants and luggage. The tire should be inflated up to 35 pounds per square inch.	

Activity 14.3 Facts About Cars

Directions: Consult an almanac or other source about automobiles in the United States, and write a short report about your findings in three of the following areas:

1. Best-selling automobiles
2. Deaths from automobile accidents
3. Drivers (by state)—number and age
4. Exports and imports
5. Fuel consumption, prices, and gasoline tax
6. Injuries
7. Invention of the automobile
8. Production of the automobile
9. Vehicle registration in your state
10. Sales of vehicles in your state
11. Seat belt laws
12. Theft of automobiles

Or other topics, as approved by your instructor, as follows:

13. _____

14. _____

15. _____

Activity 14.4 Auto Repairs and Rip-Offs

Overcharging and needless repairs cost motorists many billions of dollars according to the U.S. Department of Transportation, which concludes that at least 50 cents of every dollar spent for auto repairs is unnecessary, due to inflated prices or needless work.

Some states require repair shops to give customers written notices, and then the cost cannot be increased more than 10 percent without authorization from the customer. Many states require that the repair shop return defective or worn out parts to customers rather than discard them. Automobile repair rip-offs represent a large number of consumer complaints each year.

Travelers should beware of allowing others to check engines, tires, and other car parts. These items are often targeted for unnecessary work. It works like this: The traveler pulls into a service station for gas and asks that the oil be checked. When the attendant checks the oil, he sees faulty parts, worn out hoses, or some engine problem that needs to be fixed immediately. These repairs typically cost $100 or more. When checking tire pressure, the attendant lets out some air and then claims that the tires are wearing, defective, damaged, or otherwise need to be replaced for safe driving.

But you don't have to be a stranger to get ripped off. Dishonest mechanics find work that doesn't need to be done and add inflated time (labor charges) as well as unnecessary parts to their bills. They remove parts that are in good condition and replace them with used, rebuilt parts. The removed parts are "reconditioned" and put into other cars.

Incompetent workmanship is also a major complaint received by Better Business Bureaus. When work performed does not prove to solve the car's running problems, and may in fact make it worse, the mechanic makes no adjustments without additional charges.

Below is a list of tips from New York City's Department of Consumer Affairs to help you know what to do when you run into car trouble.

Tips from New York City's
Department of Consumer Affairs

- Look for a reliable mechanic before you are faced with an emergency. Ask friends for references.
- If you suspect your car needs repairs, have it checked before it becomes a big repair.
- For large repairs, get two estimates and compare the charges. Let the shops know that you are comparison shopping.
- List all symptoms so that you won't forget anything when you are talking to a mechanic. Give a copy of the list to the mechanic and keep a copy for yourself. Make sure that all symptoms are taken care of before you accept the work for full payment.
- Don't authorize work unless you understand what is being done. Add-on work that does not apply to the reason for your repair is suspect.
- Don't tell a mechanic to "get this car in good running order." This is a blanket opportunity for him or her to do anything, whether or not it is needed.
- Don't sign a repair order unless you understand what is being done to your car. Question each line item.
- Keep itemized bills. Good records will help you in the event work is not satisfactory and mechanics must stand behind their work. Be able to tell the mechanic, "I had this fuel pump replaced by you two months ago. It should still be working." Have the documentation with you to prove it.
- If you suspect you are being overcharged, ask to see the supplier's parts price list.
- Find out which local and state government agencies have jurisdiction over auto-repair complaints and use them to get satisfaction.

Directions: Read the following situation and then answer the questions that follow. In responding to the questions, refer to the list of tips from New York City's Department of Consumer Affairs.

Consuelo Fuentes had been having a great deal of trouble with her 10-year-old Chevrolet. The engine stalled every time she pulled up to a stoplight. She was embarrassed as impatient drivers pulled up behind her and blasted their horns.

One day, Consuelo's car stalled, and she could not get it running again. She called Santiago's Service Station for towing. Once the car was towed to the service station, the manager looked under the hood and shook his head. "Your problem is with the electrical system," he said. "Don't worry about it, though. We'll get the problem fixed tomorrow."

Consuelo called a friend for the short ride home from the service station. She assumed the manager would call her once the nature of the problem was pinpointed. She also told him to get the car in good running condition.

When she returned to the station the next day, the manager presented her with a bill for $795. "What is this?" she exclaimed. "I didn't sign for those repairs, and I thought you would call me if the bill would be high." The manager explained that the car needed a new starter, a fuel pump, and a complete tune-up. "We also thought something was wrong with the transmission. We decided that we had to tear it down," he said.

Consuelo was totally frustrated. If she did not pay the bill, the manager said that he would have to hold her car. Consuelo consented and paid with a credit card.

1. What mistake did Consuelo make?

_____

_____

_____

_____

_____

_____

_____

_____

_____

_____

2. When Consuelo was overcharged for the repair bill, what course of action could she have taken?

_____

_____

_____

_____

_____

_____

_____

_____

_____

_____

Name _____

Activity 14.5 Car Options and Their Prices

Directions: The cost of a vehicle will depend on the major options or components that are included. When you order a new car, you can choose the options that you prefer. *Consumer Reports* publishes lists of these components and their current costs. From a current issue of the magazine or from online resources, write in prices you would expect to pay if you were ordering a vehicle today. Also identify the advantages and disadvantages of each option.

Option	Price Range	Advantages	Disadvantages
Diesel engine/ hybrid engine/ electric engine			
Automatic transmission			
Manual transmission			
Power brakes			
Power steering			
Cruise control			
Full-service, full-size spare tire			
Power seats			
Tinted windows			
Power windows			
Central locking system			
Other: (Student's choice)			

Activity 14.6 Car Research Project

Directions: Complete the following project by answering each question and writing a summary report of your findings. You should consult at least three sources: a bank or credit union, a car dealership, and a person who has had experience purchasing a new or used car.

1. What type of car would you like to buy? (Be specific—list year and make, features, size of engine, color, and so on.)

   _____

   _____

   _____

2. What is the sticker price (for a new car) or Kelley Blue Book value (for a used car) of the vehicle of your choice?

   _____

3. What is the final price you are likely to pay for the vehicle? Based on this price, what would the monthly payments be, and for how long?

   _____

   _____

4. List all of the features and the cost of each feature.

   _____

   _____

   _____

   _____

5. List the expenses of operating this vehicle for the next year, including fuel and oil, regular maintenance, insurance, and other necessary costs.

   _____

   _____

   _____

   _____

6. Determine how many miles you would drive in a given year, including where you would go, how often, and the distance.

   _____

   _____

   _____

   _____

7. Compute your cost per mile of driving the car (total costs divided by miles driven).

   _____

   _____

   _____

   _____

chapter 15

Family Decisions

1 section: vocabulary

Fill in the missing word(s) in the space provided at the right.

Answers

Example: When two people decide to commit to a life together, they become _____, or formally pledged to each other.

0. ___engaged___

1. The _____ consists of the people who are active participants in the wedding ceremony.

1. _____

2. A(n) _____ wedding is one in which all participants and guests wear tuxedos and long gowns.

2. _____

3. A(n) _____ wedding may be held almost anywhere, and no special attire is required for the wedding party or guests.

3. _____

4. A(n) _____ wedding is usually held during the afternoon or early evening, with less formal wear required of guests.

4. _____

5. A(n) _____ is a listing of the couple's choice of dishes, housewares, and other products.

5. _____

6. A(n) _____ is a document specifying the division of assets agreed to by both parties involved in a divorce.

6. _____

7. A detailed list of events, times, and places to visit on a trip or vacation is called a(n) _____.

7. _____

8. A(n) _____ is an advance commitment to receive a service at a specified later date.

8. _____

9. A(n) _____ is a business that arranges transportation, accommodations, and itineraries for customers.

9. _____

10. When airlines _____ flights, this means they sell more reservations than they can fulfill.

10. _____

11. The process of reducing a body to ashes in a high-temperature oven is called _____.

11. _____

12. A wedding performed by a public official rather than a member of the clergy is called a(n) _____.

12. _____

13. _____ includes the monthly payments made by a noncustodial parent to help provide food, clothing, and shelter for children of the divorce.

13. _____

14. A divorce, or _____, is a legal process in which a judge dissolves the bonds of matrimony between two people.

14. _____

15. A(n) _____ is a group benefit that allows employees and their families to seek counseling and other services.

15. _____

16. _____ is a nonprofit program consisting of medical and support services provided by a team of professionals and volunteers for those who are dying and for their families.

16. _____

2 section:
review questions

After each of the following statements, circle *T* for a true statement or *F* for a false statement.

	Answers	For Scoring

1. A civil ceremony is performed by a public official rather than a member of the clergy.   T   F   1. _____

2. In this country, premarital counseling is always required before a couple can be married.   T   F   2. _____

3. Most long-term disability plans cover 50 to 70 percent of an employee's monthly salary.   T   F   3. _____

4. Honeymoons often begin right after the wedding and reception.   T   F   4. _____

5. Family financial decisions are the primary responsibility of the husband in today's society.   T   F   5. _____

6. Family goals are similar to individual goals; there are short-term, intermediate, and long-term goals.   T   F   6. _____

7. Once married, a couple must have a joint checking account from which all bills are paid.   T   F   7. _____

8. The steps in setting a family budget are the same steps used in creating a personal budget.   T   F   8. _____

9. Full-service travel sites often offer packaged discounts if you book both your flight and hotel.   T   F   9. _____

10. You should arrive at the airport at least two hours before a domestic flight and three hours before an international flight.   T   F   10. _____

11. It is illegal for airlines to overbook flights.   T   F   11. _____

12. Adult foster care is a facility for adults who need care beyond what their families can provide.   T   F   12. _____

13. Long-term disability insurance is available through the Social Security Administration.   T   F   13. _____

14. For safety reasons, you should take all of your credit cards with you on vacation, even if you won't be using them.   T   F   14. _____

15. All 50 U.S. states allow no-fault divorce.   T   F   15. _____

16. Custodial parents usually are required to pay child support to their former spouses.   T   F   16. _____

17. Divorce in the United States is governed by federal law.   T   F   17. _____

18. Alimony is awarded to a former spouse at the court's discretion.   T   F   18. _____

19. Cremation is typically more expensive than a traditional funeral and burial.   T   F   19. _____

20. A divorce decree is the final statement of the dissolution decisions.   T   F   20. _____

21. Hospice can be provided in the patient's home or an outside facility.   T   F   21. _____

22. Typically, the estate of the deceased is liable for any unpaid medical bills.   T   F   22. _____

23. Funeral costs include embalming, the casket, funeral services, the obituary, and cost of burial.   T   F   23. _____

On the line at the right of each sentence, print the letter that represents the word or group or words correctly completing the sentence or answering the question.

1. Life insurance benefits are (a) taxable to the beneficiaries, (b) taxable to the estate of the person who died, (c) not taxable to the beneficiaries, (d) taxable to the beneficiaries but not to the estate of the person who died.   _____ 1. _____

2. Chris and Maria have decided to have their wedding at Maria's parents' house. Chris and Maria are most likely having a(n) (a) civil ceremony, (b) formal wedding, (c) informal wedding, (d) semiformal wedding.   _____ 2. _____

3. The amount of child support payments depends on (a) the income of both parents, (b) the marital status of the custodial parent, (c) the time each parent spends with the child, (d) the employment status of the custodial parent.   _____ 3. _____

4. A couple should begin planning the wedding ceremony at least _____ before the wedding. (a) two weeks, (b) two months, (c) six months, (d) one year   _____ 4. _____

5. Which of the following costs traditionally have been considered to be the groom's responsibility? (a) wedding invitations, (b) cleric's fee, (c) groom's wedding ring, (d) bride's dress   _____ 5. _____

6. Which of the following is an example of a short-term goal for a couple? (a) whether they want children, (b) where the couple will put down roots, (c) whether both partners will work, (d) all of these   _____ 6. _____

7. Survivors' benefits include all of the following except (a) life insurance benefits, (b) veterans benefits, (c) Social Security benefits, (d) child support.   _____ 7. _____

8. The average engagement period lasts (a) less than a month, (b) between 3 and 6 months, (c) between 6 and 12 months, (d) between 12 and 18 months.   _____ 8. _____

9. The bride usually pays for which of the following? (a) marriage license, (b) bride's bouquet, (c) wedding dress, (d) bachelor dinner   _____ 9. _____

10. Guest lists are prepared by (a) the bride, (b) the groom, (c) the parents of the bride and groom, (d) all of the above.   _____ 10. _____

11. Which of the following vacation alternatives would be the least expensive? (a) camping, (b) skiing, (c) plane trip, (d) visit to amusement park   _____ 11. _____

12. An itinerary lists all of the following except (a) events, (b) times, (c) costs, (d) places.   _____ 12. _____

13. Most airlines permit each traveler to bring _____ on planes. (a) two personal items and one carry-on bag, (b) two carry-on bags, (c) one personal item and one carry-on bag, (d) one carry-on bag only   _____ 13. _____

14. Family financial goals should be (a) specific (b) realistic, (c) measurable, (d) all of these.   _____ 14. _____

15. Expenses of divorce include all of the following except (a) attorneys' fees, (b) court costs, (c) filing fees, (d) custody and visitation fees.   _____ 15. _____

16. The first step in the divorce process is (a) serving the other party with papers, (b) setting a court date, (c) meeting with an attorney and drafting the petition, (d) entering the decree.   _____ 16. _____

3 section:
problem solving

Activity 15.1 Wedding Costs

Directions: Complete the following wedding worksheet. Estimate costs based on advice from married couples or other sources of information. Plan the type of wedding you believe that you would like to have in the future. Total the costs.

Engagement Party

Invitations	$_____
Food	_____
Beverages	_____
Music	_____
Rental fees	_____
Decorations	_____
Professional services	_____
Gratuities	
Total	$_____

Stationery

Invitations	$_____
Announcements	_____
At-home cards	_____
Personal stationery	_____
Stamps	_____
Total	$_____

Clothing

Wedding dress	$_____
Headpiece/veil	_____
Shoes	_____
Accessories	_____
Personal trousseau	_____
Total	$_____

*Denotes expenses usually shared by both families.

Bridesmaids' Luncheon

Invitations and place cards	$_____
Food	_____
Beverages	_____
Rental fees	_____
Decorations	_____
Professional services	_____
*Gratuities	_____
Total	$_____

Photographs

Engagement portrait	$_____
Wedding portrait	_____
Formal photos	_____
Reprints	_____
Total	$_____

Wedding Ceremony

Sanctuary rental	$_____
Music	_____
Decorations	_____
Flowers for attendants	_____
Aisle runner	_____
Transportation to/ from ceremony	_____
*Gratuities	_____
Miscellaneous	_____
Total	$_____

Reception

Hall rental	$_____
Decorations	_____
Music	_____
Food	_____
Beverages	_____
Wedding cake	_____
Favors	_____
Professional services	_____
*Gratuities	_____
Total	$_____

Other

Bridal consultant fees	$_____
Accommodations for out-of-town attendants	_____
*Security guard	_____
Sound recording/ video of ceremony	_____
*Insurance for wedding gifts	_____
Bride's blood test (if required)	_____
Groom's ring	_____
Gift for groom	_____
Gifts for attendants	_____
Special effects	_____
Other fees	_____
Total	$_____

Grand Total $_____

Activity 15.2 Family Living Decisions

Directions: Complete the following questionnaire by talking to a couple who have been married for a year or less. Record their responses in the space that is provided.

Family Goals

1. a. What types of family goals have you set since you became a family unit?

    Short-term (this year and next): _____

    _____

    Intermediate (five to ten years): _____

    _____

    Long-term (distant future): _____

    _____

    b. How do these goals differ from those of your friends who are single?

    _____

    _____

Family Budget

2. Do you have a family budget? _____ If so, who plans it? _____

3. Have you made financial plans to meet your future goals? If so, do your plans include any of these?

    _____ Tax shelters (such as buying a home)

    _____ Tax-deferred annuities (savings plans)

    _____ Other: _____

Dividing Responsibilities

4. Are you both employed outside the home? _____ If not, are you planning to have one partner not work or work part time? Please explain.

    _____

    _____

5. How are household chores divided?

    _____

    _____

    _____

    At some time in the future (work changes, new family member), will these responsibilities change? If so, how?

    _____

    _____

    _____

6. Do you maintain separate bank accounts? _____

    How are budgeting, checking account balancing, and bill paying responsibilities divided?

    _____

    _____

    _____

    _____

Activity 15.3 Plan a Vacation

Directions: Plan a one-week vacation. First, decide what type of vacation you'd like to have. Then decide how much money you have to spend. In the space provided, plan an itinerary. List costs to the right of the itinerary and total them.

Type of vacation: _____ excitement $ _____ total amount budgeted for vacation

_____ travel

_____ adventure

_____ special event

_____ visiting relatives

_____ other: _____

Briefly describe the vacation (where you're going, what your main activities will be).

_____

_____

_____

ITINERARY				COSTS	
Date	**Time**	**Activity**		Food	$_____
Day 1				Travel	_____
				Gas	_____
Day 2				Tickets	_____
				Rentals	_____
Day 3				Purchases	_____
Day 4				_____	_____
Day 5				_____	_____
				_____	_____
Day 6				Other:	
				_____	_____
Day 7				Total	$_____

(Use additional paper if needed.)

List items to be packed.

_____

_____

List arrangements to be made (for time away from home).

_____

_____

List items to be purchased.

_____

_____

Activity 15.4 Vacation Costs

Directions: Interview a couple or a family who has recently (in the last year or two) taken a two-week (or longer) vacation. Ask them these questions and record their answers in the space provided.

1. Type of vacation (may check more than one):
   _____ excitement   _____ special event
   _____ travel   _____ visiting relatives
   _____ adventure   _____ other: _____

2. Number of days gone on the trip: _____

3. How long did it take to plan this trip? _____

4. Who was involved in the planning of the trip? _____

5. How many people went on this trip? _____

6. What travel arrangements and reservations did you make for the trip?

   _____

   _____

   _____

7. What at-home preparations did you make before leaving on your vacation?

   _____

   _____

   _____

8. What did you take with you? How many bags?

   _____

   _____

   _____

9. Please describe the following:
   a. Type of transportation _____ Cost $ _____
      Days/Time traveling to/from destination _____
   b. Type of accommodations (tents, hotel, relatives' houses, and so on) _____
   c. Food on the trip: _____ eating out _____ eating with others _____ making your own
      Food costs per day $ _____

10. a. What types of entertainment did you enjoy?

    _____

    _____

    _____

    b. What was the cost (entry fees, and so on)? $ _____

11. a. What did you buy on the trip?

    _____

    _____

    _____

    b. What was the cost? $ _____

12. What was the approximate total cost of the trip? $ _____

Activity 15.5 Divorce

Directions: Fill in the information in the space provided.

1. a. List five attorneys engaged in general legal practice in your area. (Use online resources.)

   _____

   _____

   _____

   _____

   _____

   b. How much do these attorneys charge in attorneys' fees to handle divorce cases (both contested and noncontested)?

   _____

   _____

   _____

   _____

2. a. What is the court's filing fee to file for divorce or dissolution of marriage in your county circuit court?

   _____

   _____

   b. How many days, weeks, or months does it take for a divorce to be heard before a judge in your county?

   _____

   _____

3. a. Describe the divorce or dissolution of marriage process in your state.

   _____

   _____

   _____

   _____

   b. Describe the process in your state for handling a divorce that is contested (one party does not want to get divorced).

   _____

   _____

   _____

   _____

Activity 15.6 Final Instructions

Directions: Fill in answers to the following questions based upon your personal desires, or those you think you might wish to have if you were involved in a fatal accident.

Hospital Procedures

1. Would you want to have life support if there was no hope of survival?

   _____

2. Would you want to donate organs?

   _____

Burial/Cremation

3. What would you want done with your body? (Do you want to be buried in a specific cemetery or cremated?)

   _____

   _____

4. What type of service or memorial would you want?

   _____

   _____

5. In what location (city and state) would you want to be buried, or have your ashes disposed?

   _____

6. What other memorial or funeral instructions do you have for your loved ones (e.g., what songs should be sung, who should officiate, who should act as pallbearers, and so on)?

   _____

   _____

   _____

   _____

   _____

   _____

   _____

Final Message

7. Do you have a final message for loved ones?

   _____

   _____

   _____

   _____

   _____

   _____

   _____

   _____

   _____

   _____

   _____

Activity 15.7 Death

Directions: Answer the questions below in the space provided.

1. List five funeral homes or mortuaries in your area. (Use online resources.)

_____

_____

_____

_____

2. With your instructor's permission, visit a funeral home or mortuary and report on the following information regarding (a) the total cost of the average funeral and (b) a brief description of what is included in the cost.

a. Hearse: _____

_____

_____

b. Use of facilities: _____

_____

_____

c. Casket: _____

_____

d. Embalming fees: _____

_____

e. Funeral director and staff fees: _____

_____

_____

f. Notices, folders, permits: _____

_____

_____

3. Are there prearranged funeral plans available? If so, describe one of the plans.

_____

_____

_____

_____

_____

_____

_____

_____

_____

_____

unit

3

Project

Project 3
Resource Planning and Management

Directions: After reading the Unit 3 Project in the student text, complete Worksheets 1–5.

WORKSHEET 1
Before You Buy: Rip-Offs and Warning Signals

Directions: Analyze the following situations and determine what might be wrong.

Situation 1. You receive an e-mail that says you qualify for a new mortgage. You can get a $300,000 loan for as little as $600 a month. Bad credit is no problem. You can refinance at any time. Just click the link for a free consultation.

_____
_____
_____
_____

Situation 2. You receive a telephone call that offers you free products for answering a few simple questions. All you have to do is give them your name, Social Security number, address, and other personal information, and they will send you free samples of merchandise that you use or would like to try based on your lifestyle.

_____
_____
_____
_____
_____

Situation 3. You see an ad in the classified pages where a desperate investor is seeking to unload his collection of rare baseball cards and comic books at lower-than-market prices. He needs the money right away and will sell to the highest bidder. You call to get the address, and when you show up, there are several others there who are interested in the merchandise and are bidding on it.

_____
_____
_____
_____
_____

WORKSHEET 2
Computing Loan Payments

Directions: Compute the mortgage amounts for items 1–9 by using the Monthly Mortgage Payment Factors table below.

Monthly Mortgage Payment Factors (per $1,000 of loan amount)

Loan Rate	30 Yrs.	25 Yrs.	20 Yrs.	15 Yrs.
5.0%	5.59	6.07	6.86	8.11
6.0%	5.94	6.40	7.16	8.40
6.5%	6.29	6.73	7.46	8.69
7.0%	6.64	7.06	7.76	8.98
7.5%	6.99	7.39	8.06	9.27
8.0%	7.34	7.72	8.36	9.56
8.5%	7.69	8.05	8.68	9.85
9.0%	8.05	8.39	9.00	10.14
9.5%	8.41	8.74	9.32	10.44
10.0%	8.78	9.09	9.65	10.75

What is your estimated mortgage payment for:

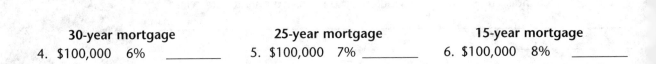

30-year mortgage	25-year mortgage	15-year mortgage
1. $50,000 8% _____	2. $70,000 6% _____	3. $80,000 7.5% _____

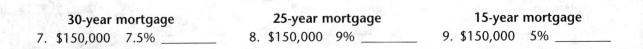

30-year mortgage	25-year mortgage	15-year mortgage
4. $100,000 6% _____	5. $100,000 7% _____	6. $100,000 8% _____

30-year mortgage	25-year mortgage	15-year mortgage
7. $150,000 7.5% _____	8. $150,000 9% _____	9. $150,000 5% _____

WORKSHEET 3
Building Your Dream Home

Directions: Answer the following questions and complete the research suggested to specify your dream home. Be sure to list your sources of information.

1. What style of house do you prefer? (two-story, ranch, Victorian, Tudor, and so on)

   _____

2. Attach a picture of a house that closely resembles the home of your dreams.

3. Prepare a floor plan that details the rooms and configuration, along with windows, doors, and so on.

4. What is the total square footage of your home? _____
   How many bedrooms? _____
   How many bathrooms? _____
   Describe the bedrooms, bathrooms, kitchen, and living area(s).

   _____

   _____

   _____

   _____

   _____

   Describe the general layout of the house, starting at the front door and ending at the back door or on the second floor.

   _____

   _____

   _____

   _____

   _____

   _____

5. Describe the lot and landscaping, including lot size and shape.

   _____

   _____

   _____

   _____

   _____

6. Describe the block—what part of town, city or country, the neighborhood or region.

   _____

   _____

   _____

7. Based on today's costs of building real estate, what would it cost to build this house? (*Hint*: You need to consult newspaper or online ads that describe similar new properties or interview a builder or other reliable source.)

   _____

8. Prepare a report of your findings, including a cover page, drawings or exhibits, narrative of information, and list of sources of information.

WORKSHEET 4
Rip-Offs and Warning Signals for Your Car

Directions: Read each of the following statements that could be a potential rip-off. Identify the warning signal (a point that makes you uncomfortable) and what you would do about it.

1. Your car is making pinging noises every time you accelerate to pass another car or go up a hill. You stop by a service station, and while your car is being filled with gas, you casually ask what could be wrong. The attendant replies that he would be happy to take a look at it when he gets off work and that he could probably fix it in his spare time. Repairs could cost as little as $50 or as much as $250.

_____

_____

_____

2. You are on vacation and driving the family car. You had it tuned up before you left, and your tires are fairly new. Along the way, you stop for gas. While checking the oil, the attendant notices that one of your hoses is loose. He fixes it (no charge) but then sees that you have an oil leak. He offers to make the repair within an hour for $100 plus parts.

_____

_____

_____

3. You take your car in for its regular tune-up and maintenance. You take a list of things that need to be done. An hour later, you receive a telephone call and are asked to authorize extra repairs that total $500. These repairs are not related to the tune-up or regular maintenance. But when the car is up on the rack, the mechanic sees that the work needs to be done.

_____

_____

_____

4. You decide you'd like to add a specialty after-market product to your new car. You visit the dealership, and the salesman quotes you $400 for parts and $200 for labor to install it. You order it and put down a deposit of $200. When you check on the part to see if it has arrived a week later, you are told that the part will now cost $600 (new price list) and labor will cost $400 because installation will be more complicated.

_____

_____

_____

5. You've driven your car less than 500 miles after purchasing it. It has a full manufacturer's warranty. When you make sharp right-hand turns, you can hear a strange scraping noise from that area of the car. You take the car back to the dealership, and the service technician tells you the right wheel bearing needs to be replaced and quotes you $1,000 to fix it. He indicates that this repair isn't covered by the warranty because it isn't part of the drivetrain. The dealer offers to sell you an extended warranty that will cover this repair, but the cost of the extended warranty is $2,500, which must be paid up front.

_____

_____

_____

WORKSHEET 5
Letter of Final Instruction

Directions: In the space below, write a letter of final instruction. Use Figure U3.3 in your textbook as an example. Consider your own personal wishes and information. You may also wish to project this data into the future, based on your long-term goals.

chapter 16 Investing for the Future

1 section: vocabulary

Fill in the missing word(s) in the space provided at the right.

Example: _____ involves making investments on a regular and planned basis.

1. _____ is a rise in the general level of prices.

2. _____ is the use of long-term savings to earn a financial return.

3. _____ is the chance that an investment's value will decrease.

4. A(n) _____ is a summary of a corporation's financial results for the year and its prospects for the future.

5. Government actions that affect investment values are types of _____ risk.

6. Newspaper sections containing investing data are called the _____.

7. A(n) _____ is any physical asset that appreciates in value over time because it is rare or desired by many.

8. Investment choices that are held for the long run are called _____.

9. _____ brokers buy and sell securities for clients for a reduced commission, but provide little or no investment advice.

10. Professionals who are trained to give investment advice are called _____.

11. The spreading of risk among many types of investments is called _____.

12. The _____ is a technique for estimating the number of years required to double your money at a given rate of return.

13. _____ is a unit of ownership in a corporation.

14. A(n) _____ is a debt obligation of a corporation or a government.

15. A(n) _____ pools money of many investors to buy a large selection of securities.

16. A(n) _____ is a contract by which you make a lump-sum payment or series of payments that earn interest and, in return, receive regular disbursements, usually after retirement.

17. A(n) _____ is a collection of investments.

18. _____ are contracts to buy and sell commodities for a specified price on a specified future date.

19. Low-priced stocks of small companies that have no track record are called _____ stocks.

20. A(n) _____ is the right, but not the obligation, to buy or sell a commodity or stock for a specified price within a specified time period.

0. Systematic investing

1. _____

2. _____

3. _____

4. _____

5. _____

6. _____

7. _____

8. _____

9. _____

10. _____

11. _____

12. _____

13. _____

14. _____

15. _____

16. _____

17. _____

18. _____

19. _____

20. _____

2 section:
review questions

After each of the following statements, circle *T* for a true statement or *F* for a false statement.

	Answers	For Scoring

1. The put-and-take account is an emergency fund. T F 1. _____
2. Public corporations are not required to publish annual reports. T F 2. _____
3. Market risk is caused by periods of economic growth or decline. T F 3. _____
4. Nonmarket risk is entirely unpredictable and uncontrollable. T F 4. _____
5. Stocks and bonds are considered low-risk/low-return investments. T F 5. _____
6. Investments that require more risk usually provide greater potential returns. T F 6. _____
7. An investment in real estate has proven to be protection against inflation. T F 7. _____
8. Initial investments should involve only long-range goals such as planning for retirement. T F 8. _____
9. Age is not a consideration in the financial planning process. T F 9. _____
10. U.S. Treasury securities are exempt from state and local income taxes. T F 10. _____

On the line at the right of each sentence, print the letter that represents the word or group of words correctly completing the sentence or answering the question.

1. Which of these risks is associated with an economic decline? (a) nonmarket risk, (b) speculative risk, (c) market risk, (d) political risk _____ 1. _____

2. The third level of investing is called (a) put and take, (b) systematic, (c) strategic, (d) speculative. _____ 2. _____

3. Treasury bills are issued for terms of (a) 1 year or less, (b) 2 years, (c) 10 years, (d) 30 years. _____ 3. _____

4. The final level of investing is called (a) put and take, (b) systematic, (c) strategic, (d) speculative. _____ 4. _____

5. Which of the following is a factor in selecting an investment? (a) liquidity, (b) growth in value, (c) safety, (d) all of the above _____ 5. _____

6. Which of the following is a high-risk/high-return investment? (a) annuities, (b) penny stocks, (c) Treasury securities, (d) bonds _____ 6. _____

7. What is the first step to wise investment practices? (a) go slowly, (b) define your financial goals, (c) follow through, (d) keep good records _____ 7. _____

8. An investor who wants low-risk investments should choose which of the following? (a) futures, (b) annuities, (c) bonds, (d) mutual funds _____ 8. _____

9. Which of the following is considered high-risk investing? (a) speculative investing, (b) systematic investing, (c) strategic investing, (d) all of these _____ 9. _____

10. Where is the most detailed data about a corporation most likely to be found? (a) the financial pages, (b) a discount broker, (c) an annual report, (d) a financial magazine _____ 10. _____

3 section:
problem solving

Activity 16.1 Risk Averse

Directions: Answer the following questions to see if you are a risk taker, a moderate investor, a cautious investor, or risk averse.

1. When I vacation, I like to (a) travel without reservations and see what happens, (b) make plans but stay flexible, (c) plan the trip in great detail, (d) stay at home to save money.

2. When I choose friends, I prefer to (a) date people I meet over the Internet, (b) go on blind dates arranged by friends or dating services, (c) meet people at social events, (d) meet people through friends or relatives.

3. When I eat at a restaurant, I prefer to (a) order my meat rare, (b) order my meat medium, (c) have vegetarian choices, (d) bring my own food.

4. When I am unprepared for an exam, I will (a) attend class and see what happens, (b) ask the teacher for an extension, (c) miss school that day, (d) study day and night until I feel prepared.

5. When I am flying, my preferred mode of travel is to (a) fly standby, (b) use electronic tickets and show up at the last minute, (c) use electronic tickets and show up early, (d) have confirmed reservations and a printed ticket, and show up an hour early.

6. When it comes to driving, I almost always (a) drive at or above the speed limit, (b) drive carefully at or below the speed limit, (c) drive only during off-peak hours, (d) prefer that someone else drive.

7. When traveling for long periods of time, I prefer to (a) stay in hostels or to camp, (b) take my chances and not make reservations, (c) make reservations as I travel, (d) have confirmed hotel reservations at every stop.

Scoring: Compute your score as follows: Answer (a) 4 points, (b) 3 points, (c) 2 points, (d) 1 point.

Interpretation: Add up your points. Here's what the totals mean: 24–28 points: Risk Taker—Go ahead and buy high-risk investments! 16–23 points: Moderate Investor—Invest only what you can afford to lose. 11–15 points: Cautious Investor—Avoid risk unless you have carefully decided to take this one-time risk. 7–10 points: Risk Averse—Do not take risks; invest in conservative investments only.

Think Critically

1. Do you think your score on this risk test accurately predicts how you would feel about investments that offer big potential profits but with a high probability of losing your money?

_____

_____

_____

_____

2. Would you be more willing to make risky investments if you had a lot of extra money than if you were living paycheck to paycheck? Why or why not?

_____

_____

_____

_____

Activity 16.2 Research Project

Directions: Go to your school or public library (or use the Internet) to locate one issue of each of the following magazines containing financial information. Also, write in a financial magazine of your choice in the last row. Complete the chart below, and then write a paragraph summarizing one major article from one of the magazines.

Name of Magazine	Number of Major Articles	Charts or Graphs (Y/N)	Types of Information Found	Subscription Price
1. Forbes				
2. Fortune				
3. Money				
4. The Economist				
5. Consumer Reports				
6. Time				
7. Business Week				
8. Newsweek				
9. Harvard Business Review				
10. Kiplinger's Personal Finance				
11.				

_____

_____

_____

_____

_____

_____

_____

_____

_____

_____

_____

_____

_____

_____

_____

_____

_____

Activity 16.3 The Annual Report, Part 1

Directions: Locate a copy of the annual report of a corporation in your area (photocopy a library copy, go online, or visit the business). Attach the annual report to this assignment sheet, and answer the following questions based on information found in the annual report.

1. Name of corporation: _____

2. Address of corporate headquarters: _____

3. Year of report: _____ How report was located: _____

4. Length of report (number of pages): _____

5. Name of president and/or CEO: _____

6. Summary of president's or CEO's message to stockholders:

   _____

   _____

   _____

   _____

   _____

   _____

   _____

7. Net profits (as shown on the income statement) earned last year: $_____

   Total shares of stock outstanding: _____

   Average return to stockholders: _____%

8. Total assets (as shown on the balance sheet): $_____

   Total stockholders' equity: $_____

9. Major actions taken during the past year:

   _____

   _____

   _____

   _____

   _____

10. Prospects for the future (industry, company, product line):

   _____

   _____

   _____

   _____

   _____

11. What did you learn about this company that most interested you?

   _____

   _____

   _____

   _____

   _____

Activity 16.4 The Annual Report, Part 2

Directions: Below are excerpts from a corporate annual report. Study the information shown and answer the questions that follow.

Statement of Income

	Year Ended December 31		
	2015	2014	2013
	(expressed in thousands)		
Revenues			
Sales	$3,820,810	$3,739,970	$3,737,220
Other income (expense), net	8,310	(4,150)	52,240
	3,829,120	3,735,820	3,789,460
Costs and expenses			
Materials, labor, and other operating expenses	2,881,800	2,925,870	2,997,570
Depreciation and cost of company timber harvested	185,600	191,360	176,320
Selling and administrative expenses	340,080	337,990	355,200
	3,407,480	3,455,220	3,529,090
Income from operations	421,640	280,600	260,370
Interest expense	(104,430)	(114,160)	(114,080)
Interest income	3,970	6,210	6,980
Foreign exchange gain (loss)	(2,940)	(550)	4,740
	(103,400)	(108,500)	(102,360)
Income before income taxes	318,240	172,100	158,010
Income tax provision	135,250	70,560	53,720
Net income	182,990	101,540	104,290
Preferred dividends	7,050	6,620	10,220
Net income available to common shareholders	$ 175,940	$ 94,920	$ 94,070
Average number of common shares outstanding	47,546	47,715	45,389
Net income per common share	$3.70	$1.99	$2.07

1. a. What were total sales in 2015? _____
   b. How much had total sales increased from 2014? _____
2. How much was paid out in preferred dividends in 2015? _____ In 2013? _____
3. What was net income per common share in 2015? _____ In 2013? _____
4. Who would be interested in the type of information found in the annual report of a corporation?

   _____

   _____

   _____

Activity 16.5 Investment Advice

Directions: Answer the following questions in the space provided.

1. What advice would you give a person (or couple) just getting started in investing about:
   a. Keeping informed? _____
   _____
   _____
   _____

   b. Initial investments? _____
   _____
   _____
   _____

   c. Managing risk? _____
   _____
   _____
   _____

2. What would you say to the person (or couple) just starting to invest about the following investments in terms of safety, liquidity, rate of return, potential for growth in value, professional management, and diversification?
   a. Stocks: _____
   _____
   _____

   b. Treasury bills: _____
   _____
   _____

   c. Mutual funds: _____
   _____
   _____

   d. Real estate: _____
   _____
   _____

3. How would you explain the following statement to the person (or couple): "The investment has good growth potential but is very illiquid."

   _____
   _____
   _____
   _____
   _____
   _____
   _____
   _____

Activity 16.6 Investment Decisions

Directions: Answer the following questions in the space provided.

1. You have a regular job, and your budget shows that you have an extra $100 a month that you can invest (beyond regular savings). You are thinking of beginning an investment program. Decide whom you will consult, and explain why.

_____

_____

_____

_____

_____

_____

_____

_____

_____

2. A young married couple has managed to save $5,000 over the last several years. What suggestions did this chapter offer to help this couple start an investment program?

_____

_____

_____

_____

_____

_____

_____

_____

3. You have decided to invest $500 a month in securities. How do the factors of safety, income, growth, liquidity, and taxation influence your investment decisions? Choose three alternatives that you might consider appropriate investments.

_____

_____

_____

_____

_____

_____

_____

_____

_____

section:
1 vocabulary

Fill in the missing word(s) in the space provided at the right.

Example: _____ represents a type of stock that pays a fixed dividend
but has no voting rights.

0. __Preferred stock__

1. A(n) _____ is a company whose stock is traded openly on stock
    markets.

    1. _____

2. When a corporation is profitable, the stockholders often receive a
    distribution of money from the corporation's earnings called _____.

    2. _____

3. _____ represents a type of stock that pays a variable dividend and
    gives the holder voting rights.

    3. _____

4. A(n) _____ is an increase in the number of outstanding shares
    of a company's stock.

    4. _____

5. _____ is the use of dividends previously earned on stock to buy
    more shares.

    5. _____

6. Stocks that have a history of consistently paying high dividends are
    called _____ stocks.

    6. _____

7. Stocks in corporations that reinvest profits into the business so that
    it can grow are called _____ stocks.

    7. _____

8. A(n) _____ is a benchmark that stock investors use to judge
    investment performance.

    8. _____

9. Stocks of large, well-established corporations are called _____ stocks.

    9. _____

10. A(n) _____ stock remains stable during an economic decline.

    10. _____

11. A(n) _____ buys and sells stock within a short period of time.

    11. _____

12. The _____ is an assigned dollar value given to each share of stock.

    12. _____

13. _____ is the price for which the stock is bought and sold in the
    marketplace.

    13. _____

14. A corporation's after-tax earnings divided by the number of common
    stock shares outstanding is _____.

    14. _____

15. A(n) _____ market is characterized by rising stock prices
    and investor optimism.

    15. _____

16. A(n) _____ market is characterized by falling stock prices
    and investor pessimism.

    16. _____

17. A marketplace where brokers buy and sell securities is called
    a(n) _____.

    17. _____

18. _____ buy and sell stocks on the trading floor of the securities exchange.

    18. _____

19. An abbreviated stock name used in stock listings is known as the
    stock's _____.

    19. _____

20. Borrowing money to buy stock is called _____.

    20. _____

![section 2] **section:**
review questions

After each of the following statements, circle *T* for a true statement or *F* for a false statement.

	Answers	For Scoring
1. Very few people (individuals) in the United States own stock.	T F	1. _____
2. With preferred stock, dividends are fixed, regardless of how the company is doing.	T F	2. _____
3. You can assign your stock voting rights to someone else by completing a proxy.	T F	3. _____
4. The par value assigned to a stock has nothing to do with the stock's market value.	T F	4. _____
5. NASDAQ is a form of auction market.	T F	5. _____
6. The securities market is where you buy and sell stocks and bonds.	T F	6. _____
7. Brokers in the over-the-counter market deal face to face with other brokers.	T F	7. _____
8. Short selling involves selling borrowed stock.	T F	8. _____
9. Buying on margin is an illegal activity.	T F	9. _____
10. Dollar-cost averaging is a short-term investment strategy.	T F	10. _____

On the line at the right of each sentence, print the letter that represents the word or group of words correctly completing the sentence or answering the question.

1. Which of the following is used to evaluate the efficiency of an investment? (a) earnings per share (EPS), (b) percent yield, (c) return on investment (ROI), (d) price/earnings (P/E) ratio _____ 1. _____

2. _____ stocks are a popular choice for retirees. (a) Growth, (b) Emerging, (c) Cyclical, (d) Income _____ 2. _____

3. Which of the following represents the cost of dividends as a percentage of the current price? (a) P/E ratio, (b) par value, (c) percent yield, (d) net change _____ 3. _____

4. Which of the following is a long-term technique whereby investors buy stock directly from a corporation? (a) dividend reinvestment, (b) stock split, (c) direct investment, (d) buy and hold _____ 4. _____

5. Which of the following investing strategies lowers the selling price of a stock and encourages investors to buy more? (a) stock split, (b) dividend reinvestment, (c) dollar-cost averaging, (d) short selling _____ 5. _____

6. Which of the following investing strategies is a short-term technique? (a) buying on margin, (b) dollar-cost averaging, (c) direct investment, (d) none of these _____ 6. _____

7. Which of the following is the oldest and most widely known stock index? (a) the Standard & Poor's 500, (b) the NASDAQ Composite Index, (c) the New York Stock Exchange, (d) the Dow Jones Industrial Average _____ 7. _____

8. Which of the following factors affects the price you will pay for a share of stock? (a) the company, (b) earnings per share, (c) stock market conditions (d) all of the above _____ 8. _____

3 section:
problem solving

Activity 17.1 Stock Dividends

Directions: Based on the information given, compute yearly total dividends as well as dividends per share paid to common and preferred stockholders.

1. There are 5,000 shares of $50 par value preferred stock outstanding, and 25,000 shares of common stock outstanding. Preferred stock has an 8 percent guaranteed rate of return. Dividends are declared of $1.25 per share of common stock, together with the guaranteed rate for preferred stock.

2. There are 10,000 shares of $20 par value cumulative 7 percent preferred stock outstanding, and 90,000 shares of common stock outstanding. Last year, the preferred stock did not receive its dividend because of a loss. This year, dividends of $50,000 are distributed to shareholders.

3. There are 7,500 shares of $10 par value participating 9 percent preferred stock outstanding, and 32,500 shares of common stock outstanding. The common stock cash dividend is $.50 per share, and total dividends of $50,000 are distributed. Remaining dividends are shared equally between common and preferred stockholders.

Activity 17.2 Computing Stock Returns

Directions: Based on the information given, compute stock returns. Refer to Figure 17.1 in your textbook for the formula for computing a stock's one-year return. (Round answers to the nearest tenth of a percent.)

1. John Adams purchased 100 shares of XYZ Corporation for $25 a share and paid a commission of $125. The current price of the stock is $32 per share. Last year, John received dividends of $1 per share.

2. Sally Clark purchased 500 shares of ABC Corporation for $10 per share and paid a total commission of $200. The current price of the stock is $12 per share. Last year, Sally received dividends of $2 per share.

3. Alice Kruse purchased 1,000 shares of Kendall Corporation for $22.50 per share and paid a total commission of $575. The current price of the stock is $25 per share. Last year, Alice received dividends of $880.

4. Mike Welch purchased 5,000 shares of Grass Roots stock for $82 per share and paid a commission of 1 percent on the purchase price. The current value of the stock is $96 per share. Mike received no dividends last year.

Activity 17.3 Buying on Margin

Directions: Based on the information given, compute the rates of return for the following margin transactions. Use Figure 17.2 in your textbook as your model. (Round answers to the nearest tenth of a percent.)

1. Rick Mendez bought stock for $5,000, using $2,500 of his own money and $2,500 borrowed from the broker. One month later, the stock is sold for $5,650. Interest owed to the broker is $30; brokerage commissions to buy and sell the stock totaled $300.

2. Julie Martin bought stock for $3,000, using $2,000 of her own money and $1,000 borrowed from the broker. One month later, the stock is sold for $3,850. Interest owed to the broker is $15; brokerage commissions to buy and sell the stock totaled $150.

Activity 17.4 Selling Short

Directions: Based on the information given, compute the rates of return for the following short transactions. Use Figure 17.3 in your textbook as your model. (Round answers to the nearest tenth of a percent.)

1. Andy Hastings borrowed 500 shares of stock from a broker. This stock is currently selling for $25 a share ($12,500). The commission was $125. Three weeks later, the price of the stock was $22.50 a share, so he bought the 500 shares. The commission was $115. He returned a stock certificate for 500 shares to the broker.

_____
_____
_____
_____
_____

2. Cindy Jacobs borrowed 100 shares of stock from her broker, and then sold the stock for $45 a share ($4,500). The commission was $65. A month later, the price of the stock was $42.50 a share, so she bought the 100 shares. The commission was $60. She returned the 100 shares to the broker.

_____
_____
_____
_____
_____

Activity 17.5 Stock Prices

Directions: Using the financial section of your local newspaper or a financial website, record the progress of five different stocks for five consecutive days, listing for each stock the closing price and net change. Fill in your information in the following chart.

	Closing Price						Net Change				
Name of Stock	Day 1	2	3	4	5		Day 1	2	3	4	5

Activity 17.6 Using the Financial Section of the Newspaper

Directions: The following is a stock listing that might appear in a financial newspaper such as the *Wall Street Journal.* Column headings are self-explanatory and contain more information than is given in most local newspapers. For example, AAR, the first stock listed, has the following information: The 52-week high was $12\frac{1}{8}$; the low, 8. The dividend is 44 cents for every $10 of stock owned; the percent yield is 6.2 percent. The price/earnings (P/E) ratio is 15, and 600 shares were sold that day. The high during the day was $6\frac{3}{4}$, the low $6\frac{5}{8}$. The closing price was $6\frac{1}{2}$, which showed a net change of $-\frac{1}{8}$ during the day's trading. Answer the questions that follow the listing.

Stock	High	Low	Close	Net Chg.	52 Week High	Low	Div.	Yld	PE	Sales 100s
AAR	$6\frac{3}{4}$	$6\frac{5}{8}$	$6\frac{1}{2}$	$-\frac{1}{8}$	$12\frac{1}{8}$	8	.44	6.2	15	6
ACF	$36\frac{1}{4}$	$37\frac{5}{8}$	37	$+\frac{3}{4}$	$49\frac{1}{2}$	$31\frac{1}{4}$	2.76	7.4	7	477
AMF	$17\frac{1}{2}$	$17\frac{1}{2}$	$17\frac{1}{2}$	$-\frac{3}{8}$	$26\frac{1}{2}$	16	1.36	6.7	7	133
ARA	$33\frac{7}{8}$	$33\frac{7}{8}$	33	-1	$6\frac{1}{8}$	$3\frac{1}{8}$	2	7	8	10
CFG	$91\frac{7}{8}$	$92\frac{1}{2}$	$92\frac{1}{4}$	$-1\frac{1}{2}$	110	$86\frac{1}{8}$	3.33	8.5	15	22
CMED	$17\frac{1}{8}$	$16\frac{1}{8}$	17	-1	$19\frac{1}{8}$	$12\frac{7}{8}$	4.40	5	2	6
Cnem	$19\frac{7}{8}$	$19\frac{3}{8}$	$19\frac{1}{2}$	$+1\frac{1}{8}$	$22\frac{3}{8}$	$6\frac{3}{8}$	.92	1.5	3	12
Coax	$11\frac{5}{8}$	$9\frac{1}{8}$	$10\frac{1}{8}$	$+2$	$12\frac{1}{2}$	$7\frac{1}{4}$	1	2	5	1

1. For the stock ACF, list the net change: _____ Closing price: _____ Sales that day: _____
   Dividend: _____

2. For the stock CMED, list the net change: _____ Closing price: _____ PE: _____
   Dividend: _____

3. Stock listings in the *Wall Street Journal* contain many columns of interest to investors. In a daily issue, locate the columns listed below and enter the information requested.

Date of *Journal*: _____

Column Heading: Information:

Trading by Markets   How many shares were traded at the New York Stock Exchange today?_____

Most Active Stocks   What were the day's most active stocks? Record stock names and today's volume for each.

a. _____

b. _____

c. _____

d. _____

e. _____

Activity 17.7 Stock Market Game

Directions: You have just inherited $10,000 cash and can use this money any way you wish. According to provisions of the will, however, you must account for how you spend the money, how much you earn on it, and the balance on hand every three weeks for the first year. Because you have adequate savings in your put-and-take account, you have decided to use the $10,000 to invest in stocks.

List your stock choices below. At the end of three weeks, record how much you have gained or lost. Turn in actual source material or photocopies of materials for verification of data.

Beginning Stock Investment: Day 1

Name of Stock	Amount Invested	Current Price	Source of Information
1.			
2.			
3.			
4.			
5.			
Total..................$10,000			

End of Week 1 (5 business days) Report:

Name of Stock	Amount Invested	Current Price	Source of Information
1.			
2.			
3.			
4.			
5.			
Total Value..................$_____	Gain (Loss) of $_____		

End of Week 2 (10 business days) Report:

Name of Stock	Amount Invested	Current Price	Source of Information
1.			
2.			
3.			
4.			
5.			

Total Value....................$_____   Gain (Loss) of $_____

End of Week 3 (15 business days) Report:

Name of Stock	Amount Invested	Current Price	Source of Information
1.			
2.			
3.			
4.			
5.			

Total Value....................$_____   Gain (Loss) of $_____

Stock Market Simulation

Directions: Following the instructions for Part 1 of the Stock Market Simulation in the student text, complete Worksheets 1–4. In Part 1, you will seek appropriate advice (as provided in the student text), make stock selections (based on Figure 1), and determine the outcome based on predetermined stock changes. Figure 1 showing the stocks from which you can choose is provided below for easy reference.

If you continue to Part 2 of the Stock Market Simulation, complete Worksheets 5–8. In Part 2, you will consult financial pages and use real stock listing values to compute real outcomes.

Figure 1 Stock Listings

Stock	Symbol	Open	High	Low	Close	52-Week High	52-Week Low	Div.	P/E	YTD % Chg.
AT&T	T	33.74	33.81	33.51	33.62	39.00	32.76	1.84	23.68	−4.38
Bank of America	BAC	16.75	16.79	16.61	16.77	16.93	10.98	0.04	25.03	+7.71
Boeing	BA	142.79	142.80	140.90	141.90	142.80	72.68	2.92	24.92	+3.96
Chevron	CVX	122.50	122.84	120.37	121.01	127.83	110.80	4.00	9.83	−3.12
Coca-Cola	KO	39.96	40.29	39.90	40.13	43.43	36.52	2.79	20.47	−2.86
Delta Airlines	DAL	31.19	31.48	30.66	31.47	31.58	13.09	0.24	12.90	+14.56
Eli Lily	LLY	51.49	52.11	51.25	51.93	58.41	47.53	1.56	11.80	+1.82
FedEx	FDX	141.20	142.74	140.41	142.63	144.39	90.61	0.60	27.32	−0.79
Ford Motor	F	16.01	16.11	15.94	16.07	18.02	12.10	0.50	11.68	+4.15
General Electric	GE	27.19	27.23	26.86	26.96	28.09	21.01	0.88	19.29	−3.82
Johnson & Johnson	JNJ	94.64	94.97	94.14	94.74	95.99	72.00	2.64	20.60	+3.44
Macy's	M	55.98	56.09	55.26	55.84	56.25	36.75	1.00	15.43	+4.57
Oracle	ORCL	37.75	38.14	37.59	38.11	38.34	29.86	0.48	16.01	−0.39
Public Storage	PSA	153.04	154.60	153.04	154.26	176.68	145.04	5.60	32.64	+2.48
Target	TGT	62.89	63.63	62.16	62.62	73.50	59.72	1.72	16.65	−1.03
Xerox	XRX	12.06	12.07	11.94	11.99	12.28	7.17	1.92	12.62	−1.48

WORKSHEET 1
Week 1: Investment Choices

Directions: Using the stock listings in Figure 1, record the name and symbol of the stock(s) you want to purchase, the closing price, the number of shares you would like to purchase, and your total investment in each stock. (*Note:* Remember that each investment must include a $10 broker fee and that your total investment amount cannot exceed $10,000.)

Stock	Symbol	Close	# of Shares	Investment Amount
_____	_____	_____	_____	_____
_____	_____	_____	_____	_____
_____	_____	_____	_____	_____
_____	_____	_____	_____	_____
_____	_____	_____	_____	_____
_____	_____	_____	_____	_____
_____	_____	_____	_____	_____
_____	_____	_____	_____	_____
_____	_____	_____	_____	_____
_____	_____	_____	_____	_____
_____	_____	_____	_____	_____
_____	_____	_____	_____	_____
_____	_____	_____	_____	_____
_____	_____	_____	_____	_____
_____	_____	_____	_____	_____
_____	_____	_____	_____	_____
_____	_____	_____	_____	_____
_____	_____	_____	_____	_____
_____	_____	_____	_____	_____
_____	_____	_____	_____	_____
_____	_____	_____	_____	_____
_____	_____	_____	_____	_____
_____	_____	_____	_____	_____
_____	_____	_____	_____	_____
_____	_____	_____	_____	_____
_____	_____	_____	_____	_____
_____	_____	_____	_____	_____

Total Investment $ _____

Name _____

WORKSHEET 2
Week 1: Gains or Losses

Directions: Record the name and symbol of the stock(s) you listed in Worksheet 1, the closing price at purchase and the closing price at the end of week 1, the difference between the closing price you paid at purchase and the closing price at the end of week 1, your gain or loss on the investment, and your new investment amount in each stock.

Stock	Symbol	Close at Purchase	Close at End of Week 1	Difference	Gain or Loss	New Investment Amount
_____	_____	_____	_____	_____	_____	_____
_____	_____	_____	_____	_____	_____	_____
_____	_____	_____	_____	_____	_____	_____
_____	_____	_____	_____	_____	_____	_____
_____	_____	_____	_____	_____	_____	_____
_____	_____	_____	_____	_____	_____	_____
_____	_____	_____	_____	_____	_____	_____
_____	_____	_____	_____	_____	_____	_____
_____	_____	_____	_____	_____	_____	_____
_____	_____	_____	_____	_____	_____	_____
_____	_____	_____	_____	_____	_____	_____
_____	_____	_____	_____	_____	_____	_____
_____	_____	_____	_____	_____	_____	_____
_____	_____	_____	_____	_____	_____	_____
_____	_____	_____	_____	_____	_____	_____
_____	_____	_____	_____	_____	_____	_____
_____	_____	_____	_____	_____	_____	_____
_____	_____	_____	_____	_____	_____	_____
_____	_____	_____	_____	_____	_____	_____
_____	_____	_____	_____	_____	_____	_____
_____	_____	_____	_____	_____	_____	_____
_____	_____	_____	_____	_____	_____	_____
_____	_____	_____	_____	_____	_____	_____

Total Investment $ _____

WORKSHEET 3
Week 2: Investment Choices

Directions: Record the name and symbol of the stock(s) you want to keep and any new stock(s) you want to purchase, the closing price at the end of week 1 [for the stock(s) you decide to hold on to and for any new stock(s) you decide to purchase], the number of shares you purchased/would like to purchase, and your total investment in each stock, including broker fees for new transactions. (*Note:* Remember that the total amount you have to invest may be greater or less than the initial $10,000 amount due to any gains or losses made.)

Stock	Symbol	Close at End of Week 1	# of Shares	Investment Amount
_____	_____	_____	_____	_____
_____	_____	_____	_____	_____
_____	_____	_____	_____	_____
_____	_____	_____	_____	_____
_____	_____	_____	_____	_____
_____	_____	_____	_____	_____
_____	_____	_____	_____	_____
_____	_____	_____	_____	_____
_____	_____	_____	_____	_____
_____	_____	_____	_____	_____
_____	_____	_____	_____	_____
_____	_____	_____	_____	_____
_____	_____	_____	_____	_____
_____	_____	_____	_____	_____
_____	_____	_____	_____	_____
_____	_____	_____	_____	_____
_____	_____	_____	_____	_____
_____	_____	_____	_____	_____
_____	_____	_____	_____	_____
_____	_____	_____	_____	_____
_____	_____	_____	_____	_____
_____	_____	_____	_____	_____

Total Investment $ _____

Name _____

WORKSHEET 4
Week 2: Gains or Losses

Directions: Record the name and symbol of the stock(s) you listed in Worksheet 3, the closing price at the end of week 1 and the closing price at the end of week 2, the difference between the closing price at the end of week 1 and the closing price at the end of the week 2, your gain or loss on the investment, and your new investment amount in each stock.

Stock	Symbol	Close at End of Week 1	Close at End of Week 2	Difference	Gain or Loss	New Investment Amount

Total Investment $ _____

WORKSHEET 5
Week 1: Investment Choices

Directions: Record the name and symbol of the stock(s) you want to purchase, the closing price, the number of shares you would like to purchase, and your total investment in each stock. (*Note:* Remember that each investment must include a $10 broker fee and that your total investment amount cannot exceed $10,000.)

Stock	Symbol	Close	# of Shares	Investment Amount
_____	_____	_____	_____	_____
_____	_____	_____	_____	_____
_____	_____	_____	_____	_____
_____	_____	_____	_____	_____
_____	_____	_____	_____	_____
_____	_____	_____	_____	_____
_____	_____	_____	_____	_____
_____	_____	_____	_____	_____
_____	_____	_____	_____	_____
_____	_____	_____	_____	_____
_____	_____	_____	_____	_____
_____	_____	_____	_____	_____
_____	_____	_____	_____	_____
_____	_____	_____	_____	_____
_____	_____	_____	_____	_____
_____	_____	_____	_____	_____
_____	_____	_____	_____	_____
_____	_____	_____	_____	_____
_____	_____	_____	_____	_____
_____	_____	_____	_____	_____
_____	_____	_____	_____	_____
_____	_____	_____	_____	_____
_____	_____	_____	_____	_____
_____	_____	_____	_____	_____
_____	_____	_____	_____	_____

Total Investment $ _____

Name _____

WORKSHEET 6
Week 1: Gains or Losses

Directions: Record the name and symbol of the stock(s) you listed in Worksheet 5, the closing price at purchase and the closing price at the end of week 1, the difference between the closing price you paid at purchase and the closing price at the end of week 1, your gain or loss on the investment, and your new investment amount in each stock.

Stock	Symbol	Close at Purchase	Close at End of Week 1	Difference	Gain or Loss	New Investment Amount
_____	_____	_____	_____	_____	_____	_____
_____	_____	_____	_____	_____	_____	_____
_____	_____	_____	_____	_____	_____	_____
_____	_____	_____	_____	_____	_____	_____
_____	_____	_____	_____	_____	_____	_____
_____	_____	_____	_____	_____	_____	_____
_____	_____	_____	_____	_____	_____	_____
_____	_____	_____	_____	_____	_____	_____
_____	_____	_____	_____	_____	_____	_____
_____	_____	_____	_____	_____	_____	_____
_____	_____	_____	_____	_____	_____	_____
_____	_____	_____	_____	_____	_____	_____
_____	_____	_____	_____	_____	_____	_____
_____	_____	_____	_____	_____	_____	_____
_____	_____	_____	_____	_____	_____	_____
_____	_____	_____	_____	_____	_____	_____
_____	_____	_____	_____	_____	_____	_____
_____	_____	_____	_____	_____	_____	_____
_____	_____	_____	_____	_____	_____	_____
_____	_____	_____	_____	_____	_____	_____
_____	_____	_____	_____	_____	_____	_____
_____	_____	_____	_____	_____	_____	_____
_____	_____	_____	_____	_____	_____	_____
_____	_____	_____	_____	_____	_____	_____
_____	_____	_____	_____	_____	_____	_____

Total Investment $ _____

WORKSHEET 7
Week 2: Investment Choices

Directions: Record the name and symbol of the stock(s) you want to keep and any new stock(s) you want to purchase, the current closing price [for the stock(s) you decide to hold on to and for any new stock(s) you decide to purchase], the number of shares you purchased/would like to purchase, and your total investment in each stock, including broker fees for new transactions. (*Note:* Remember that your total investment amount may be greater or less than the initial $10,000 amount due to any gains or losses made.)

Stock	Symbol	Close	# of Shares	Investment Amount
_____	_____	_____	_____	_____
_____	_____	_____	_____	_____
_____	_____	_____	_____	_____
_____	_____	_____	_____	_____
_____	_____	_____	_____	_____
_____	_____	_____	_____	_____
_____	_____	_____	_____	_____
_____	_____	_____	_____	_____
_____	_____	_____	_____	_____
_____	_____	_____	_____	_____
_____	_____	_____	_____	_____
_____	_____	_____	_____	_____
_____	_____	_____	_____	_____
_____	_____	_____	_____	_____
_____	_____	_____	_____	_____
_____	_____	_____	_____	_____
_____	_____	_____	_____	_____
_____	_____	_____	_____	_____
_____	_____	_____	_____	_____
_____	_____	_____	_____	_____
_____	_____	_____	_____	_____
_____	_____	_____	_____	_____
_____	_____	_____	_____	_____
_____	_____	_____	_____	_____
_____	_____	_____	_____	_____

Total Investment $ _____

Name _____

WORKSHEET 8
Week 2: Gains or Losses

Directions: Record the name and symbol of the stock(s) you listed in Worksheet 7, the closing price at the end of week 1 and the closing price at the end of week 2, the difference between the closing price at the end of week 1 and the closing price at the end of the week 2, your gain or loss on the investment, and your new investment amount in each stock.

Stock	Symbol	Close at End of Week 1	Close at End of Week 2	Difference	Gain or Loss	New Investment Amount
_____	_____	_____	_____	_____	_____	_____
_____	_____	_____	_____	_____	_____	_____
_____	_____	_____	_____	_____	_____	_____
_____	_____	_____	_____	_____	_____	_____
_____	_____	_____	_____	_____	_____	_____
_____	_____	_____	_____	_____	_____	_____
_____	_____	_____	_____	_____	_____	_____
_____	_____	_____	_____	_____	_____	_____
_____	_____	_____	_____	_____	_____	_____
_____	_____	_____	_____	_____	_____	_____
_____	_____	_____	_____	_____	_____	_____
_____	_____	_____	_____	_____	_____	_____
_____	_____	_____	_____	_____	_____	_____
_____	_____	_____	_____	_____	_____	_____
_____	_____	_____	_____	_____	_____	_____
_____	_____	_____	_____	_____	_____	_____
_____	_____	_____	_____	_____	_____	_____
_____	_____	_____	_____	_____	_____	_____
_____	_____	_____	_____	_____	_____	_____
_____	_____	_____	_____	_____	_____	_____
_____	_____	_____	_____	_____	_____	_____
_____	_____	_____	_____	_____	_____	_____
_____	_____	_____	_____	_____	_____	_____
_____	_____	_____	_____	_____	_____	_____

Total Investment $ _____

Follow-Up Assignment

Directions: As you assess your choices for Parts 1 and/or Part 2 of the simulation, answer the following questions:

1. How did the stocks that you chose perform? Did you make good choices? Explain why you would (or would not) make the same choices again.

_____

_____

_____

_____

_____

2. How did the stocks that you didn't choose perform? Which stock do you wish you had chosen? Why?

_____

_____

_____

_____

3. What information did you rely on to make your choices? What nonfinancial reasons might affect your choices?

_____

_____

_____

_____

_____

4. Do you believe that making investments in stocks is a good idea for you as an individual, considering your risk aptitude? What are the pros and cons of investing in stocks?

_____

_____

_____

_____

_____

5. How has this simulation changed your thoughts about the stock market?

_____

_____

_____

_____

_____

chapter 18 Investing in Bonds

1 section: vocabulary

Fill in the missing word(s) in the space provided at the right.

Example: The amount a bond can sell for is called the _____. 0. __market price__

1. The amount a bondholder is repaid when a bond matures is called _____. 1. _____

2. Bonds are considered _____ investments because a specified amount of interest is paid on a regular schedule. 2. _____

3. A(n) _____ bond is recorded in the owner's name by the issuer. 3. _____

4. A(n) _____ is any investment or action that helps offset against loss from another investment or action. 4. _____

5. A bond is _____ when it can be paid off before its maturity date. 5. _____

6. A(n) _____ is a corporate bond that is based on the general creditworthiness and reputation of the issuing corporation. 6. _____

7. Secured bonds, called _____, are backed by specific assets of the issuing firm. 7. _____

8. A(n) _____ bond can be exchanged for a certain number of shares of common stock. 8. _____

9. A(n) _____ tells the investor the risk category that has been assigned to a bond. 9. _____

10. When bonds sell for more than their face value, they are selling at a(n) _____. 10. _____

11. When bonds sell for less than their face value, they are selling at a(n) _____. 11. _____

12. A(n) _____ bond is a municipal bond issued to raise money for a public-works project. 12. _____

13. Bonds issued by state and local governments are called _____ bonds. 13. _____

14. A(n) _____ bond is backed by the power of the issuing state or local government to levy taxes to pay back the debt. 14. _____

15. _____ bonds are considered high-quality and safe because the issuers are stable and dependable. 15. _____

16. Bonds with a low or no investment rating, called _____ bonds, are risky and speculative. 16. _____

17. _____ are extensive tables found in financial news publications that contain information about recent trades of bonds. 17. _____

18. A(n) _____ is a group of bonds that have been bundled together and sold in shares to investors. 18. _____

19. Bond _____ occurs when the bond issuer cannot meet the interest and/or principal payments. 19. _____

20. The FHA or Ginnie Mae would issue a(n) _____ bond. 20. _____

2 section: review questions

After each of the following statements, circle *T* for a true statement or *F* for a false statement.

		Answers	For Scoring
1. The interest received on a corporate bond is taxable.		T F	1. _____
2. Capital gains result from the sale of assets such as stocks, bonds, or real estate.		T F	2. _____
3. A bond with a rating of Ba/BB would be considered an investment-grade bond.		T F	3. _____
4. The *Wall Street Journal* contains bond listings.		T F	4. _____
5. Bonds pay a variable interest rate monthly.		T F	5. _____
6. Bondholders cannot sell a bond before its maturity date.		T F	6. _____
7. The secondary market is created when stockholders buy and sell previously issued stocks and bonds from one another with the help of brokers.		T F	7. _____
8. Bonds must be repaid in full at maturity.		T F	8. _____
9. Bonds sold for more than their face value are sold at a discount.		T F	9. _____
10. Municipal bonds are issued by public corporations.		T F	10. _____

On the line at the right of each sentence, print the letter that represents the word or group of words correctly completing the sentence or answering the question.

1. _____ bonds are issued by state or local governments. (a) Savings, (b) Municipal, (c) T-bill, (d) Agency _____ 1. _____

2. A feature that allows a bond issuer to buy back bonds from current bondholders before the maturity date is known as a(n) (a) serial provision, (b) premium provision, (c) call provision, (d) revenue provision. _____ 2. _____

3. Which of these bond prices indicates it is selling at a premium? (a) 96, (b) par value, (c) 104, (d) market value _____ 3. _____

4. Which of these bonds would have a low rating? (a) junk bonds, (b) municipal bonds, (c) callable bonds, (d) convertible bonds _____ 4. _____

5. Municipal bonds (a) pay a higher rate than most corporate bonds, (b) are exempt only from state income taxes, (c) are sold by agencies of the federal government, (d) are exempt from federal income tax. _____ 5. _____

6. U.S. Treasury securities can be purchased through (a) the TreasuryDirect website, (b) brokers, (c) banks, (d) all of the above. _____ 6. _____

7. A(n) _____ bond is recorded in the owner's name by the issuing company. (a) mortgage, (b) bearer, (c) registered, (d) debenture _____ 7. _____

8. Which type of bond is sold at a deep discount and makes no interest payments? (a) callable bond, (b) zero-coupon bond, (c) secured bond, (d) convertible bond _____ 8. _____

9. The principal or face value of the bond must be paid in full at the (a) premium date, (b) capital gains date, (c) maturity date, (d) purchase date. _____ 9. _____

10. The return that an investor gets on a bond is called the (a) par value, (b) yield, (c) face value, (d) premium. _____ 10. _____

3 section:
problem solving

Activity 18.1 Computing Bond Earnings

Directions: Complete the following charts, inserting each semiannual interest payment and the total of interest payments for each bond.

1. Earnings on a 10-year, $10,000, 8 percent corporate bond.

Year	May 1 Interest	November 1 Interest
1		
2		
3		
4		
5		
6		
7		
8		
9		
10		
Total interest earned:		

2. Earnings on a 10-year, $10,000, 6.5 percent corporate bond.

Year	April 1 Interest	October 1 Interest
1		
2		
3		
4		
5		
6		
7		
8		
9		
10		
Total interest earned:		

3. Earnings on an 8-year, $5,000, 7.25 percent corporate bond.

Year	March 1 Interest	September 1 Interest
1		
2		
3		
4		
5		
6		
7		
8		
Total interest earned:		

Activity 18.2 Computing One-Year Yield

Directions: For each of the following problems, compute the amount of interest and current yield. All bonds are for one year. To determine current yield, use the following formula:

$$\frac{\text{Interest amount}}{\text{Market price}} = \text{Current yield}$$

1. $1,000 face value bond, 7% stated interest rate, sold at face value.

   a. Interest _____   b. Yield _____

2. $5,000 face value bond, 5.25% stated interest rate, sold at face value.

   a. Interest _____   b. Yield _____

3. $1,000 face value bond, 7% stated interest rate, sold at 102.

   a. Interest _____   b. Yield _____

4. $5,000 face value bond, 5.25% stated interest rate, sold at 104.

   a. Interest _____   b. Yield _____

5. $1,000 face value bond, 7% stated interest rate, sold at 96.

   a. Interest _____   b. Yield _____

6. $5,000 face value bond, 5.25% stated interest rate, sold at 94.

   a. Interest _____   b. Yield _____

7. $10,000 face value bond, 6% stated interest rate, sold at 98.

   a. Interest _____   b. Yield _____

Activity 18.3 Comparing Taxable and Tax-Exempt Bonds

Directions: Complete the following problems to find annual interest, tax on interest earned, and net interest.

1.

	Corporate Bond	Municipal Bond
Face Value (Principal)	$10,000	$10,000
Rate of Interest	8%	7%
Annual Interest		
Tax on Interest (28%)		
Net Interest		

2.

	Corporate Bond	Municipal Bond
Face Value (Principal)	$50,000	$50,000
Rate of Interest	7.75%	6.25%
Annual Interest		
Tax on Interest (28%)		
Net Interest		

3.

	Corporate Bond	Municipal Bond
Face Value (Principal)	$100,000	$100,000
Rate of Interest	6.5%	5.75%
Annual Interest		
Tax on Interest (28%)		
Net Interest		

Activity 18.4 Using the Financial Section of the Newspaper or a Website for Bond Transactions

Directions: Using the financial section of your local newspaper or a website, or the bond price section of the *Wall Street Journal*, provide the following information.

1. Choose four bonds and list the following information about the bonds:

Name of Bond	Current Yield	Coupon Rate	Last Sale	Net Change
a.				
b.				
c.				
d.				
Name of Paper/Website_____ Date_____				

2. After one week, look up the same bonds and record the following information about them:

Name of Bond	Current Yield	Coupon Rate	Last Sale	Net Change
a.				
b.				
c.				
d.				
Name of Paper/Website_____ Date_____				

3. For each bond, determine whether it has gone up, down, or remained unchanged in the one-week period. Which bond would you purchase? Explain your choice.

   a. _____

   b. _____

   c. _____

   d. _____

chapter 19
Investing in Mutual Funds, Real Estate, and Other Choices

1 section: vocabulary

Fill in the missing word(s) in the space provided at the right.

Example: A(n) _____ is an average of the price movements of certain selected securities.

0. _____index_____

1. A(n) _____ is a variety of mutual funds covering a whole range of investment objectives.

1. _____

2. A(n) _____ fund does not charge a sales fee when you buy or sell because no salespeople are involved.

2. _____

3. A(n) _____ fund invests in the stocks of companies that reinvest their profit rather than distribute dividends.

3. _____

4. The goal of a(n) _____ fund is to produce current income on a steady basis in the form of interest or dividends.

4. _____

5. A(n) _____ fund invests in a mixture of stocks and bonds rather than stocks alone.

5. _____

6. A(n) _____ fund purchases international stocks and bonds as well as U.S. securities.

6. _____

7. A legal document about a fund's investment portfolio, its objectives, and its financial statements is called the _____.

7. _____

8. A(n) _____ is a corporation that pools the money of many individuals to invest in a diversified class of real estate properties.

8. _____

9. Land or buildings, such as stores, hotels, and duplexes, that produce rental income are _____ property.

9. _____

10. A(n) _____ is a building with two separate living units.

10. _____

11. The _____ collects rent and maintains property for an owner.

11. _____

12. With _____ investing, real estate investors have a third person do the actual buying and selling of property.

12. _____

13. A(n) _____ is an investment in a pool of mortgages that have been purchased by a government agency.

13. _____

14. _____ is unimproved property that is usually considered a speculative investment.

14. _____

15. A(n) _____ is an agreement to buy or sell a commodity at a specified price on a specified future date.

15. _____

16. A(n) _____ is a sales fee paid when you buy a mutual fund through a broker.

16. _____

17. With _____ investing in real estate, the investor holds legal title to the property.

17. _____

18. Gold, silver, and platinum are examples of _____.

18. _____

19. Natural stones, such as diamonds and rubies, are examples of _____.

19. _____

20. Products that are mined or grown, such as livestock, crops, or gold, are examples of _____.

20. _____

2 section: review questions

After each of the following statements, circle *T* for a true statement or *F* for a false statement.

	Answers	For Scoring
1. Commodities are considered a risky investment.	T F	1. _____
2. A call option is the right to sell stock at a fixed price until the expiration date.	T F	2. _____
3. An option obligates the investor to buy or sell a commodity for a specified price on a specified future date.	T F	3. _____
4. Collectibles are considered a safe and relatively risk-free investment, both short- and long-term.	T F	4. _____
5. Prices of gems are high and subject to drastic change.	T F	5. _____
6. Diversification is an advantage of mutual funds.	T F	6. _____
7. An investment in real estate is generally considered a good way to combat inflation but illiquid.	T F	7. _____
8. The owner of rental property can deduct depreciation expenses when filing a tax return.	T F	8. _____
9. When money is left over after expenses are paid, a negative cash flow exists.	T F	9. _____
10. A limited partner organizes a real estate syndicate.	T F	10. _____

On the line at the right of each sentence, print the letter that represents the word or group of words correctly completing the sentence or answering the question.

1. The most popular collectibles are (a) gems, (b) antiques, (c) coins, (d) dolls. _____ 1. _____

2. Which of the following is considered an individually owned apartment? (a) duplex, (b) house, (c) condominium, (d) recreation property _____ 2. _____

3. When you pay a sales fee at the time you buy a mutual fund, you are paying a (a) front-end load, (b) back-end load, (c) no-load, (d) brokerage flat fee. _____ 3. _____

4. What type of mutual fund reacts in the same way the stock or bond markets do as a whole? (a) money market, (b) global, (c) balanced, (d) index _____ 4. _____

5. What is an example of an indirect investment? (a) futures contract, (b) vacant land, (c) limited partnership, (d) vacation property _____ 5. _____

6. A building with three separate living units is a (a) house, (b) condominium, (c) triplex, (d) quad. _____ 6. _____

7. With leverage, the homebuyer makes a down payment and then assumes a (a) family of funds, (b) mortgage, (c) positive cash flow, (d) capital gain. _____ 7. _____

8. Which of the following is a type of direct investment in real estate? (a) REIT, (b) certificate of participation, (c) duplex, (d) real estate syndicate _____ 8. _____

9. What are diamonds, rubies, and sapphires called? (a) precious metals, (b) semiprecious stones, (c) collectibles, (d) gems _____ 9. _____

10. A mutual fund that seeks both growth and income while minimizing risk is called a(n) _____ fund. (a) balanced, (b) income, (c) specialty, (d) growth _____ 10. _____

3 | section:
problem solving

Activity 19.1 Computing Fund Performance

Directions: Answer the following questions in the space provided.

1. Mutual funds are regularly reviewed and ranked by numerous financial publications—from monthly magazines to the *Wall Street Journal*. Both mutual fund companies and individual funds are ranked on their one-, five-, and even ten-year performances. The *Wall Street Journal* publishes rankings and lists the best performers in a specific fund category daily in the financial section under the heading "Mutual Fund Scorecards."

   Pick three mutual funds listed in the financial section of your newspaper or on a website. Locate these funds in monthly magazines or in the *Wall Street Journal* and report their one-, five-, and ten-year rankings, as available.

   _____

   _____

   _____

   _____

   _____

   _____

   _____

   _____

2. You can do some calculations on your own—beyond what the magazines and financial experts do. The following formula will help you determine the return you would be earning for one year. You are adding the dividend per share plus increases in share prices, and dividing by the price you paid for your initial shares.

$$\text{Return on Mutual Fund} = \frac{(\text{Number of Shares} \times \text{NAV}) + \text{Dividends}}{\text{Cost of Initial Investment}} - 1 \times 100$$

Example: You own 50 shares of PrfDm mutual fund. The net asset value (NAV) is $26.12. You have received total dividends (cash or shares) of $400 during the year. The cost of your initial investment was $1,300.

$$\text{Return} = \frac{(50 \times \$26.12) + \$400}{\$1,300} - 1 \times 100 = 1.3123 - 1 \times 100 = .3123 \times 100 = 31.23\%$$

Solve the following problems using the above formula for the one-year return on a mutual fund.

a. 100 shares, NAV $31.20, dividends of $250, initial investment of $2,900

b. 75 shares, NAV $8.40, dividends $102, initial investment $590

c. 250 shares, NAV $16.11, dividends $322, initial investment $4,000

Activity 19.2 Mutual Funds Newspaper Columns

Directions: Choose five mutual funds from the listings of mutual funds in the *Wall Street Journal.* (Use the Thursday edition for this activity.) Choose a variety of funds—for example, a growth fund, an income fund, a bond fund, a global fund, and a balanced fund. Record the following information about all five funds here:

MUTUAL FUND QUOTATIONS								
1	2	3	4	5	6	7	8	9
Name of Mutual Fund	Inv. Obj.	NAV	Offer Price	NAV Chg.	—Total Return—			
					YTD	26 wks	4 yrs	Return
1.								
2.								
3.								
4.								
5.								

If available, record the same information for the same mutual funds for a year prior (using the Internet or the library's archives). If not possible, then record the same information for the same mutual funds one week later.

One Year Earlier or One Week Later:

MUTUAL FUND QUOTATIONS								
1	2	3	4	5	6	7	8	9
Name of Mutual Fund	Inv. Obj.	NAV	Offer Price	NAV Chg.	—Total Return—			
					YTD	26 wks	4 yrs	Return
1.								
2.								
3.								
4.								
5.								

What changes have occurred?

_____

_____

_____

_____

_____

_____

_____

_____

Activity 19.3 Real Estate Investment Opportunities

Directions: Use the classified section of your local newspaper or a classifieds website for this activity. Cut or print out advertisements or photocopy requested information where possible for attachment to this page.

1. List the column headings identifying real estate for sale in your community. For example, residential owner-occupied and commercial property might appear separately, and there may be several classifications for each category. You may find columns titled "apartments," "office buildings," and so on under commercial property.

_____

_____

_____

_____

_____

2. Find a piece of real estate for sale that interests you as a potential property owner (but not owner-occupant) as a direct investment. Clip the article, or copy it exactly as it appears in the newspaper, including the name of the real estate agent or sales company offering the property.

   a. In what section of town is this property located?

   _____

   _____

   _____

   _____

   b. What attracted your attention to this property?

   _____

   _____

   _____

   _____

   c. How much money could you make from this investment in a year?

   _____

   _____

   _____

   d. How much money (cash) would it cost to purchase this property?

   _____

   _____

   _____

   _____

   e. What rate of return (percentage) would you expect to make from this investment?

   _____

   _____

   _____

   _____

Activity 19.4 Precious Metal Prices

Directions: Using a current *Wall Street Journal,* financial magazine, the financial section of your local newspaper, or online information, find the current prices for the following precious and nonprecious metals:

1. Gold   _____
2. Silver   _____
3. Platinum   _____
4. Copper   _____
5. Tin   _____
6. Zinc   _____
7. Nickel   _____

What other information can you locate about these metals? For example: City of market (London? Tokyo?) Bid? Close? Change?

_____

_____

_____

_____

_____

_____

Activity 19.5 Commodity Prices

Directions: Using a current *Wall Street Journal,* financial magazine, the financial section of your local newspaper, or online information, find the current prices for the following commodities exchange transactions:

1. Crude Oil   _____
2. Barley   _____
3. Heating Oil Futures _____
4. Cocoa (Metric Tons) _____
5. Pork Bellies   _____
6. Sugar (World)   _____

What other information can you locate about trading commodities? For example, what can you find about spot market for crude oil—current price, price a year ago? List some abbreviations used for commodities trading and explain what they mean.

_____

_____

_____

_____

_____

_____

chapter 20 — Retirement and Estate Planning

1 section: vocabulary

Fill in the missing word(s) in the space provided at the right.

Example: A(n) _____ tax is levied on an heir who receives property from the estate of a decedent.

0. ____inheritance____

1. A(n) _____ is a loan that allows homeowners age 62 or older to convert part of their home equity into income.

1. _____

2. A(n) _____ is a type of IRA where contributions are taxed, but earnings are not.

2. _____

3. A(n) _____ is a tax-deferred retirement savings plan for self-employed individuals.

3. _____

4. A retirement plan for small businesses, similar to that for self-employed individuals, is a(n) _____ plan.

4. _____

5. In a(n) _____ plan, employees receive a set monthly payment based on wages earned and number of years of service.

5. _____

6. In a(n) _____ plan, employees receive a periodic or lump-sum payment based on their account balance and investment performance.

6. _____

7. An employee is _____ after he or she has worked for an employer for a specified number of years.

7. _____

8. A(n) _____ is a defined-contribution plan available through companies that operate for a profit.

8. _____

9. A(n) _____ is a defined-contribution plan for employees of government or nonprofit organizations.

9. _____

10. All that a person owns, less debts owed, at the time of the person's death is called a(n) _____.

10. _____

11. _____ is the process of planning for the administration and transfer of property during one's lifetime and at one's death.

11. _____

12. The _____ is the person who makes a will.

12. _____

13. A(n) _____ will is one written in a person's own handwriting.

13. _____

14. A person who dies without having a valid will is said to die _____.

14. _____

15. A(n) _____ is a legal document in which a person gives a trustee control of property for eventual distribution to the beneficiary.

15. _____

16. A(n) _____ is used to make small changes to an existing will.

16. _____

17. A legal document called a(n) _____ authorizes another person to act on your behalf.

17. _____

18. _____ is a legal process of validating a deceased person's will and distributing the estate upon death.

18. _____

19. A(n) _____ is levied by the federal government on the transfer of property at death.

19. _____

section:
review questions

After each of the following statements, circle *T* for a true statement or *F* for a false statement.

		For
	Answers	Scoring

1. An estate must be worth more than a certain amount to be subject to federal estate taxes.   T F   1. _____

2. Inheritance taxes are levied against the estate of a decedent by the federal government.   T F   2. _____

3. Gift taxes are levied against the person receiving the gift, not against the estate.   T F   3. _____

4. Social Security benefits are usually sufficient to provide a comfortable retirement.   T F   4. _____

5. Appreciation is one way that the equity in your home increases.   T F   5. _____

6. With a reverse mortgage, you can receive payments equal to a percentage of your equity.   T F   6. _____

7. Insurance needs do not change with retirement.   T F   7. _____

8. Inflation is a major concern to people on fixed retirement income.   T F   8. _____

9. Any working person can make the maximum contribution to an IRA.   T F   9. _____

10. A Roth IRA offers full tax-free benefits; no tax is levied on money used for a Roth IRA.   T F   10. _____

On the line at the right of each sentence, print the letter that represents the word or group of words correctly completing the sentence or answering the question.

1. Which retirement plan is designed for self-employed individuals? (a) IRA, (b) SEP, (c) Keogh, (d) 401(k)   _____   1. _____

2. The earliest age at which (reduced) Social Security retirement benefits are payable is (a) 55, (b) 59 ½, (c) 62, (d) 65.   _____   2. _____

3. The person who is given control of a trust is called a(n) (a) trustor, (b) beneficiary, (c) legal guardian, (d) trustee.   _____   3. _____

4. The U.S. government provides health insurance to those age 65 and older called (a) Medicare, (b) probate, (c) Medicaid, (d) annuity.   _____   4. _____

5. A short document that identifies what your heirs will receive is called a (a) trust will, (b) simple will, (c) power of attorney, (d) probate.   _____   5. _____

6. An automatic way to transfer the title of property between spouses is called (a) power of attorney, (b) annuity, (c) joint tenancy, (d) probate.   _____   6. _____

7. What term describes a person who dies without a will? (a) trustee, (b) beneficiary, (c) testator, (d) intestate   _____   7. _____

8. A beneficiary of a trust could include which of the following? (a) spouse, (b) minor children, (c) friend, (d) all of the above   _____   8. _____

9. Which type of trust takes effect when a person dies? (a) inter vivos, (b) testamentary, (c) living, (d) probate   _____   9. _____

10. With a traditional IRA, you must begin making withdrawals by age (a) 55, (b) 59 ½, (c) 65, (d) 70 ½.   _____   10. _____

3 section:
problem solving

Activity 20.1 Assessing Retirement Expenses

Directions: Financial advisers predict that a retired person or couple will need between 75 and 85 percent of their net income received before retirement. While some expenses will decrease, others will remain the same, or even increase.

Fill out the following projected expenses that you would have today if you (a) are working full time; (b) own your own home; (c) have children who are grown and out of the house.

Then, compute how much expenses will change at retirement. Total your expenses and see whether they are between 75 and 85 percent of preretirement expenses. To complete this exercise, you may wish to talk to people who are nearing retirement and to people who are retired to get realistic numbers.

Items	Monthly Expenses	
	Before Retirement	**After Retirement**
Fixed Expenses:		
House Payment.............................	_____	_____
Taxes:		
Property	_____	_____
Income....................................	_____	_____
Insurance:		
Life..	_____	_____
Health	_____	_____
Automobile	_____	_____
Property	_____	_____
Car Payment.................................	_____	_____
Other: _____	_____	_____
Variable Expenses:		
Food:	_____	_____
Groceries................................	_____	_____
Eating Out	_____	_____
Utilities......................................	_____	_____
Clothing	_____	_____
Entertainment/Recreation/Travel.....	_____	_____
Phone/Internet/Cable TV	_____	_____
Gifts/Contributions	_____	_____
Other:	_____	_____
Total Expenses.................................	_____	_____

Activity 20.2 Comparing Do-It-Yourself Plans

Directions: Using your textbook and current reference material (magazine and newspaper articles, online information), complete the following chart comparing do-it-yourself retirement plans.

Type of Plan	Maximum Annual Allowed	Who Is Eligible?	Tax Deductible?
IRAs			
SEPs			
Keoghs			
401(k) Plans			
403(b) Plans			

Name _____

Activity 20.3 Retirement Income Comparisons

Directions: Using your textbook, current reference material (magazine and newspaper articles, online information), and personal interviews with retired persons, complete the following chart comparing the advantages and disadvantages of various sources of retirement income.

Source of Income	Advantages	Disadvantages
Social Security		
Employee Retirement Plans: 401(k) or 403(b)		
Individual Saving and Investing: IRAs, Keoghs, SEPs Annuities		
Working part time after retirement: 30 hours/week or less		

Activity 20.4 Social Security and Other Government Benefits

Directions: Complete group research on the questions that follow by visiting a local Social Security Administration office or going to www.ssa.gov online. Many of the questions can be answered using brochures that are available at no charge.

1. What is the retirement age for a retired person to receive full benefits? (*Hint:* There are several categories, depending on year of birth.)

   _____

   _____

   _____

   _____

2. At what age can a person "retire early" and receive 80 percent of full benefits? Why would someone want to do this? Why might they not want to do this?

   _____

   _____

   _____

   _____

3. How are retirement benefits computed by the Social Security Administration? List the factors that are considered.

   _____

   _____

   _____

   _____

4. How does a person become eligible for receiving Social Security retirement benefits?

   _____

   _____

   _____

   _____

   _____

5. What are minimum and maximum benefits that can be received?

   _____

   _____

   _____

   _____

6. What happens if you work after retirement?

   _____

   _____

   _____

   _____

   _____

Source of Information _____

Activity 20.5 Preparing a Will

Directions: Complete the following simple will by filling in the blanks, or write your own holographic will, giving your property to whomever you wish. As a guide, review the will shown in Figure 20.1 in the textbook.

LAST WILL AND TESTAMENT OF _____

     I, _____, of the City of

_____, and State of _____,

do hereby make and declare this to be my Last Will and Testament, revoking

hereby all former wills and codicils heretofore made by me.

     FIRST: I hereby declare that I am single and have no issue born to

or adopted by me now or ever living.

     SECOND: I declare that my possessions should be divided as follows:

To _____ I give, devise, and

bequeath _____; to _____

_____ I give, devise, and bequeath _____

_____; to _____ I give,

devise, and bequeath _____ .

     THIRD: All the rest, residue, and remainder of my property, where-

soever situated, I give, devise, and bequeath unto my parents, _____

_____, of the City of _____ ,

and State of _____ .

     FOURTH: In the event my parents have predeceased me at death, I

give the residue of my estate to_____ .

     LASTLY: I hereby appoint_____

to be _____ of my estate, and in the event of his/her death or

inability to serve, I appoint_____ .

     IN WITNESS WHEREOF, I have hereunto set my hand this _____

day of _____, in the year two thousand _____ .

_____
(Typed signature)

     We, the undersigned, certify that the foregoing instrument was, on
the date thereof, signed and declared by _____
as _____ Last Will and Testament, in the presence of us who, in _____
presence and in the presence of each other, have, at _____ request, hereunto
signed our names as witnesses of the execution thereof, this _____
day of _____, 20--; and we hereby certify that we believe the
said _____ to be of sound mind and memory.

_____ residing at _____

_____ residing at _____

Activity 20.6 Challenging a Will

Directions: Read the information below and then answer the questions that follow.

When you need a will, there are several ways you can do it and save money. You can go to a local stationery or office products store and buy a fill-in-the-blanks will (or download one from the Internet) that is supposed to be good in all states. Or you can simply sit down and write out your wishes in your own handwriting—a holographic will—which is legal in many states. But while the above choices may be legal, can these wills stand up in court if they are contested?

A person can contest the validity of another person's will if he or she feels excluded or forgotten, or believes the testator was mentally incompetent or under undue influence. A person who makes decisions under pressure from another person is said to be "influenced." The will may contain provisions that were not truly the "will" of the decedent. The court may agree with the person contesting the validity of a will in any of these circumstances. In addition, if you wait to draw your will until you are seriously ill, it could be contested based on your mental condition at the time.

If you want to disinherit a person who would ordinarily be entitled to an inheritance, you'll need a well-drawn will that will stand up to a court challenge. The most common challenge is from a possible heir who was omitted because of an outdated will. A child not mentioned in the will nor specifically disinherited will automatically share in the distribution of the decedent's estate. Adopted children inherit the same as do birth children.

How do you know for sure you have a will that can withstand a court challenge? The best way is to have an attorney prepare your will according to the laws of your state or have an attorney check a will you create from a kit or will-making software. You must mention all individuals who would normally inherit from you, and specifically disinherit any of them. To overcome a claim of insanity, undue stress, or physical illness impairing your ability to make decisions, many attorneys videotape the signing of your will. On the tape, you clearly state your intentions and your understanding of their consequences.

1. Have you considered to whom you would like to leave your property should something happen to you? Why is this important to consider?

_____

_____

_____

2. Under what conditions would you attempt to challenge the will of another person?

_____

_____

_____

_____

3. Why might you choose to have a will drawn by an attorney?

_____

_____

_____

_____

Project 4
Assessing Your Financial Security

unit 4

Project

Directions: Following the instructions in the Unit 4 Project in the student text, complete Worksheets 1–6. Figures U4.1 and U4.2, Future Value tables, are provided here for easy reference.

Fig. U4.1 Future Value (Compound Sum) of $1

Period					Percent				
	3%	4%	5%	6%	7%	8%	9%	10%	11%
1	1.03000	1.04000	1.05000	1.06000	1.07000	1.08000	1.09000	1.10000	1.11000
2	1.06090	1.08160	1.10250	1.12360	1.14990	1.16640	1.11810	1.21000	1.23210
3	1.09273	1.12486	1.15723	1.19102	1.22504	1.25971	1.29503	1.33100	1.36763
4	1.12551	1.16986	1.21551	1.26248	1.31080	1.36049	1.41158	1.46410	1.51807
5	1.15927	1.21665	1.27628	1.33823	1.40255	1.46933	1.53862	1.61051	1.68506
6	1.19405	1.26532	1.34010	1.41852	1.50073	1.58687	1.66710	1.77156	1.87042
7	1.22987	1.31593	1.40710	1.50363	1.60578	1.71382	1.82804	1.94872	2.07616
8	1.26677	1.36857	1.47746	1.59385	1.71819	1.85093	1.99256	2.14359	2.30454
9	1.30477	1.42331	1.55133	1.68948	1.83846	1.99901	2.17189	2.35795	2.55804
10	1.34392	1.48024	1.62890	1.79085	1.96715	2.15893	2.36736	2.59374	2.83942
11	1.38423	1.53945	1.71034	1.89830	2.10485	2.33164	2.58043	2.05312	3.15176
12	1.42576	1.60103	1.79586	2.01220	2.25219	2.51817	2.81266	3.13843	3.49845
13	1.46853	1.66507	1.88565	2.13203	2.40985	2.71962	3.06581	3.45227	3.88328
14	1.51259	1.73168	1.97993	2.26090	2.57853	2.93719	3.34173	3.79750	4.31044
15	1.55797	1.80094	2.07893	2.39656	2.75903	3.17217	3.64248	4.17725	4.78459
16	1.60471	1.87298	2.18288	2.54035	2.95216	3.42594	3.97031	4.59497	5.31089
17	1.65285	1.94790	2.29202	2.69377	3.15882	3.70002	4.32763	5.05447	5.89509
18	1.70243	2.02582	2.40662	2.54035	3.37993	3.99602	4.71712	5.55992	6.54355
19	1.75351	2.10685	2.52695	3.02560	3.61653	4.31570	5.14166	6.11591	7.26334
20	1.80611	2.19112	2.65330	3.20714	3.86968	4.66096	5.60441	6.72750	8.06231

Fig. U4.2 Future Value (Compound Sum) of an Annuity of $1

Period					Percent				
	3%	4%	5%	6%	7%	8%	9%	10%	11%
1	1.00000	1.00000	1.00000	1.00000	1.00000	1.00000	1.00000	1.00000	1.00000
2	2.03000	2.04000	2.05000	2.06000	2.07000	2.08000	2.09000	2.10000	2.11000
3	3.09090	3.12160	3.15250	3.18360	3.21490	3.24640	3.27810	3.31000	3.34210
4	4.18363	4.24646	4.31013	4.37462	4.43994	4.50611	4.57313	4.64100	4.70973
5	5.30914	5.41632	5.52563	5.63709	5.75074	5.86660	5.98471	6.10510	6.22780
6	6.46841	6.63298	6.80191	6.97532	7.15329	7.33593	7.52334	7.71561	7.91286
7	7.66246	7.89829	8.14201	8.39384	8.65402	8.92280	9.20044	9.48717	9.78327
8	8.89234	9.21427	9.54911	9.89747	10.25980	10.63663	11.02847	11.43589	11.85943
9	10.15911	10.58280	11.02656	11.49132	11.97799	12.48756	13.02104	13.57948	14.16397
10	11.46388	12.00611	12.57789	13.18080	13.81645	14.48656	15.19293	15.93743	16.72201
11	12.80780	13.48635	14.20679	14.97164	15.79360	16.64549	17.56029	18.53117	19.56143
12	14.19203	15.02581	15.91713	16.86994	17.88845	18.97713	20.14072	21.38428	22.71319
13	15.61779	16.62684	17.71298	18.88214	20.14064	21.49530	22.95339	24.52271	26.21164
14	17.08632	18.29191	19.59863	21.10507	22.55049	24.21492	26.01919	27.97498	30.09492
15	18.59891	20.02359	21.57856	23.27597	25.12902	27.15211	29.36092	31.77248	34.40536
16	20.15688	21.82453	23.65749	25.67253	27.88805	30.32428	33.00340	35.94973	39.18995
17	21.76159	23.69751	25.84037	28.21288	30.84022	33.75023	36.97371	40.54470	44.50084
18	23.41444	25.64541	28.13239	30.90565	33.99903	37.45024	41.30134	45.59917	50.39594
19	25.11687	27.67123	30.53900	33.75999	37.37897	41.44626	46.01846	51.15909	56.93949
20	26.87037	29.77808	33.06595	36.76339	40.99519	45.76196	51.16012	57.27500	64.20283

WORKSHEET 1
Future Values

Directions: For numbers 1–4, use Figure U4.1 to compute the value of each deposit at the rate given. For numbers 5–8, use Figure U4.2 to compute the value of each annuity at the given rate.

Future Value (Compound Sum) of $1

Deposit	Time	Annual Rate	Value
1. $5,000 Compounded quarterly	4 years	12%	$_____
2. $1,000 Compounded semiannually	10 years	6%	$_____
3. $7,500 Compounded annually	8 years	8%	$_____
4. $3,850 Compounded semiannually	2 years	8%	$_____

Future Value (Compound Sum) of an Annuity

Deposit	Time	Annual Rate	Value
5. $500/year	5 years	6%	$_____
6. $100/year	10 years	9%	$_____
7. $900/year	2 years	8%	$_____
8. $250/year	10 years	5%	$_____

WORKSHEET 2
Your Savings Plan

Directions: In the spaces, project what you could save presently (either lump sum or monthly payment), and calculate the future value in 5, 10, and 20 years at the interest rate shown. Then project what you would like to be able to save (lump sum or monthly payment) in 5, 10, and 20 years.

Savings Amount	Interest Rates	Future Value
$_____ What you could set aside today	6% per year, compounded annually, in 5 years	$_____
	6% per year, compounded annually, in 10 years	$_____
	6% per year, compounded annually, in 20 years	$_____
$_____ What you want to be able to save 5 years from now	8% per year, compounded semiannually, in 10 years	$_____
	6% per year, compounded annually, in 20 years	$_____
$_____ What you want to be able to save 10 years from now	5% per year, compounded annually, in 20 years	$_____
	6% per year, compounded semiannually, in 5 years	$_____

Make a plan for the amount of money you will set aside now and in the future.

Directions: In the spaces below, write when you will set aside money, how much you will set aside and how often, your goal amount, and the future purpose of the amount saved.

Date	Amount Set Aside/How Often/Goal	Future Purpose of Saved Amount
_____	$_____/_____/_____	_____
_____	$_____/_____/_____	_____
_____	$_____/_____/_____	_____

WORKSHEET 3
Risk Aptitude Test

Directions: Answer the following questions, recording your answers in the spaces provided. Then compute your risk aptitude score as shown.

_____ 1. You have an extra $100 left over from your year-end bonus. Would you rather (a) put it all in savings, (b) spend some and save a little, (c) bet it on a lottery.

_____ 2. You are ready to buy a new car. Will it be a (a) small economy car, (b) conventional, standard car with a variety of options, (c) sports car emphasizing speed, style, or performance.

_____ 3. You have won a weekend trip of your choice. Will you (a) take the cash value of the prize instead, (b) go on a cruise or sightseeing trip, (c) fly to a mountain lodge for skiing.

_____ 4. You are looking for a job. Which of these is most important to you? (a) job security (permanent employment), (b) higher salary with moderate security, (c) higher pay and less job security.

_____ 5. You are betting on a horse race. Which wager will you make? (a) bet on the favorite, even though winnings will be small, (b) select a horse with a good chance of winning and moderate payback if it does, (c) pick a long shot with a high payback.

_____ 6. You have a mortgage on your home. Will you (a) make regular payments, paying off the loan on schedule, (b) repay the loan quicker than required so you can save interest, (c) refinance the loan and use the extra cash for other investments.

_____ 7. You are considering changing jobs. Which sounds best? (a) joining a well-established firm and doing similar work, (b) associating with a new company in a newly created position, (c) going into business for yourself.

_____ 8. You have a schedule conflict. The following three events are all scheduled for the same day and time. Which will you choose? (a) attending a seminar, (b) working on a committee, (c) giving a speech to a group of students.

_____ 9. Your dinner is "on the house." Which will you choose? (a) cold turkey sandwich and salad, (b) enchilada with hot peppers, (c) rare sirloin with fries.

_____ 10. You have a delayed flight, and your plane will be four hours late. Will you (a) read a book and wait, (b) take in a short sightseeing trip, (c) book another flight.

Scoring: Give yourself 1 point for each question you marked (a); 3 points for each (b); and 5 points for each (c). Scores 40 and above indicate a willingness to take risk (you are a risk taker); scores between 25 and 40 indicate a willingness to take moderate risk; and scores below 25 show high risk aversion. A score of 30 is average.

Analyzing your score:
Based on your score, what are some investments that have the amount of risk you are willing to take? (See Chapter 16.)

_____

_____

_____

WORKSHEET 4
Investment Analysis

Directions: Calculate the average gain per year and average rate of return on investments shown, and rank the investments in order of desirability.

Asset Purchased	Original Price	Years Held	Current Value	Dividends or Interest Received	Avg. Yearly Gain	Avg. Rate of Return	Rank
H&H Stock 25 shares	$14.00/sh	10	$16.00	$.30/share/ year	_____	_____	_____
Time CD	$5,000	5	$5,000	$1,055	_____	_____	_____
Mutual Funds 33 shares	$18.50/sh	7	$17.50	$.35/share/ year	_____	_____	_____
Gold 50 troy oz.	$1,325/oz.	3	$1,262/oz.	0	_____	_____	_____
ATZ Stock 50 shares	$29.50/sh	5	$35.50	$.50/share/ year	_____	_____	_____

WORKSHEET 5
Investment Plan

Directions: Complete the following worksheet by listing your investments and how much you expect to invest, how long you will keep the investments, and your potential return.

	Investment Choice	Initial Cost	Time Kept	Expected Return
Example:	Time CD	$1,000	1 year	$80

Initial Investments
1. _____
2. _____
3. _____

Systematic Investments
1. _____
2. _____
3. _____

Strategic Investments
1. _____
2. _____
3. _____

Speculative Investments
1. _____
2. _____
3. _____

WORKSHEET 6
Retirement Plan

Directions: Fill in the amounts you project for each category in the spaces provided. In order to obtain realistic amounts, you may need to talk to a retired person or other person about projected benefits and costs.

1. **Projected Income (monthly)**
   a. Anticipated benefits:

Social Security	$ _____
Pensions	$ _____
Annuities	$ _____
Part-time work	$ _____
Other	$ _____

   b. Assets used for income:

Savings accounts	$ _____
IRAs	_____
Investments	_____
Other	_____

Total projected	_____
monthly income	$ _____

2. **Projected Costs (monthly)**
   a. Fixed costs:

Property taxes	$ _____
Insurance premiums	_____
Other	_____

   b. Variable costs:

Food	$ _____
Utilities	
Gas or oil	_____
Electricity	_____
Phone	_____
Household maintenance	_____
Transportation	_____
Clothing and cleaning	_____
Personal care	_____
Health care and medical	_____
Recreation/entertainment	_____
Miscellaneous	_____
Other	_____

   Total projected expenses $ _____

Projected Income – Projected Costs = Surplus (Shortage)

_____ – _____ = $ _____

chapter 21

Introduction to Risk Management

1 section: vocabulary

Fill in the missing word(s) in the space provided at the right.

Answers

Example: _____ is a method of spreading individual risk among a large group of people to make losses more affordable for all.

0. _____Insurance_____

1. A(n) _____ is a pure risk that is faced by a large number of people and for which the amount of the loss can be predicted.

1. _____

2. A(n) _____ is any interest in life or property such that, if it were lost or harmed, the insured would suffer financially.

2. _____

3. An organized strategy for controlling financial loss from pure risks is called _____.

3. _____

4. _____ is a chance of loss with no chance for gain.

4. _____

5. _____ is the process of accepting the consequences of risk.

5. _____

6. _____ lowers the chances of loss by taking measures to lessen the frequency or severity of losses that may occur.

6. _____

7. A(n) _____ is the specified amount of a loss that the insured must pay.

7. _____

8. _____ is a state of uncertainty where certain situations may result in loss or another undesirable outcome.

8. _____

9. A fee, called the _____, is paid at regular intervals by the insurance policyholder.

9. _____

10. _____ is the process of putting the policyholder back in the same financial condition he or she was in before the loss occurred.

10. _____

11. Making an investment to help offset against loss is called _____.

11. _____

12. The chance of loss or harm to personal or real property is called _____.

12. _____

13. _____ is the chance of loss involving income and standard of living.

13. _____

14. A(n) _____ is the chance of loss that may occur when your errors or actions result in injuries to others or damages to their property.

14. _____

15. A(n) _____ may result in either gain or loss.

15. _____

16. _____ lowers the chance for loss by not engaging in the activity that could result in the loss.

16. _____

17. _____ may result in gain or loss because of changing economic conditions.

17. _____

18. _____ is the likelihood that something will or will not happen.

18. _____

19. With a(n) _____, you identify risks, assess their financial impacts, and list the techniques that you plan to use to manage each risk.

19. _____

2 | section:
review questions

After each of the following statements, circle *T* for a true statement or *F* for a false statement.

	Answers	For Scoring
1. Speculative risks are random, meaning they can happen to anyone.	T F	1. _____
2. Insurance companies collect premiums with the expectation that only a few policyholders will have financial losses at any given time.	T F	2. _____
3. Insurance companies set premiums based on statistical probability.	T F	3. _____
4. The higher the probability of loss occurring, the lower the premium for insuring against it.	T F	4. _____
5. Exclusions are specified losses not covered by an insurance policy.	T F	5. _____
6. An unearned premium is not refunded to the policyholder when a policy is canceled.	T F	6. _____
7. Premiums for individual plans are usually much lower than for group plans.	T F	7. _____
8. Insuring more than one vehicle with the same company can result in a multi-line discount.	T F	8. _____
9. Uncertainty is the likelihood that something will or will not happen.	T F	9. _____
10. Accepting a higher deductible will reduce your insurance premium.	T F	10. _____

On the line at the right of each sentence, print the letter that represents the word or group of words correctly completing the sentence or answering the question.

1. Those who self-insure are engaging in (a) risk shifting, (b) risk assumption, (c) risk avoidance, (d) risk reduction. _____ 1. _____

2. Which of the following is not a major insurable risk? (a) liability risk, (b) personal risk, (c) economic risk, (d) property risk _____ 2. _____

3. A policyholder's request for reimbursement for a loss is called a (a) deductible, (b) premium, (c) peril, (d) claim. _____ 3. _____

4. Defective wiring in a house is an example of (a) a peril, (b) a hazard, (c) a loss, (d) an exclusion. _____ 4. _____

5. The first step of the risk management process is to (a) identify potential risks, (b) assess the seriousness of risks, (c) handle risks, (d) prioritize risks. _____ 5. _____

6. The amount of money payable to a policyholder upon discontinuation of a life insurance policy is called (a) benefits, (b) the face amount, (c) cash value, (d) the unearned premium. _____ 6. _____

7. A fire, storm, explosion, and robbery are examples of (a) losses, (b) perils, (c) hazards, (d) exclusions. _____ 7. _____

8. Which of the following can be used to help offset speculative losses? (a) hedging, (b) risk shifting, (c) self-insuring, (d) none of these _____ 8. _____

9. A _____ risk may involve damages to your car. (a) personal, (b) speculative, (c) property, (d) liability _____ 9. _____

10. Buying insurance is an example of (a) risk avoidance, (b) risk reduction, (c) risk assumption, (d) risk shifting. _____ 10. _____

3 section:
problem solving

Activity 21.1 Insurance Needs

Directions: Answer the following questions to assess your current and future insurance needs.

1. What kinds of risks do you take daily, weekly, monthly, or at any time during the year (such as sports, recreation, driving)?

   _____

   _____

   _____

   _____

   _____

2. If you were injured, how would the costs of taking care of you be paid (e.g., parents, insurance, self)?

   _____

   _____

   _____

   _____

   _____

3. Do you engage in any activities that could cause injuries to other persons (i.e., could you be held responsible for what happens to someone else)? List such activities.

   _____

   _____

   _____

   _____

   _____

4. What types of insurance do you or your family currently carry to meet losses you might incur? For example, do you have life insurance, auto insurance, health insurance, or any other type of coverage?

   _____

   _____

   _____

   _____

   _____

5. What types of risk do you anticipate taking in the next five years for which you will likely purchase insurance?

   _____

   _____

   _____

   _____

   _____

Activity 21.2 Insurance Action Plan

Directions: Assess the types of risks you are facing and expect to encounter in the next few years. Write a sentence about how each type of risk might affect your life.

1. Loss of income (for you personally)
   a. Death _____
   _____

   b. Illness _____
   _____

   c. Accident _____
   _____

   d. Unemployment _____
   _____

2. Loss of income (for a family member)
   a. Illness _____
   _____

   b. Disability
   _____

   c. Death _____
   _____

3. Loss of property (real or personal)
   a. Fire _____
   _____

   b. Theft _____
   _____

   c. Damage or vandalism _____
   _____

4. Loss of savings due to personal liability
   a. Causing damages to another person: _____
   _____

   b. Damaging another person's property: _____
   _____

Activity 21.3 Business Cycle

Directions: Based on Figure 21.2 in the textbook, conduct online research to answer the following questions. (Suggested resources: Federal Reserve System, Council of Economic Advisers, *Monthly Labor Review, Survey of Current Business, The Economist*, and other business news magazines.)

1. What phase of the business cycle is the U.S. economy currently experiencing? Explain your answer.

_____

_____

_____

_____

2. How does the phase of the business cycle that the U.S. economy is currently experiencing affect consumers? Explain.

_____

_____

_____

_____

3. What actions have been taken by the Federal Reserve Board in the past six months (for example, raising or lowering interest rates)?

_____

_____

_____

_____

4. Describe leading, lagging, and coincidental economic indicators (look up these words on the Internet). Cite indicators currently present in the economy. Based on those indicators, explain what you think the economy will do next. Cite any sources of information used.

_____

_____

_____

_____

_____

Activity 21.4 Choosing an Insurance Agent

Directions: Read the following material and then answer the questions that follow.

When you purchase insurance, you can either buy insurance directly from an insurance company or buy insurance through an agent. There are two types of insurance agents: captive and independent. Captive agents work exclusively for one company and sell only policies offered by that company. Independent agents work for an insurance brokerage and sell the policies of several companies. They match your needs with the companies that offer the best rates and coverage. Choosing an insurance agent is an important decision because he or she explains your options and helps you plan for your insurance needs. The agent should:

1. Be available to you locally. You should be able to reach the agent by telephone and have a personal visit every few years to keep your insurance needs current.
2. Give you full-service counseling for all of your insurance needs, including advice about when you do *not* need insurance.
3. Not exert pressure on you or try to sell you coverage or policies that are not appropriate. He or she should also inform you of when to reduce coverage (when property values decrease) and when to drop coverage.
4. Be professional, knowledgeable, and up to date about insurance. In addition, the agent should be able to explain to you, in language you can understand, exactly what is covered and what is not, and how policies work.
5. Be willing and able to answer your questions and keep you informed as to company changes and laws that affect you and your insurance policies.

1. What are some advantages of working with an insurance agent?

_____

_____

_____

_____

2. Would you consider buying insurance from an out-of-state or online-only company if the premiums were considerably less but the company did not have any local agents? Why or why not?

_____

_____

_____

_____

3. Describe the kind of person you would like to have as your insurance agent.

_____

_____

_____

_____

Activity 21.5 Risk Management Process

Directions: List the steps of the risk management process in the following flowchart from memory.

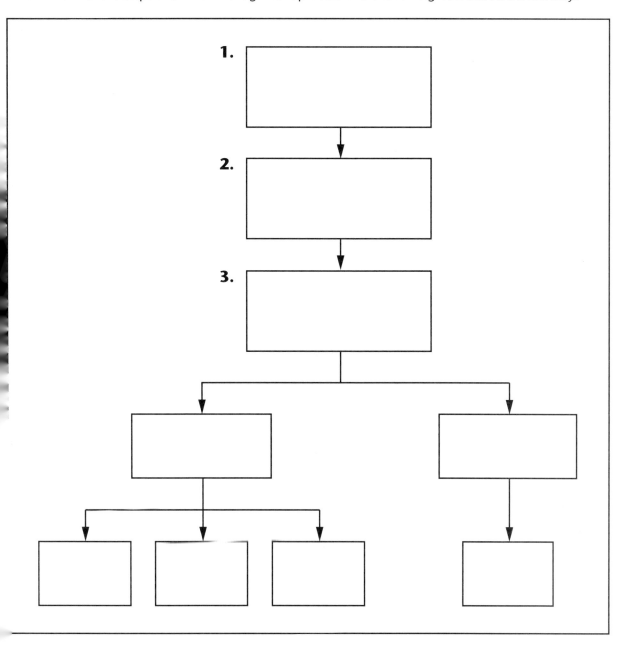

Activity 21.6 Insurance Companies

Directions: From your local *Yellow Pages*, online resources, or newspaper ads, complete the following information.

1. List four insurance companies or agencies in your area that sell health insurance.

   a. _____

   b. _____

   c. _____

   d. _____

2. List three insurance companies in your area that sell more than one type of insurance policy (e.g., auto and life, property and health, and so on).

   a. _____

   b. _____

   c. _____

3. List three life insurance companies that are national companies served either by independent agents or through insurance companies (e.g., New York Life Insurance Company).

   a. _____

   b. _____

   c. _____

4. List five insurance companies or agencies (national or local) that sell auto insurance.

   a. _____

   b. _____

   c. _____

   d. _____

   e. _____

5. What is the penalty in your state if you are caught driving an automobile without insurance and you are involved in an accident that is your fault?

   _____

   _____

   _____

   _____

6. In your state, which of the following can reduce auto insurance premiums?

   _____ good grades

   _____ driver's education courses

   _____ good driving record

   _____ more than one car insured

7. Are there any other actions that you can take to reduce your premiums?

   _____

   _____

   _____

   _____

chapter

22 Property and Liability Insurance

1 section: vocabulary

Fill in the missing word(s) in the space provided at the right.

Answers

Example: _____ insurance protects property owners from property and liability risks.

0. ___Homeowners___

1. _____ coverage is insurance to protect against claims for bodily injury to another person or damage to another person's property.

1. _____

2. _____ protects renters from property and liability risks.

2. _____

3. A(n) _____ is a dangerous place, condition, or object that is especially attractive to children.

3. _____

4. _____ coverage is auto insurance that protects your own car against damage from accidents or vehicle overturning.

4. _____

5. _____ coverage is auto insurance that protects you from damage to your car from causes other than collision or vehicle overturning.

5. _____

6. A(n) _____ is a written amendment to an insurance policy for an additional premium.

6. _____

7. A person who is presumed to have permission to be on your property is a(n) _____.

7. _____

8. The _____ is the cost of replacing an item regardless of its actual cash (market) value.

8. _____

9. _____ is auto insurance that pays for medical, hospital, and funeral costs of the insured and his or her family and passengers, regardless of fault.

9. _____

10. _____ coverage is auto insurance that pays for your injuries when the other driver is legally liable but unable to pay.

10. _____

11. A(n) _____ clause requires policyholders to insure their building for a stated percentage of its replacement value in order to receive full reimbursement for a loss.

11. _____

12. A(n) _____ is additional insurance coverage for valuable items not covered by the basic policy.

12. _____

13. Serious traffic offenses that may incur fines as well as jail time are called _____.

13. _____

14. _____ is auto insurance in which drivers receive reimbursement for their expenses from their own insurer, regardless of who caused the accident.

14. _____

15. A(n) _____ is any violation of the law committed by the driver of a vehicle while it is in motion.

15. _____

16. Every state has a(n) _____ that consists of people who are unable to obtain auto insurance due to the high risk they present.

16. _____

17. _____ supplements basic auto and personal liability coverage by expanding limits and including additional risks.

17. _____

2 section:
review questions

After each of the following statements, circle *T* for a true statement or *F* for a false statement.

	Answers	For Scoring
1. Standard auto insurance policies cover theft of the vehicle.	T F	1. _____
2. A surcharge effectively increases your premium for three years or longer.	T F	2. _____
3. Landlords can insure the property of their tenants as a part of their liability policy.	T F	3. _____
4. Common types of homeowners insurance include theft and vandalism coverage.	T F	4. _____
5. Insurance investigators determine the value of the property destroyed or damaged by a covered hazard.	T F	5. _____
6. An insurance policy endorsement does not cost an additional premium.	T F	6. _____
7. Coinsurance effectively prevents people from underinsuring their property.	T F	7. _____
8. Homeowners insurance also covers trees, plants, and fences on the property.	T F	8. _____
9. Homeowners will be held liable for injuries caused by attractive nuisances.	T F	9.

On the line at the right of each sentence, print the letter that represents the word or group of words correctly completing the sentence or answering the question.

1. Generally, people insure the contents of their home for at least _____ the value of the building. (a) one-fourth, (b) half, (c) three-fourths, (d) one-third   _____ 1. _____

2. A house's replacement value is $100,000, and it is insured for $150,000. If it is completely destroyed by a fire, the insurance company will pay (a) nothing, (b) $100,000, (c) $150,000, (d) $250,000.   _____ 2. _____

3. With an 80 percent coinsurance clause, a house valued at $100,000 must be insured for at least (a) $50,000, (b) $75,000, (c) $80,000, (d) $100,000.   _____ 3. _____

4. To cover a very expensive piece of jewelry, the insured would add (a) extended coverage, (b) liability coverage, (c) a personal property floater, (d) a coinsurance clause.   _____ 4. _____

5. A minor traffic ticket is called a(n) (a) infraction, (b) misdemeanor, (c) felony, (d) hazard.   _____ 5. _____

6. Most states require all drivers to at least carry _____ coverage. (a) collision, (b) liability, (c) comprehensive, (d) uninsured/underinsured motorist   _____ 6. _____

7. Buying a car with extra airbags and antilock brakes can reduce the cost of which type of auto insurance? (a) liability, (b) collision, (c) comprehensive, (d) personal injury protection   _____ 7. _____

8. Which of the following drivers would most likely pay the most for auto insurance? (a) Jenelle, who is age 21 and married, (b) Ben, who is age 23 and single, (c) Leah, who is age 25 and single, (d) Nathan, who is age 74 and married   _____ 8. _____

9. An increased insurance premium you must pay because you caused an accident is called a(n) (a) exception, (b) endorsement, (c) surcharge, (d) floater.   _____ 9. _____

Name _____

3 section:
problem solving

Activity 22.1 Items Not Insured

Directions: Based on Figure 22.2 in the textbook, make a list of property you own that would not be covered if it were stolen or destroyed.

Name of Item	Where It Is Located

Make a list of property that a family might own that would need special coverage (personal property floater) because its value would exceed normal limits provided by homeowners insurance.

Name of Item	Cost or Value

Activity 22.2 Household Inventory

Directions: Based on Figure 22.3 in the textbook, prepare a household inventory for the contents of one room in your home. (Suggestion: Use your own room as an example.)

Room	Type of Property	Replacement Cost	Receipt or Proof of Ownership

Do you have pictures or video as evidence of these items of property? _____

How are you able to determine replacement costs? _____

_____

_____

_____

_____

Activity 22.3 Reducing Auto Insurance Premiums

Directions: There are many things drivers can do to minimize the amount of auto insurance premiums. In each category below, explain what you could do to reduce auto insurance premiums.

1. Type of car driven (including model, style, color, engine size, and so on)

2. Driving record

3. Driving habits

4. Safety features on vehicle

5. Coverages chosen (deductibles, limits)

6. Use of vehicle

Activity 22.4 Anti-Theft Devices

Directions: Consult current magazines and other library or online sources and make a list of anti-theft devices that car owners can purchase to reduce the chances of their vehicles being stolen. Briefly describe how the device works and list its cost. (Examples: steering wheel locks, ignition-kill switches, alarm systems)

Name of Device	How It Works	Cost

Activity 22.5 Auto Insurance Coverages

Directions: The following chart shows the types of losses possible and types of coverage available in auto insurance policies. Place an X in the column of the coverage(s) if it covers the type of loss shown.

The abbreviations are as follows: LIAB. = liability coverage; COLL. = collision coverage; COMP. = comprehensive coverage; PIP = personal injury protection; UN = uninsured/underinsured motorist coverage.

	LIAB.	COLL.	COMP.	PIP	UN
Example: Covers repairs to the insured's car as a result of a falling rock			**X**		
1. Covers the insured against claims for bodily injury to another person					
2. Described using a series of numbers, such as 100/300/50					
3. Covers loss from fire to the insured's vehicle					
4. Protects the insured against claims for property damage caused by the insured's car					
5. Type of auto insurance required in most states					
6. Covers damage to the insured's car resulting from severe weather					
7. Usually has a deductible clause					
8. Covers risk of loss from theft of or from the insured's vehicle					
9. Pays for medical and hospital costs of the insured and his or her family					
10. Coverage(s) provided on a full-coverage policy					
11. Protects you as a pedestrian if you are hit by an uninsured vehicle					
12. Pays for funeral costs of insured or passengers, regardless of fault					

Activity 22.6 Understanding an Insurance Policy

Directions: Read the material below and then answer the questions that follow.

An insurance policy is a legal contract between the insurance company (the insurer) and the person(s) or business being insured (the insured). Reading a policy helps you verify that it meets your needs and that you understand your responsibilities, as well as your insurance company's responsibilities, if a loss occurs. However, insurance policies can be difficult to read and understand. Most insurance policies contain the following standard parts:

1. *Declaration.* This page is usually the first part of an insurance policy. It states the name and address of the insured, the dates that the policy will be in effect, the property that is being insured, the dollar amounts of coverage and deductibles, and other basic information that applies specifically to one person's insurance policy.
2. *Insuring Agreement.* This section specifies what the insurance company has agreed to pay for or to provide in exchange for the premium. It also states what coverages are specifically included in the policy.
3. *Definitions.* This section defines common words that appear throughout a policy that have special meaning within the context of insurance. In order to understand the terms used in the policy, it is important to read this section.
4. *Conditions.* This section explains the duties of the insured and of the insurer. For example, it is the insured's responsibility to pay premiums on time and to meet conditions that were agreed upon in the setting of premiums. The insurer will collect premiums, process claims, and pay the cost of damages as agreed.
5. *Exclusions.* This section describes perils, property, and types of losses that will not be covered. For example, a homeowners insurance policy generally does not cover damage caused by perils such as floods or earthquakes and does not cover personal property such as pets or jewelry. An auto insurance policy does not cover damage due to wear and tear.
6. *Endorsements.* Any modification to the insurance agreement is included as an endorsement. For example, the insured may decide to either add a coverage or delete a coverage. Endorsements can be made at a later date.

Your best protection is to read and understand all of this information prior to signing and agreeing to pay the premiums. Having an insurance agent can be a valuable resource in analyzing your policy.

1. Why would the declaration be different for every policy?

_____

_____

_____

2. Why do you think some situations are excluded from coverage?

_____

_____

_____

3. For what kinds of things might a policyholder use endorsements?

_____

_____

_____

chapter 23 Health and Life Insurance

1 section: vocabulary

Fill in the missing word(s) in the space provided at the right.

Answers

Example: _____ coverage provides protection against the catastrophic expenses of a serious injury or illness.

0. __Major medical__

1. _____ insurance is a plan for sharing the risk of high medical costs resulting from an accident or illness.

1. _____

2. _____ is a group health insurance provision that specifies how the insurers will share the cost when more than one policy covers a claim.

2. _____

3. _____ insurance provides funds to the beneficiaries when the insured dies.

3. _____

4. People who will receive the benefits of an insurance policy are called _____.

4. _____

5. With a(n) _____ clause, the insurer cannot dispute a policy's validity after a specified period of time.

5. _____

6. _____ term insurance gives the insured the right to renew the policy each year, without having to pass a physical exam.

6. _____

7. A(n) _____ is a small insurance addendum that modifies the coverage of the main policy.

7. _____

8. A(n) _____ is a group of health care providers who band together to provide health services for set fees.

8. _____

9. A(n) _____ is a group health insurance plan offering prepaid medical care to its members.

9. _____

10. _____ means that the beneficiary is paid double the face amount of the insurance policy.

10. _____

11. _____ coverage includes medical, hospital, and surgical costs.

11. _____

12. To predict the probability of death occurring, insurance companies use _____ tables.

12. _____

13. _____ riders give a policyholder the right to renew a policy or buy additional coverage regardless of changes in health.

13. _____

14. _____ allows people who have been diagnosed with a serious medical condition that will likely lead to their death in 12 or 24 months (or other specified time period) to collect a portion of their life insurance benefits before death.

14. _____

15. _____ is the savings accumulated in a permanent life insurance policy that you would receive if you canceled your policy.

15. _____

16. A(n) _____ is any medical condition that a person has before being enrolled in an insurance plan.

16. _____

2 | section:
review questions

After each of the following statements, circle *T* for a true statement or *F* for a false statement.

	Answers	For Scoring
1. Most health insurance is issued in the form of group health insurance.	T F	1. _____
2. Vision insurance usually pays for sunglasses and contact lenses.	T F	2. _____
3. Portability allows you to convert a group policy to an individual policy.	T F	3. _____
4. Basic health coverage often has a coinsurance provision requiring the insured to pay some portion of the bills.	T F	4. _____
5. Not everyone is eligible to buy an individual life insurance policy.	T F	5. _____
6. Workers' compensation pays workers only when they are injured on the job.	T F	6. _____
7. A traditional fee-for-service plan is less expensive than a managed care plan.	T F	7. _____
8. Health maintenance organizations encourage preventive care, such as routine physical exams.	T F	8. _____
9. Medicare insurance is provided for people age 65 or older through the Social Security Administration.	T F	9. _____
10. Disability insurance is the most commonly purchased type of insurance.	T F	10. _____

On the line at the right of each sentence, print the letter that represents the word or group of words correctly completing the sentence or answering the question.

1. Which of the following is a supplemental private insurance policy?
   (a) Medicare, (b) Medicaid, (c) Medigap, (d) Minimed   _____ 1. _____

2. Which of the following is a standard provision usually found in all life insurance policies? (a) beneficiary clause, (b) incontestable clause, (c) suicide clause, (d) all of these   _____ 2. _____

3. Which of the following types of insurance is "temporary"? (a) level term, (b) whole life, (c) limited-pay life, (d) universal life   _____ 3. _____

4. Which type of insurance plan has a premium and a death benefit that are not fixed? (a) level term, (b) whole life, (c) universal life, (d) limited-pay   _____ 4. _____

5. Which type of insurance plan has an investment feature? (a) level term, (b) whole life, (c) universal life, (d) variable life   _____ 5. _____

6. Which of the following is often offered as part of a cafeteria-style plan? (a) supplemental health insurance, (b) dental insurance, (c) a Flex 125 Plan, (d) a health savings account   _____ 6. _____

7. What type of plan is available to people who qualify under state welfare and public assistance programs? (a) Medicaid, (b) Medigap, (c) Medicare, (d) Medicare Advantage   _____ 7. _____

8. The waiting period for disability benefits can range from _____ days or longer. (a) 5 to 10, (b) 15 to 30, (c) 30 to 60, (d) 30 to 90   _____ 8. _____

9. An insurance clause that caps or sets a maximum that the insured has to pay out of pocket is called (a) coinsurance, (b) stop-loss provision, (c) double indemnity, (d) Medigap.   _____ 9. _____

10. Which of the following would not be covered by basic health insurance? (a) doctor office visit, (b) physical exam, (c) organ transplant, (d) X-rays   _____ 10. _____

3 section:
3 **problem solving**

Activity 23.1 Cutting Medical Costs

Directions: Explain how each category below can help cut medical costs and provide for better health.

1. Prevention: Regular physical examinations, checkups, vaccinations, and screenings

_____

_____

_____

_____

_____

_____

_____

2. Nutrition: Eating balanced meals, exercising regularly, and maintaining proper weight

_____

_____

_____

_____

_____

_____

_____

3. Getting a second opinion on all required and elective surgeries or medical procedures

_____

_____

_____

_____

_____

_____

_____

4. Analysis of personal habits (drinking, smoking) and family history

_____

_____

_____

_____

_____

_____

_____

Activity 23.2 A Good Health Care Plan

Directions: Complete the following chart comparing three health care plans in your local area. One plan should be a traditional fee-for-service plan, one should be a preferred provider organization, and one should be a health maintenance organization. Ask parents, teachers, or others who have group coverage to help you fill in the information below.

COMPANY 1: _____

Are physical exams provided? _____ How often? _____

Is there a yearly deductible? _____ Co-pay?_____

Are prescriptions covered?_____

Can you choose your own physician?_____

Is dental coverage provided? _____ Is there a maximum benefit?_____

Is vision coverage provided? _____ Is there a maximum benefit? _____

What are the policy limits on major medical coverage?_____

What is the maximum out of pocket (stop-loss) per year? (This is the most that the insured would have to pay.)_____

COMPANY 2: _____

Are physical exams provided? _____ How often? _____

Is there a yearly deductible? _____ Co-pay?_____

Are prescriptions covered?_____

Can you choose your own physician?_____

Is dental coverage provided? _____ Is there a maximum benefit?_____

Is vision coverage provided? _____ Is there a maximum benefit? _____

What are the policy limits on major medical coverage?_____

What is the maximum out of pocket (stop-loss) per year? (This is the most that the insured would have to pay.)_____

COMPANY 3: _____

Are physical exams provided? _____ How often? _____

Is there a yearly deductible? _____ Co-pay?_____

Are prescriptions covered?_____

Can you choose your own physician?_____

Is dental coverage provided? _____ Is there a maximum benefit?_____

Is vision coverage provided? _____ Is there a maximum benefit? _____

What are the policy limits on major medical coverage?_____

What is the maximum out of pocket (stop-loss) per year? (This is the most that the insured would have to pay.)_____

Activity 23.3 Alternative Medicine

Directions: Read the material below and then answer the questions that follow.

Alternative medicine is any practice that is put forward as having the healing effects of medicine, but is not based on evidence gathered using the scientific method. It consists of a wide range of practices, products, and therapies. Some examples of alternative medicine practices include naturopathy, acupuncture, and biofeedback.

Naturopathy is the use of natural medicines and procedures to remove toxins (poisons) from the body. Naturopaths suggest ways to build immunity by taking natural supplements. Naturopathy's goal is to promote or restore health by support of the individual's self-healing process.

Acupuncture is the use of needles inserted into the body at specific points to relieve pain. It is a Chinese medicine but is used around the world to treat conditions ranging from depression to obesity.

Biofeedback is a form of treatment that helps patients gain some control over normally involuntary body functions. It is based on the idea that the mind and the body are linked and that the mind can control the body. Patients are hooked up to a monitoring device that provides feedback on functions such as heart rate and blood pressure. Patients can then practice techniques that favorably affect these functions. For example, they can use relaxation techniques to lower blood pressure.

The majority of alternative medicine services are paid for out of pocket. Although consumer demand is causing more insurance companies to cover alternative medicine, coverage remains limited. Thus, you should understand the financial aspect of alternative medicine before committing to this treatment option.

1. Do you take vitamins? Why or why not?

_____

_____

_____

_____

_____

_____

_____

2. Do you believe there is a mind/body connection that can help you stay healthy? Explain.

_____

_____

_____

_____

_____

_____

3. Would you ever consider trying a form of alternative medicine? Why or why not?

_____

_____

_____

_____

_____

_____

Activity 23.4 Disability Needs

Directions: Prepare the following chart based on what you think your needs would be if you were working and became disabled. You can interview a person who is working full time and ask him or her to help you come up with the needed numbers.

	Monthly Expenses	
	Today	When Disabled
Projected expenses:		
Rent or mortgage payment	_____	_____
Utilities	_____	_____
Food	_____	_____
Clothing	_____	_____
Insurance: Auto	_____	_____
Homeowners	_____	_____
Life	_____	_____
Health	_____	_____
Installment payments (such as car)	_____	_____
Gas, oil, parking, repairs	_____	_____
Medical and dental care (deductibles and co-pays)	_____	_____
Recreation, entertainment	_____	_____
Miscellaneous	_____	_____
Total expenses	_____	_____

	Monthly Income	
	Today	When Disabled
Projected income:		
Disability insurance (employer or union)	_____	_____
Social Security Disability Insurance	_____	_____
Workers' compensation	_____	_____
Other income (spouse, rental, interest, dividends, and so on)	_____	_____
Total income	_____	_____

If these numbers are equal, then you do not need to purchase additional disability insurance. If, however, there is a significant difference, then you should check your options.

Activity 23.5 Life Insurance Companies

Directions: Using online resources or the *Yellow Pages*, make a list of the life insurance companies and insurance agencies that sell life insurance in your area. List the name, address, telephone number, and agent's name (if applicable) for each company or agency in the space provided.

	Company/Agency	Address	Phone	Agent Name
1.				
2.				
3.				
4.				
5.				
6.				
7.				
8.				
9.				
10.				

Activity 23.6 Survey of Insurance Costs

Directions: Interview as many people as possible who can give you cost estimates for the insurance coverages listed below. Ask people who have purchased insurance recently, people who have had coverage for many years, and insurance agents who sell these types of coverage.

1. Health insurance: (group plans)
   Traditional fee-for-service coverage,   Monthly premium: $ _____
   20 percent co-pay, $250 to $500 deductible
   Other features: _____
   _____
   _____

   Health maintenance organization   Monthly premium: $ _____
   $25 or more co-pay, no deductible
   Other features: _____
   _____
   _____

   Medicare   Monthly premium: $ _____
   Other features: _____
   _____
   _____

2. Disability insurance:
   Long-term disability   Monthly premium: $ _____
   70 percent of salary, 90-day waiting period
   Other features: _____
   _____
   _____

3. Life insurance:
   Level term insurance   Monthly premium: $ _____
   $100,000 face value, age 25, male, 5-year renewable term
   Other features: _____
   _____
   _____

   Universal life   Monthly premium: $ _____
   $100,000 face value, age 25, male, 20-year pay
   Other features: _____
   _____
   _____

Project 5
Managing Risk

Directions: After reading the Unit 5 Project in the student text, complete Worksheets 1–5. (Note that you will need to refer to tables on pages 574–575 in your textbook to complete Worksheet 1.)

WORKSHEET 1
Computing Future Value

Assume that you purchased a whole life policy for $100,000 and your premiums were $300 a year, with $150 covering insurance and $150 directed to your savings plan. The insurance cost increases by $3 every year. You are guaranteed 5 percent interest on your savings for the first five years but will not earn interest until the end of the second year.

Required:

1. Prepare a table that lists how much total premium you will have paid in five years, total insurance cost for five years, and the balance in your savings portion at the end of five years for the whole life policy.

2. How much would you have had in savings if you had bought a term policy for $150/year (for 5 years) and put the remainder in a savings account at your bank with interest compounding at the rate of 4 percent a year?

WORKSHEET 2
Insurance Claim Form

Directions: Fill out the claim form below based on the following information. The insured is Mary B. Ownbey, who lives at 845 Oak Street, Wellington, Ohio 44090. Her phone number is (440) 555-0180. Her policy number is KN338-44-2281, and her agent is G. Smiley. Her home was broken into sometime between 8 p.m. and 2 a.m. (Friday evening) while she was away. The kitchen was vandalized (spray paint on the walls and eggs thrown on the floor); the carpeting in the dining room was stained as well. A police report was filed (Case 95-2288) by Officer K. Bridges. There were no witnesses. The walls in the kitchen must be scraped and painted; the carpeting must be cleaned or replaced if the stain cannot be removed. The value of the damage is estimated at $500. The house was painted last year ($100 for the kitchen walls); the carpet was new a year ago ($2,000 for the damaged carpeting). Both were purchased at Excel Interiors, and she has a receipt. The property is located in the home at the above address. Use today's date.

Claim No. _____

Name of Insured _____

Address _____

_____ Phone _____

Policy No. _____ Agent _____

Describe what happened: _____

_____

_____

_____

_____

Was a police report filed? _____ Case No. _____

Police officer taking report _____

Were there any witnesses? _____ List their names and addresses:

_____

_____

_____

_____

Description of property damaged _____

Value of property_____

Date purchased _____ Purchase price_____

Where purchased _____ Receipt?_____

Where is property now located (for inspection)? _____

_____

_____   _____
Date   Signature of Insured

WORKSHEET 3
Reducing Health Care Costs

Directions: Answer the following questions about ways you can reduce health care costs.

1. Do you eat well-balanced meals and exercise regularly?

   _____

   _____

2. Do you get sufficient rest and relaxation?

   _____

   _____

3. Do you know your health insurance coverages, limitations, and exclusions?

   _____

   _____

4. Do you use generic prescriptions when possible? (Generic drugs are less expensive versions of brand-name drugs. Because there is no advertising or other expenses of mass marketing, the cost is lower.)

   _____

   _____

5. Do you shop around for the best prices for (a) dental work, (b) vision care and glasses, (c) prescriptions, (d) charges for office visits, and (e) supplies, vitamins, and other health care purchases?

   _____

   _____

   _____

6. List some things you and your family can do to reduce health care costs.

   _____

   _____

   _____

   _____

   _____

   _____

   _____

7. Explain why it is important to ask questions when you visit your doctor.

   _____

   _____

   _____

   _____

   _____

   _____

   _____

   _____

WORKSHEET 4
Using Mortality Tables

Directions: Based on the mortality table on page 580 in your textbook, answer the following questions.

1. At the bottom of the Life Expectancy column, what does the number 13.0 mean?

_____

2. On average, people who are 50 years old now could be expected to live to be what age?

_____

3. In the Deaths per 1,000 column, what does the number 1.2 mean?

_____

4. In a group of 10,000 males, all age 40, an average of how many could be expected to die in the next year? _____

WORKSHEET 5
Personal Insurance Plan

1. Explain the purpose of each of the following types of insurance.
   a. Homeowners insurance: _____

   _____

   b. Automobile insurance: _____

   _____

   c. Liability insurance: _____

   _____

   d. Health insurance: _____

   _____

   e. Disability insurance: _____

   _____

   f. Life insurance: _____

   _____

2. Based on your current situation, what types of insurance do you currently purchase?
   a. Homeowners insurance: _____
   b. Automobile insurance: _____
   c. Liability insurance: _____
   d. Health insurance: _____
   e. Disability insurance: _____
   f. Life insurance: _____
3. How do you anticipate that your need for each of these insurance coverages will change in the next five years?
   a. Homeowners insurance: _____
   b. Automobile insurance: _____
   c. Liability insurance: _____
   d. Health insurance: _____
   e. Disability insurance: _____
   f. Life insurance: _____
4. List several guidelines for building a plan for purchasing all types of insurance.

_____

_____

chapter 24 Role of Consumers in a Market Economy

1 section: vocabulary

Fill in the missing word(s) in the space provided at the right.

Answers

Example: _____ are the manufacturers or makers of goods and services for sale. 0. ___Producers___

1. A(n) _____ economy is one in which both market forces (based on individual freedoms) and government decisions determine which goods and services are produced and how they are distributed. 1. _____

2. A(n) _____ system is one where the government or central authority controls most of the production decisions. 2. _____

3. _____ is an illegal sales technique in which a seller advertises a product with the intention of persuading consumers to buy a more expensive product. 3. _____

4. The measurement of something's usefulness is called _____. 4. _____

5. _____ are government grants to some citizens paid with money collected from other citizens. 5. _____

6. _____ is the willingness and ability of consumers to purchase goods and services at various prices. 6. _____

7. The value of money, measured in the amount of goods and services that it can buy is called _____. 7. _____

8. Consumer _____ means that consumers have the ultimate power in a market economy. 8. _____

9. _____ is a remedy to a problem. 9. _____

10. A scam in which a con artist convinces people to give up their money in return for a share of a larger sum of money is called a(n) _____. 10. _____

11. Advertising an item at special savings when in reality it is selling at regular price is called a(n) _____. 11. _____

12. The basic economic problem, called _____, means that consumers' wants are unlimited while resources to satisfy them are limited. 12. _____

13. A(n) _____ is a market with many buyers but only one seller. 13. _____

14. _____ is an illegal agreement among competitors to sell a good or service for a set price. 14. _____

15. _____ refers to actions of the government to stimulate or slow the economy. 15. _____

16. The quantity of goods and services that producers are willing and able to provide at various prices is known as the _____. 16. _____

17. _____ is the rivalry among sellers in the same market to win customers. 17. _____

18. _____ occurs when false or misleading claims are made about the quality, price, or purpose of a particular product. 18. _____

2 section:
review questions

After each of the following statements, circle *T* for a true statement or *F* for a false statement.

			Answers	**For Scoring**
1.	Most nations today have a market economy.		T F	1. _____
2.	Demand is the quantity of goods and services available for sale.		T F	2. _____
3.	Whenever consumers purchase a product, they are casting "dollar votes" for that product.		T F	3. _____
4.	Three essential parts of a market economy are competition, purchasing power, and informed consumers.		T F	4. _____
5.	The government shifts purchasing power among citizens by making transfer payments.		T F	5. _____
6.	With the bait-and-switch sales technique, the "bait" is the customer.		T F	6. _____
7.	It is wise to wait at least 24 hours before making a major purchase.		T F	7. _____
8.	Low-balling results when the consumer is promised a great deal of money with little effort.		T F	8. _____
9.	Senior citizens are often subject to the schemes of con artists.		T F	9. _____
10.	Infomercials are advertisements involving product demonstrations and testimonials.		T F	10. _____

On the line at the right of each sentence, print the letter that represents the word or group of words correctly completing the sentence or answering the question.

1. A scam whereby a person is convinced to use his or her checking account to assist in the transfer of an international deposit in return for a portion of the money is an example of (a) a Ponzi scheme, (b) a pigeon drop, (c) a pyramid scheme, (d) low-balling. _____ 1. _____

2. In a _____ scheme, distributors are promised commissions from their own sales and those of other distributors they recruit. (a) Ponzi, (b) pyramid, (c) pigeon drop, (d) low-balling _____ 2. _____

3. Probably the most common of all consumer frauds is (a) Internet fraud, (b) bait and switch, (c) low-balling, (d) the fake sale. _____ 3. _____

4. Which of the following items is the best buy when unit prices are computed? (a) 3/$.89, (b) 4/$1.00, (c) 5/$1.29, (d) 6/$1.33 _____ 4. _____

5. Which of the following is not a form of competition in a market economy? (a) monopoly, (b) pure competition, (c) profit competition, (d) oligopoly _____ 5. _____

6. Which of the following is not a transfer payment? (a) interest income, (b) Social Security, (c) welfare, (d) veterans' benefits _____ 6. _____

7. Which of the following types of economic systems is not considered a hands-off system? (a) traditional, (b) socialism, (c) capitalism, (d) all of these _____ 7. _____

8. _____ have the final say in what is produced and at what price in a market economy. (a) Producers, (b) Governments, (c) Consumers, (d) Retailers _____ 8. _____

3 | section:
problem solving

Activity 24.1 Calculating Unit Prices

Directions: To compute unit prices, reduce the selling price to the lowest possible unit. For example, if a product costs $1.00 and a package contains 8 ounces, the price per unit is $1.00 divided by 8 ounces, or 12.5 cents per ounce.

Calculate the unit prices to the nearest penny in the questions below.

1. a. The cost of gasoline is $48.50 to fill up a tank containing 14 gallons. What is the cost per gallon?

   b. There are 3.785 liters per gallon. You bought 33 liters of gasoline and paid $32.70. What is the price per gallon?

2. You are purchasing the following items. Calculate unit prices to the nearest penny:
   a. 6/$1.00   b. 3/$1.09

   c. 5/$.99   d. 6/$.89

   e. 4/$1.00   f. 8/$3.99

3. Compute the following prices per ounce to the nearest penny:
   a. 8 oz./$1.49   b. 12 oz./$1.33

   c. 31 oz./$2.29   d. 48 oz./$3.89

   e. 1 lb./$3.29   f. 1 lb. 6 oz./$4.49

   g. 2 lbs. 12 oz./$3.99   h. 3 lbs. 6 oz./$4.99

4. After reading the following problems, which of the following cars should you buy?
   (Car A or Car B) _____
   a. Car A uses regular gasoline at $3.77 a gallon and gets 19 miles per gallon (mpg) in town. Assume that you drive 100 miles a week, or 400 miles a month. What is your gas bill each month?

   b. Car B uses premium unleaded gasoline at $3.97 a gallon and gets 24 mpg in town. If you drive 100 miles a week, or 400 miles a month, what will be your gas bill each month?

Activity 24.2 Reading the Label

Directions: The following label represents a consumer product. Read the label carefully and answer the questions in the right-hand column.

NUTRITION INFORMATION

The potato is America's favorite vegetable. Potato chips are a favorite energy food for many active Americans. Potato chips provide protein, vitamins, and minerals needed to maintain good health.

Because we quick-fry our potato chips, we make sure that important vitamins are sealed in. A one-ounce serving contains 10% of the Recommended Daily Allowance of Vitamin C plus measurable amounts of protein, thiamine, and niacin. No preservatives added!

Only the finest natural ingredients are used in GRIPMAN'S potato chips. EAT THEM FOR ENJOYMENT. EAT THEM FOR ENERGY. EAT THEM FOR NUTRITION.

Serving Size: 1 ounce
Number of Servings: 10

Calories	150
Protein	2g
Carbohydrates	14g
Fat	10g
Cholesterol** (0mg/100g)	0mg
Sodium (800mg/100g)	225mg

Percentage of U.S. Recommended Daily Allowances (U.S. RDA)

Protein	2	Riboflavin	*
Vitamin A	*	Niacin	6
Vitamin C	10	Calcium	*
Thiamine	4	Iron	2
Vitamin B$_6$	4		

**Information on cholesterol content is provided for individuals who, on the advice of a physician, are modifying their total dietary intake of cholesterol.

*Contains less than 2% U.S. RDA for this nutrient.

INGREDIENTS: POTATOES, VEGETABLE OIL (CONTAINS ONE OR MORE OF THE FOLLOWING: COTTONSEED OIL, CORN OIL, PALM OIL, SUNFLOWER OIL, SOYBEAN OIL OR PARTIALLY HYDROGENATED SOYBEAN OIL), SALT.

THIS PACKAGE IS PACKED AND SOLD BY WEIGHT, NOT BY VOLUME. SOME SETTLING OF CONTENTS MAY OCCUR DURING SHIPMENT.

GRIPMAN'S FINE SNACK FOODS, Alexandria, VA 22310-2511

Gripman's
America's Favorite Snack Food

1. What general information is given about potatoes and potato chips?

_____

_____

_____

_____

_____

_____

_____

_____

_____

_____

2. How large is one serving size? _____

3. How many calories are contained in 10 servings? _____

4. How much cholesterol is contained in an ounce of potato chips? _____

5. What percentages of the RDA are provided in:

a. Protein _____

b. Thiamine _____

c. Calcium _____

d. Vitamin B6_____

6. List the ingredients.

_____

_____

_____

_____

_____

7. Is the package sold by weight or volume?

_____

8. List the name of the producer and the address.

_____

_____

9. Are preservatives contained in this product?

_____

Activity 24.3 Correcting an Error

Directions: Information about the correct procedures to follow in solving errors in bank statements or credit card statements is usually sent to bank and credit card customers at least once a year. Following is a leaflet, sometimes sent with a monthly bank reconciliation, for you to review. The purpose of this leaflet is to inform customers of the procedures to follow in case of errors or inquiries about electronic transfers. Answer the questions that follow.

Nature of Error Resolution Procedures Concerning Electronic Transfers

In Case of Errors or Inquiries About Electronic Transfers

Call us (collect if necessary) at 203-555-0124 or call your branch of account or write us at Metro First Bank of New Haven, Connecticut, P.O. Box 1711-09, New Haven, CT 06511-3023 if you think your checking or savings account statement or Automated Teller Machine (ATM) receipt is wrong or if you need more information about an ATM transaction or a preauthorized deposit or payment listed on your statement or receipt.

You must contact us within 60 days after the first checking or savings account statement reflecting the error was mailed and give us your name, account number, and a description of the error, including the dollar amount.

If you notify us in the time and manner provided above, we will then investigate and contact you by phone or mail within 10 business days of receipt of your notice. We may credit the checking or savings account in question for the amount you think is in error while we are investigating the error. If we do, we have up to 45 days to investigate and make a determination.

If your notice of error is not in writing, we may require you to put it in writing within 10 business days of your oral notice. If we do not receive that written notice within 10 business days of requesting it, we need not provisionally credit your account and have up to 45 days to investigate and make a determination.

If we determine an error was made, we will correct it within one business day.

If we determine there was no error, we will mail an explanation within three business days after our investigation, and if you ask, we'll send you copies of the documents we relied upon to reach our conclusions.

For the purpose of any notice to us about electronic transfers, our business days are Monday through Friday, except holidays.

Member FDIC
MISC-679 7-89

|| **Metro First Bank** ||

1. What should you do if you suspect an error in an ATM receipt?

_____

_____

_____

2. How soon after suspecting an error must you contact the bank?

_____

_____

3. How soon will the bank acknowledge your complaint?

_____

4. How many days will the bank take to investigate and respond to your complaint?

_____

5. If your complaint is not in writing, what may the bank require you to do?

_____

_____

_____

_____

6. If the bank agrees there is an error, what will it do?

_____

_____

_____

7. If the bank does not find an error, what will it do?

_____

_____

_____

_____

_____

_____

8. What is the name of the bank? Is the bank federally insured?

_____

_____

Activity 24.4 Reading the Warranty—No. 1

Directions: Read the following warranty carefully and answer the questions.

ONE-YEAR LIMITED WARRANTY

This Evans-Powell electronic calculator warranty extends to the original purchaser of the calculator.

WARRANTY DURATION

This Evans-Powell electronic calculator is warranted to the original purchaser for a period of one (1) year from the original purchase date.

WARRANTY COVERAGE

This Evans-Powell electronic calculator is warranted against defective materials or workmanship. THIS WARRANTY IS VOID IF (i) THE CALCULATOR HAS BEEN DAMAGED BY ACCIDENT OR UNREASONABLE USE, NEGLECT, IMPROPER SERVICE, OR OTHER CAUSES NOT ARISING OUT OF DEFECTS IN MATERIAL OR WORKMANSHIP, (ii) THE SERIAL NUMBER HAS BEEN ALTERED OR DEFACED.

WARRANTY PERFORMANCE

During the above one-year warranty period, your calculator will either be repaired or replaced with a reconditioned model of an equivalent quality (at E-P's option) when the calculator is returned, postage prepaid and insured to an Evans-Powell Service Facility listed below. In the event of replacement with a reconditioned model, the replacement unit will continue the warranty of the original calculator or 90 days, whichever is longer. Other than the postage and insurance requirement, no charge will be made for such repair, adjustment, and/or replacement

WARRANTY DISCLAIMERS

ANY IMPLIED WARRANTIES ARISING OUT OF THIS SALE, INCLUDING BUT NOT LIMITED TO THE IMPLIED WARRANTIES OF MERCHANTABILITY AND FITNESS FOR A PARTICULAR PURPOSE, ARE LIMITED IN DURATION TO THE ABOVE ONE-YEAR PERIOD. EVANS-POWELL SHALL NOT BE LIABLE FOR LOSS OF USE OF THE CALCULATOR OR OTHER INCIDENTAL OR CONSEQUENTIAL COSTS, EXPENSES, OR DAMAGES INCURRED BY THE PURCHASER.

Some states do not allow the exclusion or limitation of implied warranties or consequential damages; therefore, the above limitations or exclusions may not apply to you.

LEGAL REMEDIES

This warranty gives you specific legal rights, and you may also have other rights that vary from state to state.

EVANS-POWELL CONSUMER SERVICE FACILITIES

United States residents write to:

P.O. Box 851
Chicago, Illinois 60611-4160

Canadian residents write to:

P.O. Box 841
Toronto, Canada M4C 1P1

Evans-Powell
INCORPORATED
Chicago, Illinois

Printed in U.S.A.   0930185-1

---

1. What type of equipment or merchandise is represented by this warranty?

   _____

2. Who is the manufacturer of the equipment? Where is the manufacturer located?

   _____

3. How long does the warranty last?

   _____

4. To whom is the warranty extended?

   _____

5. How is the warranty made void?

   a. _____

   _____

   _____

   _____

   b. _____

   _____

   _____

6. Do you have to return the merchandise for repair or replacement?

   _____

7. How long is the warranty on a replaced (reconditioned) model?

   _____

8. What is the address for the Canadian service facility of this manufacturer?

   _____

9. Where should Pennsylvania residents write to this manufacturer?

_____

10. What are the limits to the warranty on this product?

_____

_____

_____

Activity 24.5 Reading the Warranty—No. 2

Directions: From the limited warranty below, answer the questions that follow.

CALL-ON-TIME RECORDERS, INC., RECORDER II, Telephone Answering Systems
LIMITED WARRANTY
Model Nos. 70C, 70CA, 70CB Ninety Days Labor/One-Year Parts

Call-on-Time Recorders, Inc., warrants your Recorder II to be free from factory defects in material and workmanship for a period of one (1) year for parts and ninety (90) days for labor from the date of the original purchase. The obligation under this warranty is limited to repairing or replacing any defective part for one (1) year, and providing all necessary labor for the first ninety (90) days in connection with the correction of any defect. Tapes and accessories are not covered under this warranty, and all transportation charges or shipping expenses shall be the sole responsibility of the purchaser. The exchange of any factory defective Recorder II is at the exclusive option of Call-on-Time Recorders, Inc., and in no event does Call-on-Time Recorders, Inc., assume liability for any damage beyond the refund of the purchase price of its nonconforming products, or the repair or replacement of same.

ALL IMPLIED WARRANTIES IN RESPECT TO THE RECORDER II PRODUCTS, EXCEPT TO THE EXTENT PROHIBITED BY APPLICABLE LAW, SHALL HAVE NO GREATER DURATION THAN THE WARRANTY PERIODS SET FORTH HEREIN. NO WARRANTIES, WHETHER EXPRESSED OR IMPLIED, INCLUDING WARRANTIES OF THE MERCHANTABILITY OR FITNESS SHALL APPLY TO THE RECORDER II PRODUCT AFTER THE WARRANTY PERIODS HAVE EXPIRED. UNDER NO CIRCUMSTANCES SHALL THE COMPANY BE HELD LIABLE FOR ANY LOSS OR DAMAGE, DIRECT OR CONSEQUENTIAL, ARISING OUT OF THE USE OF, OR INABILITY TO USE, RECORDER II PRODUCTS. SOME STATES DO NOT ALLOW LIMITATIONS ON HOW LONG AN IMPLIED WARRANTY LASTS, AND EXCLUSIONS OR LIMITATION OF INCIDENTAL OR CONSEQUENTIAL DAMAGES; THEREFORE, THE ABOVE LIMITATIONS OR EXCLUSIONS MAY NOT APPLY TO YOU. THIS WARRANTY GIVES YOU SPECIFIC LEGAL RIGHTS, AND YOU MAY HAVE OTHER RIGHTS WHICH VARY FROM STATE TO STATE.

To obtain repairs under the terms of this warranty, pack your Recorder II product carefully in the original packing, or its equivalent, and carry in, or ship to, your nearest authorized Service Center* or directly to Call-on-Time Recorders, Inc., together with a copy of the original bill of sale.

This warranty extends only to the original purchaser and is not assignable or transferable. This warranty shall not apply to any Recorder II product which has been improperly maintained or repaired, including the installation of parts or accessories that do not conform to the quality and specifications of the original components or parts, or that may have been subject to alterations, abuse, misuse, neglect (including improper installation), accidental or intentional damage, or to any product which may have had serial numbers or model name altered, defaced, or removed.

No informal dispute settlement mechanism as allowed under the Magnuson-Moss Warranty/Federal Trade Commission Improvement Act, Public Law 93-637 (1975) is available under this warranty.

Although it is not mandatory, to avoid unnecessary difficulties in determining your eligibility for warranty work, we suggest you fill out your warranty and registration card and mail it to Call-on-Time Recorders, Inc., National Service Department, 4821 Blair Boulevard, San Francisco, California 94162-0001, within ten (10) days after purchase of the Recorder II product.

NO OTHER WARRANTY, WRITTEN OR VERBAL, IS AUTHORIZED BY CALL-ON-TIME RECORDERS, INC., WITH RESPECT TO THE RECORDER II PRODUCT.

Call-on-Time Recorders, Inc., or its authorized representative will either repair or replace the unit, at its option, and return the repaired or new unit to any address in the United States at no charge. If a unit is to be returned to any address outside of the United States, shipping charges must be paid in advance by the owner. In addition, Call-on-Time Recorders, Inc., assumes no responsibility for compliance with laws and regulations other than those of the United States pertaining to the usage of telephone answering devices and/or their connection to or with telephone systems in countries other than the United States. Any usage in connection with electrical systems other than those for which the unit was designed will void this warranty.

*Requests for warranty information and questions regarding the location of authorized Service Centers should be directed to the National Service Department of Call-on-Time Recorders, Inc., at the following telephone numbers: toll free 800-555-0111, and in California (213) 555-0178 collect.

---

1. How long does the warranty extend for labor? For parts?

   _____

2. How must the original equipment be returned to the manufacturer?

   _____

3. Is the warranty transferable or assignable to anyone other than the original purchaser?

   _____

4. What public law is cited in this warranty?

   _____

5. To what address should you send the warranty and registration card?

   _____

6. How long after the purchase should you send in the warranty and registration card?

   _____

7. List the toll-free number that can be called with questions regarding authorized service centers for this product.

   _____

Activity 24.6 Monetary and Fiscal Policy

Directions: Conduct research online and at the library to answer the following questions about monetary and fiscal policy.

Section 1. Monetary Policy

Monetary policy refers to actions taken by the Federal Reserve System to regulate the economy by managing interest rates, the availability of loans, and the supply of money.

1. What actions has the Federal Reserve Board taken in the last six months? What is their rationale?

   _____

   _____

   _____

   _____

2. If the Fed were to raise (or lower) the discount rate now, what would be the effect on the economy? Explain.

   _____

   _____

   _____

   _____

3. Explain what is meant by "open market operations." How does this affect the economy?

   _____

   _____

   _____

   _____

Section 2. Fiscal Policy

Fiscal policy refers to actions taken by the government (U.S. Congress and the President) to stimulate or slow down the economy, such as lowering tax rates or increasing its own spending.

1. What actions are currently being proposed by the President or the Congress? What is the rationale?

   _____

   _____

   _____

   _____

2. Explain how a tax cut or a tax rebate will affect the economy.

   _____

   _____

   _____

   _____

1 section: vocabulary

Fill in the missing word(s) in the space provided at the right.

Answers

Example: The _____ oversees the U.S. commercial aviation industry for the Department of Transportation.

0. _____FAA_____

1. _____ are medications with the same composition as the equivalent brand-name drugs, but they are generally less expensive.

1. _____

2. A(n) _____ is a request for consumers to return a defective product to the manufacturer for a refund or repair.

2. _____

3. The _____ updated the Meat Inspection Act of 1906 and provided stricter standards for meat processing facilities.

3. _____

4. _____ give instructions for the care of clothing and fabrics.

4. _____

5. The _____ is an agency within the Department of Commerce that develops and rewards standards of excellence in business.

5. _____

6. Products that are resistant to tampering by young children are _____.

6. _____

7. The _____ enforces laws and regulations preventing distribution of mislabeled foods, drugs, cosmetics, and medical devices.

7. _____

8. _____ is the capacity for catching on fire.

8. _____

9. The _____ regulates interstate and international communications by radio, television, wire, satellite, and cable.

9. _____

10. The _____ regulates unfair competition, false or deceptive advertising, and deceptive product labeling.

10. _____

11. The _____ is a federal law enforcement agency that investigates consumer complaints regarding illegal use of the mail.

11. _____

12. The _____ is a nonprofit organization focused on creating a more trusting relationship between businesses and customers.

12. _____

13. _____ is a nonprofit organization best known as the publisher of *Consumer Reports*.

13. _____

14. A(n) _____ is a person who actively promotes consumer causes.

14. _____

15. The _____ was proposed by President Kennedy, and it outlines basic consumer rights.

15. _____

16. A(n) _____ is a reasonable, untrained person in a similar position.

16. _____

17. _____ allows media stored on one device to be accessed from another place through another device.

17. _____

18. Consumers are _____ when they record video or audio for later viewing or listening.

18. _____

section: 2 review questions

After each of the following statements, circle *T* for a true statement or *F* for a false statement.

	Answers	For Scoring

1. Most of the major consumer protection laws in this country have been passed since 1960. — T F   1. _____
2. The Food, Drug, and Cosmetic Act of 1938 requires truthful labeling on foods, drugs, and cosmetics. — T F   2. _____
3. The Flammable Fabrics Act of 1953 requires that children's sleepwear not catch fire when exposed to a match or small fire. — T F   3. _____
4. The Kefauver-Harris Drug Amendment of 1962 established the modern system of generic drugs. — T F   4. _____
5. Airlines are required to compensate passengers who are "bumped" from a flight that is oversold or if the flight is canceled due to bad weather. — T F   5. _____
6. The FDA has the power to test and approve all new drugs. — T F   6. _____
7. The FCC oversees the U.S. National Do Not Call Registry. — T F   7. _____
8. Consumers Union established the right of aggrieved consumers to picket businesses. — T F   8. _____
9. The FTC regulates broadcast communications. — T F   9. _____
10. The Better Business Bureau is a government agency with the legal authority to accept and process complaints against merchants. — T F   10. _____

On the line at the right of each sentence, print the letter that represents the word or group of words correctly completing the sentence or answering the question.

1. The most immediate way to reach a public official is by (a) e-mail, (b) letter, (c) phone, (d) visiting in person. _____ 1. _____
2. The Fair Packaging and Labeling Act requires product labels to contain accurate (a) names, (b) quantities, (c) weights, (d) all of these. _____ 2. _____
3. A flame-retardant finish used on garments must last for _____ washings and dryings. (a) 10, (b) 25, (c) 50, (d) 100 _____ 3. _____
4. Which of the following agencies has the power to ban products that are dangerous? (a) FTC, (b) FCC, (c) FDA, (d) CPSC _____ 4. _____
5. Which of the following is one of the four basic rights of consumers outlined in the 1962 Consumer Bill of Rights? (a) the right to satisfaction of basic needs, (b) the right to be heard, (c) the right to a healthy environment, (d) all of these _____ 5. _____
6. The Children's Online Privacy Protection Act of 1998 applies to the online collection of personal information from children under _____ years of age. (a) 12, (b) 13, (c) 16, (d) 18 _____ 6. _____
7. The _____ requires that warning labels appear on all household products that are potentially dangerous to the consumer. (a) Fair Packaging and Labeling Act, (b) Hazardous Substances Act, (c) Care Labeling Rule, (d) Food, Drug, and Cosmetic Act _____ 7. _____
8. The USDA is responsible for developing and executing federal government policy on all of the following except (a) alcohol and tobacco, (b) food, (c) farming, (d) forestry. _____ 8. _____

3 section: problem solving

Activity 25.1 Labels

Directions: For the following statements, cut and attach labels, or copy them exactly as they are, word for word, in the space provided.

1. Provide a label from a garment containing wool. Include the fabric content and the care instructions.

2. Find a label for a garment that is supposed to be dry-cleaned only. From your example, note what fabric(s) are dry-cleaned and compare your findings with a permanent press fabric.

3. Obtain a label from a child's sleepwear garment. Include the fabric contents, chemicals added, and care instructions. Also, explain how the label is attached to the clothing.

4. Find a label from a garment that is at least two years old. Explain where the label is attached. Notice if the label is still readable. What does the label tell you?

5. Read the label on a prescription bottle. Include the information contained on the label, such as warnings, precautions, or directions for use of the medicine. Also, note any additional information supplied, such as a leaflet, with the prescription.

Activity 25.2 Matching Consumer Protection Laws

Directions: Match the descriptions in Column A with the lettered items in Column B by placing the correct letter on the blank provided.

Column A

_____ 1. Requires that foods be safe, pure, and wholesome; that drugs and medical devices be safe and effective; and that cosmetics be safe

_____ 2. Requires product labels to contain accurate names, quantities, and weights

_____ 3. Established national safety standards for automobiles

_____ 4. Requires that warning labels appear on all household products that are potentially dangerous to the consumer

_____ 5. Requires that clothing and fabrics be labeled permanently with laundering and care instructions

_____ 6. Protects the privacy of student education records

_____ 7. Requires drug manufacturers to test drugs for safety and effectiveness before they are sold to consumers

_____ 8. Sets flammability standards for clothing, children's sleepwear, carpets, rugs, and mattresses

_____ 9. Requires states to have meat inspection programs equal to that of the federal government

_____ 10. Sets rules about who can see your health information

_____ 11. Imposes strict labeling laws for manufacturers and retailers of children's toys that may present a danger to small children

_____ 12. Details what a website must include in a privacy policy, when and how to seek verifiable consent from a parent or guardian, and the responsibilities of the website to protect children's privacy and safety online

_____ 13. Established the modern system of generic drugs

_____ 14. Bans the sale of toys and children's articles that contain hazardous substances

_____ 15. Requires poultry to be inspected for harmful contaminants

Column B

a. Wholesome Meat Act of 1967

b. Care Labeling Rule of 1971

c. Child Protection and Toy Safety Act of 1969

d. Drug Price Competition and Patent Term Restoration Act of 1984

e. Food, Drug, and Cosmetic Act of 1938

f. Children's Online Privacy Protection Act of 1998

g. Kefauver-Harris Drug Amendment of 1962

h. Child Safety Protection Act of 1994

i. National Traffic and Motor Vehicle Safety Act of 1966

j. Health Insurance Portability and Accountability Act of 1996

k. Family and Educational Rights and Privacy Act of 1974

l. Fair Packaging and Labeling Act of 1967

m. Hazardous Substances Act of 1960

n. Flammable Fabrics Act of 1953

o. Poultry Inspection Act of 1957

Activity 25.3 New Laws

Directions: At any given time, there are thousands of bills before the U.S. Congress. Of those, only about 5 percent become law. The GovTrack.us website (www.govtrack.us) helps citizens find and track bills that are currently pending in the U.S. Congress or have recently been enacted by the President. Use the GovTrack.us site to browse currently pending or enacted bills by subject. Choose one of the bills listed and answer the following questions.

1. What is the name of the bill?

_____

_____

2. What is the purpose of the bill?

_____

_____

_____

_____

_____

3. Who is the sponsor of the bill? (Include the sponsor's name, state, and party affiliation.)

_____

_____

_____

4. When was the bill introduced? What is its current status?

_____

_____

_____

_____

5. If the bill is still pending:

a. What is the bill's prognosis, according to GovTrack.us?

_____

_____

_____

_____

_____

b. Would you vote to pass this bill if you were a member of the U.S. Congress? Why or why not?

_____

_____

_____

_____

_____

Activity 25.4 Elected Officials

Directions: How many of the following elected officials can you name? Write in the correct answers in the spaces provided. Use library or online resources if necessary. Your parents may also be able to help you with the answers.

1. President of the United States _____

2. Vice president of the United States _____

3. U.S. senators representing your state _____

   _____

4. U.S. representative(s) representing your state _____

   _____

   _____

5. Your state officials:

   a. Governor _____

   b. Secretary of the state _____

   c. Treasurer _____

   d. Attorney general _____

   e. Senator from your district _____

   f. Representative from your district _____

6. Your local officials:

   a. Mayor _____

   b. City Council members _____

   _____

   _____

   c. City manager _____

   d. Sheriff _____

   e. County commissioners _____

   _____

   _____

   f. Tax assessor _____

7. List the addresses for one national elected official, one state elected official, and one local elected official:

   a. _____

   _____

   b. _____

   _____

   c. _____

   _____

Activity 25.5 Letter to a Public Official

Directions: Below is an example of a letter written to a public official. In the space provided on the next page, write a letter to a public official expressing your concerns or opinions about an issue. When writing about a bill, identify it by the proper name and number; clearly state the purpose of the letter, your position, and your reasoning. Be specific and courteous.

```
          458 Washington Street #12
          Eugene, OR 97401-4501
          January 15, 20—-



          The Honorable John Doe
          U.S. Congressman from Oregon
          United States House of Representatives
          Washington, DC   20515-3205

          Dear Congressman Doe

          I am a resident of Oregon and of the congressional
          district that you represent. I am very concerned about
          a current bill before Congress, HB#261, that would
          change the funding basis for local districts.

          The current system is, in my opinion, adequate
          and fair. The new method of distributing funds would
          reallocate on the basis of population, rather than
          geographic area. Because rural areas have lower
          population, they would receive fewer funds and
          therefore would not be able to keep current with
          improvements and recreational enhancements.

          Even though rural areas have fewer permanent
          residents, they do attract many state and out-of-state
          tourists. To reduce their funding would serve as a
          disadvantage to all.

          I urge you to vote "NO" on HB#261.

          Sincerely yours



          Jacquee B. Meekins
```

chapter 26
Dispute Resolution

1 section: vocabulary

Fill in the missing word(s) in the space provided at the right.

Answers

Example: A(n) _____ is a request to a higher court to review the decision of a lower court.

0. _____appeal_____

1. _____ generally means that you are asking the credit issuer to reverse the charge on your account.

1. _____

2. _____ is a process in which a neutral third person, a negotiator, assists two parties in reaching a compromise that is acceptable to both sides.

2. _____

3. A(n) _____ is one in which a large number of people with similar complaints against the same defendant join together to sue.

3. _____

4. A(n) _____ is a court of limited jurisdiction that resolves cases involving small amounts.

4. _____

5. A(n) _____ case involves a person who has a dispute with another person or entity.

5. _____

6. A(n) _____ case involves a government unit that is accusing an individual of committing a crime.

6. _____

7. The _____ is the presiding officer in the court and is either elected or appointed.

7. _____

8. A body of citizens known as the _____ is sworn by a court to hear the facts submitted during a trial and to render a verdict.

8. _____

9. _____ is the process of gathering and sharing evidence in a lawsuit.

9. _____

10. _____ is a system of laws based on decisions made in court cases.

10. _____

11. The _____ is a document outlining the issues of a case and the relief (damages) that the plaintiff requests.

11. _____

12. A(n) _____ is a legally defined time limit in which a lawsuit may be filed for various complaints.

12. _____

13. The person who brings a lawsuit by filing a complaint is called the _____.

13. _____

14. The person against whom a lawsuit is filed is the _____.

14. _____

15. In a _____ trial, the judge decides the matter.

15. _____

16. A(n) _____ is the sworn statement of a witness that is recorded by the court reporter and put into written form for later use in court.

16. _____

17. _____ is a general term covering several methods of settling disputes without using the court system.

17. _____

18. A(n) _____ is the final court ruling that resolves the trial's key issues and establishes the rights and obligations of each party.

18. _____

2 section:
review questions

After each of the following statements, circle *T* for a true statement or *F* for a false statement.

	Answers	For Scoring

1. Some courts are empowered to decide all types of cases or classes of cases. — T F 1. _____
2. The U.S. district courts are the trial courts of the federal court system. — T F 2. _____
3. No formal record is made of a small claims court hearing. — T F 3. _____
4. In deciding civil cases, the burden of proof required by prosecutors is called *beyond a reasonable doubt*. — T F 4. _____
5. The authority of the federal courts comes directly from the U.S. Constitution and the laws enacted by Congress. — T F 5. _____
6. Federal courts may hear a dispute between citizens of two different states, but only if the dispute involves $75,000 or more. — T F 6. _____
7. Each state has one federal district court that handles civil and criminal matters. — T F 7. _____
8. The Fifteenth Amendment to the U.S. Constitution grants each state the sovereign power to enact and enforce state laws. — T F 8. _____
9. While mediators may be specialists in certain areas, they do not have to be legal authorities. — T F 9. _____
10. A lawsuit generally involves four phases: pleadings, discovery, trial, and appeals. — T F 10. _____

On the line at the right of each sentence, print the letter that represents the word or group of words correctly completing the sentence or answering the question.

1. Issues that can be heard in either state or federal courts are said to be under _____ jurisdiction. (a) exclusive, (b) appellate, (c) original, (d) concurrent   _____ 1. _____
2. Geographically, the United States is divided into _____ federal districts. (a) 12, (b) 25, (c) 50, (d) 94   _____ 2. _____
3. Which of the following is not one of the purposes of the discovery process? (a) to preserve evidence, (b) to lead to settlement, (c) to discredit evidence, (d) to eliminate surprise   _____ 3. _____
4. A counterclaim is filed by the (a) plaintiff, (b) defendant, (c) judge, (d) losing party.   _____ 4. _____
5. All of the following issues are tried exclusively in a state court except (a) divorce, (b) adoption, (c) bankruptcy, (d) inheritance.   _____ 5. _____
6. How many people make up the jury for a criminal case? (a) 6, (b) 6 to 12, (c) 8 to 10, (d) 12   _____ 6. _____
7. The form of dispute resolution in which an independent third person has the power to impose a decision that both parties must accept is called (a) mediation, (b) voluntary arbitration, (c) binding arbitration, (d) negotiation.   _____ 7. _____

3 section:
problem solving

Activity 26.1 The Court System and the Courthouse Personnel

Directions: Use the *Yellow Pages*, library, or online sources to answer the following questions.

1. In what city is your state supreme court located?

   _____

2. Name the justices or judges for your state supreme court.

   _____

   _____

   _____

3. Where is the circuit and district court nearest you? (city, county)

   _____

4. Name the judges for either the circuit or district court.

   _____

   _____

   _____

   _____

5. List the county and city courts in your area.

   _____

   _____

   _____

   _____

6. Name the judges for the county and city courts.

   _____

   _____

   _____

7. Provide the telephone numbers for the following county officials who are usually located in the county courthouse.
   a. Tax assessor _____
   b. County clerk _____
   c. County recorder _____
   d. County court docket clerk _____
   e. Sheriff _____

8. What is the address of the nearest county courthouse?

   _____

   _____

9. What is the telephone number(s) for calling the courthouse for information about trial dates, time, and location?

   _____

   _____

Activity 26.2 The Complaint

Directions: Read the following complaint and answer the questions on the next page.

IN THE CIRCUIT COURT FOR THE STATE OF TEXAS, COUNTY OF WADE

```
JOHN M. PRESCOTT, aka        )        CIVIL
JOHNNY M. PRESCOTT,          )        CASE NO. 89- _____
                             )
              Plaintiff,     )
                             )
     vs.                     )        COMPLAINT
                             )
LYDIA D. EARLE and           )
EARLE MANUFACTURING CO.,     )
              Defendant.     )
_____)
```

COMES NOW plaintiff and alleges as follows:

I

Plaintiff and defendants herein are residents of said county and state for at least six months prior to the filing of this lawsuit.

II

Defendant, Lydia D. Earle, is employed by Earle Manufacturing Co., and was so employed on the first day of January, 20--. At or about 1:00 p.m. on said date, defendant was acting in the course and scope of work in behalf of said company.

III

Said defendant, Lydia D. Earle, did carelessly and recklessly operate her automobile, which is the property of Earle Manufacturing Co., so as to cause injuries to plaintiff in an automobile collision that occurred at 1250 Oak Street on said date and time.

IV

As a result of said accident, plaintiff has suffered specific damages for medical expenses of Twelve Thousand Eight Hundred Forty Dollars ($12,840) and general damages for loss of income of Thirty Thousand Dollars ($30,000).

WHEREFORE, plaintiff prays that judgment be entered against said defendants in favor of plaintiff in the amount of Twelve Thousand Eight Hundred Forty Dollars ($12,840) for specific damages, Thirty Thousand Dollars ($30,000) for general damages, and for plaintiff's attorneys' fees and court costs, Three Thousand Two Hundred Dollars ($3,200).

DATED: _____, 20--.

_____
Attorney for Plaintiff

ATTESTATION BY PLAINTIFF

1. Who is the plaintiff in this court action?

_____

2. What is the court in which this action is filed? For what county and state?

_____

3. Is this a criminal or civil action?

_____

4. What do the letters "aka" stand for?

_____

5. Who are the defendants in this action?

_____

6. What is the name (title) of this action?

_____

7. What is the general nature of the complaint? (What happened? What action or relief is desired?)

_____

_____

_____

8. Who signs the complaint?

_____

9. When the plaintiff attests this document, he or she swears that the statements contained in it are true. Following is a typical attestation clause that would appear in a complaint. Read it and tell why it is necessary to have the attestation clause.

_____

_____

_____

_____

_____

```
STATE OF TEXAS     )
                   )  SS.
County of Wade     )

        On the date last above written, _____,

did appear before me and swore the foregoing to be his free and willful act,

and acknowledge that all facts contained therein are true and correct.


                              _____
                              Notary Public for Texas
                              My Commission Expires: _____

    (NOTARY SEAL)
```

10. What happens now that the complaint is filed?

_____

_____

_____

_____

_____

Activity 26.3 Remedies

Directions: Match the descriptions on the left with the answers on the right. Write your answers in the space provided.

_____ 1. A process whereby the decision of a neutral third person must be accepted by both parties of a dispute

_____ 2. A process in which a neutral third person assists two parties in reaching a compromise that is acceptable to both sides

_____ 3. A procedure whereby the customer refuses to pay a bill until a dispute is settled

_____ 4. A state trial court that hears civil cases involving large sums of money, criminal matters with major penalties, and cases that are appealed from local courts

_____ 5. A court that has the authority to review the decision of a lower court

_____ 6. Filed when many people are affected by the act of one defendant

_____ 7. A court of limited jurisdiction that resolves cases involving small amounts

_____ 8. A consumer protection group that files lawsuits on behalf of others

_____ 9. A request to a higher court to review the decision of a lower court that is filed by the losing party of a lawsuit

_____ 10. The final ruling of the court that establishes the rights and obligations of each party

a. district court
b. binding arbitration
c. judgment
d. withholding payment
e. voluntary arbitration
f. negotiation
g. mediation
h. American Civil Liberties Union
i. small claims court
j. appellate court
k. appeal
l. class action lawsuit

Activity 26.4 Seeking Redress

Directions: You have purchased a product and are not satisfied with it. You charged it to your account, and it has been less than ten days. The product does not do what it was advertised to do, but it was on sale and the tag was marked "all sales final." Based on this information, answer the questions that follow.

1. Explain the self-help remedies that you can pursue.

2. Assuming you are unable to reach a settlement, what other options remain open to you? Choose one option and describe the process you would follow.

3. What are the advantages of using a credit card to make a purchase if you have a problem with the merchandise later?

Activity 26.5 Alternative Dispute Resolution

Directions: Alternative dispute resolution (ADR) is a general term covering several formal methods of settling disputes without using the court system. ADR has gained widespread acceptance among both the general public and the legal profession in recent years. Many states now have ADR programs in place to alleviate the overuse of the court system. In fact, in some states these programs are mandatory before a court will consider hearing a case. Review the discussion on ADR in your textbook and answer the questions that follow.

1. What are the three forms of ADR?

    a. _____

    b. _____

    c. _____

2. What are three advantages of using ADR rather than taking a matter to court?

    a. _____

    b. _____

    c. _____

3. Explain why mediation is a higher level of ADR than negotiation.

    _____

    _____

    _____

    _____

    _____

    _____

4. What are the two forms of arbitration? How are they different?

    _____

    _____

    _____

    _____

    _____

    _____

5. Many contracts (such as credit card agreements) require arbitration of disputes that arise. Why do you think these contract provisions are important? Do you agree or disagree? Explain.

    _____

    _____

    _____

    _____

    _____

    _____

Project 6
Philanthropy and Ethics

Directions: After reading the Unit 6 Project in the student text, complete Worksheets 1–6.

WORKSHEET 1
My Philanthropy Plan

Answer the following questions about yourself and what you can do to help others who are less fortunate than you are. Then make a commitment to give during your lifetime, so that you can help make the world a better place.

1. If you had money to spare, far beyond your wants and needs, how would you choose to spend it? Be specific.

_____

_____

2. What is your favorite charitable organization or cause? Why?

_____

_____

3. What do you consider to be your greatest gift (talent)? How could you use that gift to help others?

_____

_____

4. If you had enough time to spare and didn't need to work for a living, what would you do?

_____

_____

5. Looking back at your life, 100 years after your death, for what would you like to be remembered?

_____

_____

6. List organizations you would like to help and the ways you can help.

_____

_____

WORKSHEET 2
Cutting It Close

Valerie wanted to earn extra money over the summer, so she decided to start a lawn-mowing business in her neighborhood. To advertise her business, she composed a flyer to put in her neighbors' mailboxes. On the flyer, she listed her services: mowing, trimming, and blowing grass clippings off the driveway and sidewalk when she finished. She offered all of these services for one low price.

Several neighbors wanted her service. In fact, more people asked than she had time to serve. Not wanting to pass up the opportunity to earn so much money, Valerie agreed to do the lawns of all who asked. She figured she would find some way to mow them all. Since she was dealing with neighbors, she did not offer any written contracts. They just agreed verbally.

For three weeks, Valerie worked very hard but still could not finish all the lawns she had agreed to mow. She realized, though, that if she didn't trim the lawns, she could mow one additional lawn each weekend, so that's what she decided to do. Valerie reasoned that her mower could cut grass very close to trees and walls, so the trimming didn't really seem necessary. She was giving her customers a very low price, so it was a good deal even without the trimming. Besides, she could now satisfy more customers who otherwise would have to mow their own lawns or take the time to find someone else to do them.

1. Since Valerie and her neighbors did not sign a written contract, is Valerie obligated to perform the services she listed on her flyer? Why or why not?

2. Valerie is 16, so she is a minor. Does this fact affect her legal and ethical obligations to her neighbors?

3. Do you agree with Valerie's reasons for not trimming? Why or why not?

4. Are the benefits she is offering her neighbors worth giving up the trimming service?

5. If you were in Valerie's situation, what would you do? Why?

WORKSHEET 3
I'm Anonymous

Hiroto has met many people online, and he uses several screen names. He visits chat rooms and reads personal ads frequently and sometimes responds to them. He never provides correct information because he doesn't want anyone finding out who he really is. On several occasions, Hiroto made arrangements to meet someone, but often he did not show up as agreed.

As a joke, Hiroto sometimes sends insulting or vaguely threatening e-mail messages to coworkers he doesn't like. He enjoys hearing them talk about the messages at work. Because Hiroto doesn't mean them any real harm, he believes the messages don't hurt anybody. And because he's anonymous, he doesn't think he's taking any risks.

1. Do you think Hiroto is acting appropriately on the Internet? Why or why not?

2. Have you ever acted in similar ways toward people on the Internet? Explain.

3. How would you feel if you received an insulting or threatening e-mail from an anonymous sender?

4. What suggestions would you make to Hiroto about behaving appropriately and staying safe on the Internet?

5. Are there any laws that protect users from actions such as Hiroto's? If so, what are they?

WORKSHEET 4
Something for Nothing

Mahir and Kayla work together at a fast-food restaurant. They are both good workers and have been employed for over a year. Each Christmas, the company they work for has a big party for all employees. Gifts are given away to employees who provide outstanding service during the year.

Mahir and Kayla's manager has worked for the company for over ten years. She discovered a way to falsify information in the computer to her advantage. She gets more than her fair share of gifts while others in the company do not get as much. Mahir and Kayla accidentally discovered this scam. The manager encouraged Mahir and Kayla to participate in the scheme. "You two can get more gifts if you participate. If you try to turn me in, I'll have both of you fired," she said.

1. What is the ethical problem involved in this situation?

_____

_____

_____

_____

_____

2. What are Mahir and Kayla's options?

_____

_____

_____

_____

_____

3. What would you do if you were in this situation? Why?

_____

_____

_____

_____

_____

4. How is this case an example of employee theft in the workplace?

_____

_____

_____

_____

5. Are there employment laws that would protect Mahir and Kayla? If so, what are they?

_____

_____

_____

_____

WORKSHEET 5
It's a Good Deal

When Reynaldo flew to see his relatives last year, he was able to earn enough air miles for a free ticket. The frequent flyer club rules are clear: The ticket is nontransferable.

Reynaldo bought a ticket for a flight across the country but later discovered he couldn't go. A friend of his was planning a similar trip, so Reynaldo offered him the ticket for $100—much cheaper than the cost of a full fare.

When Reynaldo's friend tried to use the ticket, the agent discovered that the ticket belonged to someone else. The airline refused to allow him on the plane without paying the full price for a new ticket. When he told Reynaldo about the problem, Reynaldo said it wasn't his concern.

1. Discuss the issues involved in Reynaldo's dilemma.

_____
_____
_____
_____
_____

2. What's wrong with the owner of a ticket giving or selling it to someone else?

_____
_____
_____
_____
_____

3. Would you participate in this type of deal? Why or why not?

_____
_____
_____
_____
_____

4. If offered a similar deal, what should you do before accepting it?

_____
_____
_____
_____
_____

WORKSHEET 6
Nobody Got Hurt

Lori bought a new dress to wear for a special occasion. During the course of the evening, she spilled some juice on the dress and was unable to remove all of the stain. The stain was small and not really visible at first glance.

The next day, Lori decided that she would probably never wear the dress again. The dress didn't fit as well as she would have liked, so she decided to get her money back. That afternoon she returned the dress to the store. She claimed the dress was a gift that she didn't like. The store gave her credit for the dress, and Lori bought something else. When asked how she could do something like that, Lori replied, "Why not? Nobody got hurt."

1. Was there anything wrong with what Lori did? Did anybody get hurt? Who?

_____

_____

_____

_____

_____

2. Why do some stores have lenient return policies? Why do some stores have "no return" policies? What store policies would you recommend to avoid this kind of activity?

_____

_____

_____

_____

_____

3. What would you do if you worked in the store and knew what Lori had done?

_____

_____

_____

_____

_____

4. Discuss the ethical principles involved in this case.

_____

_____

_____

_____

_____

Activity 1 Philanthropy

Directions: Each person can develop a personal plan for giving. In some cases, it is encouraged through employment. Other people give money to religious and charitable organizations that they support in their communities. However, philanthropy doesn't always mean giving money. It also includes giving time, goods, and effort to support a cause. Answer the following questions based on your personal ideals and values.

1. Does your employer sponsor a giving program (such as payroll deductions for charities in the local area)? If so, describe the plan.

_____

_____

_____

_____

_____

2. What individual plan of giving do you have? For example, do you give money to local charities, religious organizations, or other groups? Is it a planned giving based on your income and your commitment? Explain.

_____

_____

_____

_____

_____

3. Philanthropy is a lifetime commitment. Describe your plans for philanthropy (a) as you go along through life and (b) at the end of life (inheritances).

   a. Through your lifetime:

_____

_____

_____

_____

_____

   b. At the end of life:

_____

_____

_____

_____

_____